Outsourcing US Intelligence

Series Editors: Richard J. Aldrich, Rory Cormac, Michael S. Goodman and Hugh Wilford

This series explores the full spectrum of spying and secret warfare in a globalised world.

Intelligence has changed. Secret service is no longer just about spying or passively watching a target. Espionage chiefs now command secret armies and legions of cyber warriors who can quietly shape international relations itself. Intelligence actively supports diplomacy, peacekeeping and warfare: the entire spectrum of security activities. As traditional inter-state wars become more costly, covert action, black propaganda and other forms of secret interventionism become more important. This ranges from proxy warfare to covert action; from targeted killing to disruption activity. Meanwhile, surveillance permeates communications to the point where many feel there is little privacy. Intelligence, and the accelerating technology that surrounds it, have never been more important for the citizen and the state.

Titles in the *Intelligence, Surveillance and Secret Warfare* series include:

Published:

The Arab World and Western Intelligence: Analysing the Middle East, 1956–1981
Dina Rezk

The Twilight of the British Empire: British Intelligence and Counter-Subversion in the Middle East, 1948–63
Chikara Hashimoto

Chile, the CIA and the Cold War: A Transatlantic Perspective
James Lockhart

The Clandestine Lives of Colonel David Smiley: Code Name 'Grin'
Clive Jones

The Problem of Secret Intelligence
Kjetil Anders Hatlebrekke

Outsourcing US Intelligence: Contractors and Government Accountability
Damien Van Puyvelde

Forthcoming:

The Snowden Era on Screen: Signals Intelligence and Digital Surveillance
James Smith

The CIA and the Pursuit of Security: History, Documents and Contexts
Hew Dylan

https://edinburghuniversitypress.com/series-intelligence-surveillance-and-secret-warfare.html

Outsourcing US Intelligence

Contractors and Government Accountability

Damien Van Puyvelde

EDINBURGH
University Press

For Ana

Edinburgh University Press is one of the leading university presses in the UK. We publish academic books and journals in our selected subject areas across the humanities and social sciences, combining cutting-edge scholarship with high editorial and production values to produce academic works of lasting importance. For more information visit our website: edinburghuniversitypress.com

Edinburgh University Press Ltd
The Tun – Holyrood Road,
12(2f) Jackson's Entry,
Edinburgh EH8 8PJ

First published in hardback by Edinburgh University Press 2019

Typeset in 11/13 Adobe Sabon by
IDSUK (Dataconnection) Ltd, and
printed and bound by CPI Group (UK) Ltd,
Croydon CRO 4YY

A CIP record for this book is available from the
British Library

ISBN 978 1 4744 5022 5 (hardback)
ISBN 978 1 4744 5024 9 (webready PDF)
ISBN 978 1 4744 5025 6 (epub)

Contents

Figures

Acknowledgements

This book would not have been possible without financial support from Aberystwyth University (Postgraduate Research Studentship and Caroline Adams Travel Bursary), the British International Studies Association (Founders Fund Award), and the University of Texas at El Paso. I am truly indebted to all these sources of funding.

This project started as an essay inspired by a discussion with Peter Jackson ten years ago. Since then, a number of colleagues and friends have been kind enough to provide guidance and support. Alastair Finlan and Gerry Hughes commented on early drafts as they shepherded me through my PhD thesis. Peter read the full manuscript and provided useful comments. Richard Aldrich, Stephen Coulthart, Rhodri Jeffreys-Jones, Michael Landon-Murray, Liam Mcvay, Roberto Noriega, Mark Phythian and the anonymous reviewers offered comments that helped me improve various sections. My friend, the late Chikara Hashimoto, was essential in shaping my understanding of intelligence practices. His passion for the study of intelligence was boundless and contagious!

Field research in the United States was essential to the completion of this project. I am indebted to all the individuals who agreed to share their knowledge and experiences with me. Loch K. Johnson welcomed me in Athens, GA, in July 2011. His scholarly contribution to the field of intelligence studies, our conversations about intelligence oversight, and his generosity are a source of inspiration. I also thank Etienne Linard and Cameron Roberts for hosting me in Washington, DC.

Over the course of this project, I worked at Aberystwyth University, the University of Texas at El Paso and the University of

Glasgow. The research communities at these institutions and the broader community of intelligence scholars across the world always provided an inspiring, friendly and supportive environment. Thanks go to all the colleagues and friends who shared some thoughts and drinks along the way, and to my family for their unconditional support.

Abbreviations

ACLU	American Civil Liberties Union
ASBCA	Armed Services Board of Contracts Appeal
BENS	Business Executives for National Security
CBO	Congressional Budget Office
CIA	Central Intelligence Agency
CIFA	Counterintelligence Field Activity
COR	Contracting Officer's Representative
COTR	Contracting Officer's Technical Representative
CRS	Congressional Research Service
D/CIA	Director of the Central Intelligence Agency
DFARS	Defense Acquisition Regulation Supplement
DCI	Director of Central Intelligence
DIA	Defense Intelligence Agency
DNI	Director of National Intelligence
DoD	Department of Defense
DOS	Department of State
FAIR	Federal Activities Inventory Reform
FAR	Federal Acquisition Regulation
FISC	Foreign Intelligence Surveillance Court
FISA	Foreign Intelligence Surveillance Act
FOIA	Freedom of Information Act
FTE	Full Time Equivalent
GAO	General Accounting Office; Government Accountability Office
HPSCI	House Permanent Select Committee on Intelligence
HUMINT	Human Intelligence
I&A	Office of Intelligence and Analysis
IC	Intelligence Community
ICD	Intelligence Community Directive

IG	Inspector General
IMINT	Imagery Intelligence
INSA	Intelligence and National Security Alliance
INSCOM	US Army Intelligence and Security Command
IOB	Intelligence Oversight Board
IT	Information Technology
ITAR	International Traffic in Arms Regulation
MASINT	Measurement and Signature Intelligence
MEJA	Military Extraterritorial Jurisdiction Act
MID	Military Intelligence Division
MIP	Military Intelligence Program
NGA	National Geospatial-Intelligence Agency
NIE	National Intelligence Estimate
NIP	National Intelligence Program
NRO	National Reconnaissance Office
NSA	National Security Agency
NSC	National Security Council
ODNI	Office of the Director of National Intelligence
OFPP	Office of Federal Procurement Policy
OIG	Office of Inspector General
OLC	Office of Legal Counsel
OMB	Office of Management and Budget
OSINT	Open Source Intelligence
OSS	Office of Strategic Services
PDB	President's Daily Brief
PIAB	President's Intelligence Advisory Board
PSC	Private Security Company
QIC	In-Q-Tel Interface Center
R&D	Research and Development
SAIC	Science Applications International Corporation
SIGINT	Signals Intelligence
SSCI	Senate Select Committee on Intelligence
UCMJ	Uniform Code of Military Justice
US	United States
USC	United States Code
USML	United States Munitions List
VCF	Virtual Case File

Introduction

Today, close to a million contractors hold a security clearance in the United States. This is a quarter of all cleared personnel, and more than the total population of the District of Columbia, where most major federal government institutions are located. Tens of thousands of contractors contribute to core intelligence functions like collection and operations, analysis and production, and even mission management.[1] This situation is not new, but has gained visibility in the last decade since interactions between the US intelligence community and the private sector have multiplied and made headlines.[2]

In January 2017, the online media company *Buzzfeed* published a series of private intelligence reports containing allegations of misconduct and conspiracy between the presidential campaign of Donald Trump and the government of Russia. A former British intelligence officer, David Steele, had compiled this dossier for the company Fusion GPS, which was conducting political research on Trump in the run-up to the 2016 presidential elections.[3] The 'Steele dossier' was eventually shared with the British and American intelligence services. Following the election of President Trump, the Federal Bureau of Investigation (FBI) reached an agreement with Steele to continue his work. However, this agreement was terminated when the dossier became public in January 2017, and President Trump denounced the revelations as 'fake'.[4] Since he first took office, tensions have escalated between President Trump and the US intelligence community. The President does not believe the assessment of the intelligence community that Russia sought to influence his election, and has mounted a series of verbal attacks on the FBI and the Justice Department.[5]

In late 2017 the administration of Donald Trump was reportedly considering whether to 'privatise the CIA' as a means to counter the 'deep state'.[6] These news stories raise important questions about the evolving role of public and private intelligence in US democracy. They also demonstrate how private intelligence contractors can be viewed as both a problem and a solution in the public debate on national security intelligence.

In the twenty-first century, more than ever before, government intelligence agencies collaborate with the private sector to counter diverse security threats. Speaking at an industry conference in the mid-2000s, an official from the then newly established Office of the Director of National Intelligence (ODNI) recognised how essential the private sector has become to the national intelligence effort, stating: 'We can't spy if we can't buy.'[7] In the last decade, the US intelligence community has disbursed hundreds of billions of dollars to acquire goods and services from the industry and intensified its efforts to liaise with the private sector. The extent to which American spies interact with the private sector is unparalleled and comes as a shock to outsiders, yet it is a severely underrepresented subject in the literature on intelligence.

Broadening the Study of Intelligence

This book aims to move Intelligence Studies beyond the narrow governmental frame within which it has mostly been situated and explore the roles contractors play in the US intelligence effort. In doing so, the book challenges the state centrism that has dominated the study of intelligence. Consensual definitions of intelligence illustrate this state centrism. National security intelligence is often defined as 'secret state activity aiming to understand or influence foreign threats and entities'.[8] From this perspective, national security intelligence differs from competitive or business intelligence, the process through which commercial entities gather, analyse and distribute information about their competitors.[9] While competitive intelligence serves corporate interests across the globe, national security intelligence serves the public interest. Occasionally public and private interests overlap. State intelligence activities include the collection, analysis and dissemination of information about threats to national security, the protection of that information and the implementation of covert actions to influence foreign actors. The conduct of these core intelligence activities requires capabilities to research and develop new technologies, provide administrative support and manage the daily operations of 17 US government agencies.[10] The study of national security intelligence has mostly focused on these agencies, but US intelligence has long involved a vast network of private entities and individuals who provide the agencies with goods and services. Exploring the evolving role of these private providers in supporting government intelligence can further our understanding of the scope and limits of national security and inform debates about the reconfiguration of public authority in a modern liberal democracy.

In privatisation theory, the nature of the goods and services under consideration determines the preferred mode of public-private engagement.[11] National security intelligence can be considered as a public good that benefits the nation as a whole. The public interest in national security creates a need for government officials to determine objectives and manage the national intelligence effort. Officials can decide whether a good or service is best provided in-house, or produced by another institution of society. Privatisation occurs when there is a shift 'from an arrangement with a government producer to one with a private producer'.[12] Such a shift affects the role of the government and the institutions of society in the provision of national security. Privatisation by divestment, when the government sells public assets and no longer owns or supervises a function, has not occurred in the field of intelligence. Privatisation by delegation, when the government maintains ultimate responsibility for the function, is the norm. When government agencies delegate functions to another organisation, the role played by public officials changes and their ability to manage their external partners becomes crucial. Privatisation by delegation can take many forms. The US intelligence community has used grants to harness the research and educational capabilities of hundreds of universities and companies.[13] Not-for-profit organisations like the Intelligence and National Security Alliance (INSA) and Business Executives for National Security (BENS) have worked on a voluntary basis for the intelligence community, conducting research and audits, and organising networking events to improve the relationships and exchange of ideas between intelligence officials and industry professionals.[14]

This book focuses on the most common type of privatisation by delegation: outsourcing or contracting out.[15] Today, the intelligence community outsources all sorts of services and products including simple functions like catering and janitorial services, and more complex ones like the development and operation of satellite systems and the provision of intelligence analysis. When the government outsources an activity, it delegates a series of tasks to contractors but retains some responsibilities toward the public. Government officials arrange the national intelligence effort and decide what goods and services are needed, who can best provide them, at what cost, and how.[16] If contractors fail to deliver a product or if they misbehave, the government is expected to reaffirm its control and hold them to account. However, the extent to which government officials have been able to maintain control over intelligence contracts and contractors is not clear, mostly because it has not been studied thoroughly.

The Debate about Intelligence Outsourcing

Examining the relationship between the intelligence community and its contractors is essential to draw lessons that can inform the conduct of cross-sector collaboration. Researchers have written a lot about private security contractors, but much less about the more specific case of intelligence contracting. The academic literature on private security has much to offer at a conceptual level, especially when authors discuss the reconfiguration of the roles played by the public and the private sectors in contemporary security settings. Initial research on this phenomenon explained the development of different types of companies and the services they provide in the market for security.[17] Scholars were quick to reach a consensus that distinguishes private security companies (PSC) from mercenaries who tend to work more independently and for their own profit. The most relevant and lively debates in this field focus on the consequences of privatising security. Researchers have analysed the impact of privatisation on state control of force,[18] and the extent to which the growth of the private security industry is redefining the structures and identities at the core of civil-military relations.[19] Their findings suggest that the privatisation of security is not an abdication but a reconfiguration of public authority.[20] This reconfiguration raises important policy questions about how to guarantee respect for liberal democratic values such as government transparency, the rule of law and human rights, as well as acceptable levels of government efficiency and effectiveness. These concerns are apparent throughout the history of intelligence outsourcing and will be addressed in this book. However, the growth of the market for national security intelligence differs to a degree from the broader privatisation of security and the history of defence contracting.[21]

The strong culture of secrecy and the deniability that surrounds spy agencies makes intelligence outsourcing a far more delicate issue. Military forces operate under the rules of international law and benefit from its protection. This is not the case with intelligence agencies, which typically operate within the rule of law at home, and often operate illegally and covertly abroad. The literature on private security tends to focus on PSC, some of which analyse and disseminate the intelligence they collect on multiple theatres of operation. Ensuring the physical security of US government personnel on specific sites and convoys, for instance, requires an intelligence capability to make well-informed decisions.[22] Private security scholarship mentions intelligence in this context, but does not really delve into the specificities of the market for national security intelligence. In practice, public-private intelligence arrangements encompass companies from a broader range of sectors, like information and communications technology, that do not have the same history as PSC and have never been considered as mercenaries.[23]

Few scholars have studied the evolving scope and limits of the relationship between the US intelligence community and its contractors. Hamilton Bean divides the nascent body of literature on intelligence outsourcing into two camps: critics and defenders. Defenders present outsourcing as 'a mere shift in the way that government fulfils intelligence responsibilities'.[24] They tend to emphasise the necessity of cross-sector collaboration and the flexibility provided by the private sector, while acknowledging some of the costs of outsourcing and the need for clear regulation.[25] Critics focus on the lack of government oversight and the inherent risks of public-private collaboration, including waste, fraud and abuse. Their arguments have dominated the public debate on intelligence contractors in the last decade. When intelligence outsourcing boomed in the decade following the 9/11 attacks, they argued that the US government appeared to be losing control over its private partners. Sensationalist books such as journalist Jeremy Scahill's *Blackwater* described the rise of 'mercenaries' supporting CIA activities on the frontline of the Global War on Terrorism.[26] Journalists like Dana Priest and William Arkin reported on a shadowy world of private spies 'growing out of control', and – in what remains the most comprehensive account of the post-9/11 boom in intelligence outsourcing – Tim Shorrock detailed a number of government shortcomings in the oversight of 'spies for hire'.[27]

Critics argue that government officials have become captive of private interests. They point out that big companies thrive on government intelligence contracts and waste taxpayers' money. During the post-9/11 period these companies also engaged in sensitive activities that were inherently public, such as intelligence analysis and interrogation. Indeed, some of the most prominent intelligence scandals of the early twenty-first century, such as the Abu Ghraib prisoner abuses and the leaks orchestrated by former National Security Agency (NSA) contractor Edward Snowden, directly involved contractors and seemed to confirm the view that contractors were out of control.[28] In light of these incidents, commentators did not hesitate to conclude that outsourcing threatened some of the core tenets of liberal democracy, such as human rights and government transparency.[29] Opinion pieces published in the *New York Times* urged: 'Don't Privatize Our Spies' and 'Put the Spies Back under One Roof'.

The behaviour of intelligence contractors in the global war on terrorism and beyond has questioned the extent to which government institutions have been able to remain in control of the multiple actors and processes at the core of national security. However, the involvement of contractors in a series of intelligence controversies does not demonstrate the existence of a causal relationship between the outsourcing of intelligence and weak accountability. Outsourcing does not necessarily leave national security in the hands of private interests, and government action does not guarantee the public interest will prevail.[30] The debate on intelligence outsourcing needs to overcome such assumptions, focus on all the evidence that is publicly available and discuss practices. What is the evidence that outsourcing intelligence impedes on *and* supports the government's ability to serve the public interest in national security? How does the US system of intelligence accountability affect outsourcing and contractors' behaviour? To answer these questions, this study explores the relationship between intelligence outsourcing and government accountability. The core of the book focuses on the evolution of intelligence as a tool of government and the ability of government officials to uphold the public interest in national security when intelligence is outsourced. Following this approach, most of the problems with private intelligence contractors can be linked to shortfalls in the US system of intelligence accountability.

Given the institutional secrecy that characterises the world of intelligence, inferences about the relationship between outsourcing and accountability can only be drawn tentatively. Intelligence agencies use secrecy to protect the sources and methods they use to acquire and understand information about the threats they confront. Disclosing these sources and methods can benefit rival countries and organisations.[31] As a result, governments prefer to keep a significant part of their intelligence activities secret, and severely punish unauthorised disclosures of information. Private sector organisations use confidentiality clauses and information security procedures to protect proprietary information.[32] When the intelligence community outsources sensitive activities, information about public-private collaboration is protected both by government and private sector policies. In these conditions, empirical evidence on the government's oversight of intelligence contractors is hard to come by for an outsider. The quality of outsourcing depends on a host of factors that are not publicly accessible, such as government contracts and performance reviews. References to some government intelligence contracts can be found in the trade press and tracked on government websites such as the federal procurement data system, but these sources do not provide much detail beyond the broad category of services that are outsourced – for instance, 'intelligence analysis' and 'information assurance'.[33]

To overcome data limitations, this study relies on extensive empirical research drawing upon hundreds of government and private sector documents, memoirs, and media coverage by well-established newspapers and specialised media including trade publications. A number of successful freedom of information act requests – all of them to the ODNI – have also provided new material. These documentary sources provide a significant amount of information on outsourcing, especially when compared to other Western countries. A French parliamentary report notes that the number of contractors working at the *Direction Générale des Services Extérieurs* rose from 17.5 per cent in 2008 to 25 per cent in 2015.[34] The 2011–12 annual report of the Intelligence and Security committee of the British Parliament mentions that 'the agencies spend hundreds of millions of pounds of public money every year with the industry'.[35] Beyond these figures, very little information is publicly available on intelligence outsourcing in France and the United Kingdom. The American intelligence community is uniquely transparent, which can largely be related to political culture and the quality of its system of intelligence accountability.

To complement documentary sources on the US case, over thirty-five semi-structured interviews and a dozen informal discussions with intelligence experts and practitioners working in government and the private sector have been conducted since 2011.[36] A number of practitioners who agreed to talk have crossed the revolving door separating public and private sectors during their career. They were able to share their perspectives both as (former) government officials and as contractors. The data gathered during these interviews drew my attention to specific examples and processes, and reinforced a number of key points made in this study. The diverse personal trajectories and different levels of experience of these informants further confirmed the significant scope of intelligence outsourcing in the United States. In turn, while all these sources of information are insufficient to represent the entire universe of intelligence contracting, they provide a window into governmental practices of intelligence accountability and outsourcing, and shed light on related risks and opportunities.

The Relationship between Intelligence Outsourcing and Accountability

The core argument of this book is that intelligence outsourcing and intelligence accountability are two interdependent phenomena, for better *and* for worse. Provided that the government finds ways to effectively leverage contractors, mutual interdependence can lead to national security successes. Public-private successes, like the development of the U-2 spy plane in the 1950s and the information technology (IT) investments made by the Central Intelligence Agency (CIA) in the last two decades through the venture capital firm In-Q-Tel, prove that outsourcing can give a competitive edge to the intelligence community without causing major accountability problems. In some situations, such as the aftermath of the 9/11 attacks, contracting out specific functions can also help the government achieve its national security objectives by rapidly plugging multiple capability gaps.

The government does not lose its responsibilities when it outsources intelligence functions, but its role changes – from implementing to overseeing activities – and this requires adaptation. Outsourcing poses risks of fraud, waste and abuse that need to be managed by government officials and overseen by outsiders in Congress and beyond. Following the latest boom in intelligence outsourcing, public authorities initially failed to gather information on intelligence contractors, adapt regulations and acquisition capabilities, and intelligence contractors became involved in a series of incidents. Some critics focused on these incidents and concluded that intelligence should not be outsourced. However, this argument overlooks the need for cross-sector collaboration and the government's national security responsibilities, which do not disappear but evolve when functions are outsourced.

A number of incidents involving intelligence contractors are examined throughout this book. All of these accountability failures involve government employees who were unable to maintain the ascendancy between public interest and private means, and contractors who underperformed or misbehaved. Examining outsourcing in practice, through examples of success and failure, provides an opportunity to reconsider the role of public authorities in a realm where commentators often seem to assume that the presence of government officials guarantees respect for the public interest in national security. The point is not to argue that this is never the case, but to research in what conditions government officials can maintain the ascendancy of the public interest over private means.

One of the key objectives of this book is to develop a more comprehensive understanding of intelligence accountability. This is essential to answer how and by whom the public interest in national security should be determined. In modern democracies, people expect government accountability holders to defend the public interest in national security. Government accountability holders have the authority to change rules and regulations and adapt their capabilities to better oversee public and private intelligence professionals. The literature on the democratic oversight of intelligence – which is reviewed extensively in Chapter 1 – largely focuses on the role of elected officials in the executive and legislative branches of government and political appointees.[37] These officials are essential to the democratic oversight of intelligence services, but their role is part of a broader system of accountability that brings together a number of public and private actors. In some circumstances, private actors, including intelligence contractors, can also contribute to upholding the public interest in national security.

Besides the role of contractors in intelligence accountability, critics have overlooked the government's efforts to respond to the accountability problems that have plagued intelligence outsourcing. While the government's adaptation efforts have not been perfect, key accountability holders have demonstrated a willingness to rectify some of the problems of outsourcing. They have developed procedures to track and understand the scope of the contractor workforce and limit its involvement in core intelligence activities such as collection and analysis. Contractors have also contributed to the democratic accountability of intelligence services in their own way. These contributions suggest that outsourcing and accountability can reinforce each other to better serve the public interest in national security.

Outline

This book explores the evolving relationship between the US intelligence community and its contractors. Chapter 1 develops a conceptual model of intelligence accountability as a relationship between accountability holders and holdees, or principals and agents. This model identifies three conditions for accountability to occur: access to information, existence of adequate standards, and authority and willingness to use them. The model posits that the existence of these conditions and the broader relationship between accountability holders and holdees are not fixed in time. When one or more of these conditions is not satisfied, accountability problems emerge and might trigger responses that may or may not fill accountability gaps. This conceptual model is used to broaden the study of intelligence accountability – which has largely focused on the role of the three branches of government – and take into account the place of contractors in the US system of intelligence accountability. The construct serves as a lens that structures my analysis of the relationship between the intelligence community and its contractors throughout the book.

Chapter 2 provides an in-depth account of the relationship between the US intelligence apparatus and its private outriders, from the earliest days of the Republic to the late twentieth century. Covering such a large period sheds light on the deep roots, the broad evolution, and the multiple opportunities and risks accompanying intelligence outsourcing. In the United States, the legitimacy of the federal government has always been entwined with the private sector, and this is related to the values underpinning American political culture. As a result, the private intelligence industry continued to thrive, deepen and diversify its involvement in national security affairs when the federal government established itself more firmly in this realm following the Second World War. The institutionalisation of intelligence in the twentieth century was accompanied by the diversification and formalisation of the ties between the intelligence community and its contractors. Contractors and their government sponsors share the responsibility for some of the greatest achievements and controversies in US intelligence history, from the success of the U-2 spy plane to the excesses of Project MKUltra in the early Cold War. These opportunities and challenges need to be managed by government officials using adequate accountability channels. Overall, the history of US intelligence is characterised by successive movements of expansion and regulation through which outsourcing and government accountability have become increasingly intertwined.

Chapter 3 charts and explains the rise of intelligence contracting in the post-Cold War era. In the 1990s, the private sector led the IT revolution and became an indispensable asset for the intelligence community. Meanwhile government policies downsized the government intelligence workforce and a number of experienced officials moved to the private sector. Intelligence contracting boomed in the aftermath of the 9/11 attacks because the private sector offered a pool of knowledge and capabilities that intelligence managers deemed necessary at the time. The government hired thousands of contractors to intensify the national intelligence effort rapidly, and the outsourcing of intelligence services diversified to an unprecedented level. In the atmosphere of emergency that characterised the early days of the global war on terrorism, this expansion was not planned, and a variety of contractors related to the intelligence community in ways that were not always harmonious or economically viable.

The post-9/11 trend toward intelligence outsourcing was accompanied by the emergence of a series of accountability problems. Chapter 4 evaluates the accountability regime for contractors in the early 2000s and finds that this regime was imperfect but not non-existent. Six examples of accountability failure shed light on three types of accountability problems involving contractors: inefficiencies, human rights abuses, and conflicts of interest. The chapter finds that intelligence contractors have not always been efficient, effective or respectful of the law, but they do not bear sole responsibility for the accountability problems in which they have been involved. These problems were caused by inadequate standards and deficient management on both sides of the public-private divide. While outsourcing can limit intelligence accountability, government accountability shortfalls also affect the outsourcing of intelligence. I argue that outsourcing and accountability are mutually interdependent. This interdependence does not need to be negative; under the right conditions, outsourcing can make the intelligence community more effective without causing major accountability problems.

Chapter 5 examines how, from the mid-2000s onwards, the executive and legislative branches of government made substantial efforts to palliate gaps in the accountability regime for intelligence contractors. This chapter sheds a more positive light on the relationship between intelligence accountability and outsourcing, and emphasises the progress government accountability holders made in four main areas: government access to information on contractors; acquisition management; the definition of core government functions; and balancing the public and private components of the intelligence workforce.[38] In Chapter 6, I consider the outcome of these government responses and argue that further efforts are and will be needed to continue to fill accountability gaps and adapt the national intelligence effort to the security environment. To avoid past mistakes and provide greater coherence to this effort, adaptation should focus on three essential questions: What to outsource? When to outsource? How to outsource? The answers to these questions emphasise the need for more coherent government policies and planning in the domain of human resources, and in particular a more stable pool of government personnel to cope with the ebb and flow of intelligence requirements.

The history of intelligence outsourcing highlights the strengths and the shortcomings of the US system of intelligence accountability, and raises questions about the factors influencing government officials' ability to anticipate problems and uphold high standards of accountability. While remedial measures can be identified and implemented, a long-term, political commitment to government intelligence capabilities and intelligence accountability is needed to maximise public-private intelligence collaboration. This commitment might go unheeded, but this much is certain: the futures of intelligence accountability and intelligence outsourcing will remain interlinked, for better *and* for worse.

Notes

1. Office of the Director of National Intelligence, National Counterintelligence and Security Center, 2015 Report on Security Clearance Determinations, 28 June 2016, p. 5; Office of the Director of National Intelligence, *FY 2013 Congressional Budget Justification, Vol. I: National Intelligence Program*, February 2012, p. 69.
2. A search on the Nexis database reveals that, from 1 January 2000 to 1 January 2018, the expression 'intelligence contractor' appeared in 193 *Washington Post* newspaper articles and 207 *New York Times* newspaper articles.
3. The Steele dossier, a thirty-five-page compilation of company intelligence reports dated June–December 2016, is available at <https://www.documentcloud.org/documents/3259984-Trump-Intelligence-Allegations.html> (accessed 13 June 2018).
4. Tom Hamburger and Rosalind S. Helderman, 'FBI Once Planned to Pay Former British Spy Who Authored Controversial Trump Dossier', *Washington Post*, 28 February 2017, available at <https://www.washingtonpost.com/politics/fbi-once-planned-to-pay-former-british-spy-who-authored-controversial-trump-dossier/2017/02/28/896ab470-facc-11e6-9845-576c69081518_story.html?utm_term=.a84606d10045> (accessed 29 May 2018).
5. Julie Hirschfeld Davis, 'Trump Calls Justice Department and FBI Conduct "a Disgrace"', *New York Times*, 2 February 2018, available at <https://www.nytimes.com/2018/02/02/us/politics/trump-blames-justice-department-and-fbi-for-conduct-he-says-was-a-disgrace.html> (accessed 13 June 2018).
6. Matthew Cole, Jeremy Scahill, 'Trump White House Weighing Plans for Private Spies to Counter "Deep State" Enemies', *The Intercept*, 5 December 2017, available at <https://theintercept.com/2017/12/04/trump-white-house-weighing-plans-for-private-spies-to-counter-deep-state-enemies/> (accessed 28 May 2018).
7. Terri Everett, Office of the Director of National Intelligence, 'Procuring the Future: 21st Century Acquisition', presentation given at conference organised by the DIA, Boulder, Colorado, 14 May 2007, available at <http://www.fas.org/irp/dni/everett.ppt> (accessed 28 May 2018).

8. This definition is based on Warner, 'Wanted: A Definition of "Intelligence"', 21.
9. On competitive intelligence, see Javers, *Broker, Trader, Lawyer, Spy.*
10. Lowenthal, *Intelligence: From Secrets to Policy*, pp. 70–251.
11. Savas, *Privatization and Public-Private Partnerships*, p. 45.
12. Ibid. p. 104.
13. See for example the case of the Intelligence Community Centers for Academic Excellence, a programme currently managed by the Defense Intelligence Agency, available at <http://www.dia.mil/Training/IC-Centers-for-Academic-Excellence/> (accessed 28 May 2018).
14. INSA staff, interviews with author, 14–15 June 2011, Arlington, VA; Business Executive for National Security (hereafter BENS) staff, interview with author, 16 June 2011, Washington, DC; Intelligence and National Security Alliance, 'About Us', available at <http://www.insaonline.org/index.php?id=79> (accessed 28 May 2018); BENS, 'About Us', available at <http://www.bens.org/our-work/principles-tenets.html> (accessed 28 May 2018).
15. Forrer et al., *Governing Cross-Sector Collaboration*, pp. 16, 86.
16. For a similar argument, see Savas, *Privatization and Public-Private Partnerships*, p. 65.
17. Singer, *Corporate Warriors*; Kinsey, *Corporate Soldiers and International Security.*
18. Avant, *The Market for Force*, pp. 40–80; Verkuil, *Outsourcing Sovereignty.*
19. See for example Krahmann, *States, Citizens and the Privatization of Security*; Bruneau, *Patriots for Profit*; Dunigan, *Victory for Hire.*
20. See for example Abrahamsen and Williams, *Security Beyond the State*; Jacqueline Best and Alexandra Gheciu, 'Introduction', in Best and Gheciu, *Return of the Public in Global Governance*, pp. 1–37.
21. See Nagle, *A History of Government Contracting*; Jones, *Arming the Eagle.*
22. See for example Steve Fainaru and Alex Klein, 'In Iraq, a Private Realm of Intelligence-Gathering; Firm Extends US Government's Reach', *Washington Post*, 1 July 2007, A1.
23. Strachan-Morris, 'The Future of Civil-Military Intelligence Cooperation', p. 274; Thomson, *Mercenaries, Pirates and Sovereigns*; Percy, *Mercenaries.*
24. Bean, 'Privatizing Intelligence', p. 82.
25. Voelz, *Managing the Private Spies*; Michaels, 'All the President's Spies'.
26. Scahill, *Blackwater.*

27. Priest and Arkin, *Top Secret America*; Shorrock, *Spies for Hire*.
28. Epstein, *How America Lost Its Secrets*.
29. Walter Pincus, 'Increase in Contracting Intelligence Jobs Raises Concerns', *Washington Post*, 20 March 2006, A3; Tim Shorrock, 'The Corporate Takeover of US Intelligence', *Salon*, 1 June 2007, available at <http://www.salon.com/2007/06/01/intel_contractors/> (accessed 28 May 2018); Jeff Stein, 'Rent-A-Spy; Three Quarters of the US Intelligence Budget Now Goes to Outside Contractors', *Washington Post*, 1 June 2008, BW3; Robert O'Harrow, Jr., 'Post-9/11 Outsourcing of US Intelligence Raises Risks', *Washington Post*, 10 June 2013, A2; Editorial Board, 'Prying Private Eyes', *New York Times*, 20 June 2013, A26.
30. On bureaucratic discretion, see Lipsky, *Street-level Bureaucracy*.
31. Warner, 'Sources and Methods for the Study of Intelligence', p. 17; Van Puyvelde, 'Qualitative Research Interviews and the Study of National Security Intelligence'.
32. Peltier, *Information Security Policies, Procedures, and Standards*.
33. See for example Allison Berliner, 'NCI Wins Several Homeland Security, Intelligence Contracts', *Newsbytes*, 15 July 2004. The existence of some contracts, to conduct intelligence analysis for instance, can be verified on the Federal Procurement Data System website, available at <https://www.fpds.gov/ezsearch/fpdsportal?indexName=awardfull&templateName=1.4.4&s=FPDSNG.COM&q=%20PRODUCT_OR_SERVICE_CODE%3A%22B538%22> (accessed 28 May 2018).
34. André Trillard and Jeanny Lorgeoux, au nom de la commission des affaires étrangères, de la défense et des forces armées, *Projet de loi de finances pour 2016: Défense: environnement et prospective de la politique de défense*, Avis no. 166 (2015–16), 19 November 2015.
35. Intelligence and Security Committee, *Annual Report 2011–2012*, pp. 68–9.
36. A number of interviews and discussions are not mentioned in the notes to respect the anonymity of those who have agreed to engage with this project.
37. See for example Johnson, *A Season of Inquiry*; Andrew, *For the President's Eyes Only*; Goldman and Rascoff, *Global Intelligence Oversight*.
38. The intelligence workforce includes the military, civilian and contractor personnel working for the intelligence community.

1 Broadening Intelligence Accountability

Questions of accountability have dominated the public debate on intelligence in the twenty-first century. In the age of terrorism and social media, Western societies are increasingly concerned by the rapid expansion of intelligence activities. People are questioning the effect of these changes on core democratic norms such as human rights, civil liberties and government transparency. Such concerns have also affected much of the contemporary debate on intelligence outsourcing. Understanding how intelligence accountability works is essential to identify why, when and how outsourcing succeeds and fails. This chapter explores intelligence accountability in two ways. The first section builds a conceptual model of intelligence accountability as an evolving relationship between accountability holders and accountability holdees. This model is used throughout the book to analyse the relationship between government officials, societal actors and intelligence contractors. The conception of accountability is a deliberately broad one, in order to expand and refine the study of intelligence accountability. The second half of the chapter provides an overview of the US system of intelligence accountability and emphasises the intricate system of checks and balances that limits government intelligence activities. This section not only focuses on the role of the three branches of government, but also considers the role of societal actors in intelligence accountability. An important aspect of this model is that government employees and contractors can both act as accountability holders and holdees.

Accountability as a Relationship

The analytical framework that drives this book draws inspiration from the principal-agent problem and defines accountability as a relationship between an accountability holder or principal who delegates specific tasks and authorities to an accountability holdee, or agent.[1] Accountability holders cannot always know what their agents are doing, and this can be particularly problematic if their goals differ. While accountability holders have the authority to oversee the holdees' actions, the holdees benefit from a level of discretion when they implement the tasks they have been delegated. This discretion can be particularly prominent in the realm of intelligence, where activities such as the development of a new collection platform are often complex and obscured by security procedures that restrict most officers' access to information.

The accountability system seeks to recalibrate the relationship between accountability holders and holdees by creating an obligation for the holdee to explain and justify their conduct to the holder. The holders use their authority to access information, review the holdees' performance and pass judgements based on standards or objectives. If the behaviour of the holdees does not correspond to certain standards, they will have to explain this discrepancy to the holder, who might redirect them or even impose some sanctions.[2]

In practice, intelligence accountability occurs in a variety of settings that bring together multiple accountability holders and intelligence providers.[3] The accountability process is political when intelligence officers answer to political appointees, and elected officials to their constituents. Accountability is administrative when it relies on the hierarchical lines of authority that connect senior executives to their employees.[4] The accountability regime applying to intelligence professionals depends on the rules, culture and priorities of the organisation they work for.[5] For example, the accountability regimes that applied to a CIA operator working in the Middle East under non-official cover in the weeks following the 9/11 attacks and an IT contractor for the Department of Energy's Office of Intelligence and Counterintelligence in the mid-1990s vary because of the different rules and procedures, institutional settings and threat environments they work in. The existence of multiple reporting channels complicates the task of these accountability holdees who need to manage the expectations of various holders, sometimes both at the political and administrative levels. What constitutes appropriate and effective conduct in the eyes of a CIA officer might not be considered as such by her chief of station, a political appointee working at the Department of Energy or a congressional staffer. The significance these various actors give to democratic values and national security imperatives has a decisive impact on the conduct of intelligence. On the whole, the interplay between their decisions determines their accountability relationship and the broader relation between democracy and national security.

Accountability as a Process

Accountability relationships evolve and are best understood as a process that encompasses the following phases (represented in Figure 1.1): first, an issue or a problem affects the relationship between the holder and the holdee; second, the accountability holder responds to this problem; and third, this leads to specific outcomes. An accountability problem occurs when one or more of three basic conditions for accountability is not satisfied: the holder needs to have access to information on the holdee's conduct, adequate standards of conduct are well defined, and he needs to be able and willing to refer to and implement these standards. Based on available information, an accountability holder refers to moral, political and legal standards to judge the

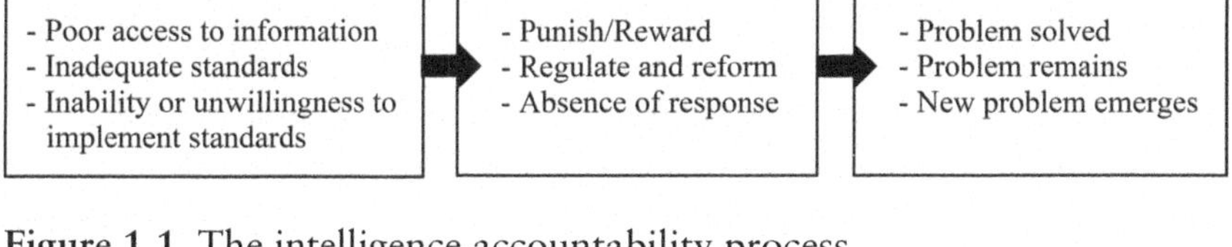

Figure 1.1 The intelligence accountability process.

accountability holdee's conduct and apply available sanctions. According to the situation, each accountability holder has different access to relevant information, adopts a specific position regarding existing standards, and holds enough authority to enforce his position if he wishes to do so. New developments in the practice of intelligence or on the political arena can cause a lapse in these conditions and lead to accountability problems. Depending on the conditions in which these problems emerge, accountability holders might fail to identify them.

Accountability holders need expertise, human and financial resources and the appropriate legal authority, or need to know, to access relevant information and make sense of it in a timely manner. When access to information is secured, the holder takes a position regarding the trade-off between national security and liberal democracy. This trade-off comes down to the dialectic of means and ends, and – in a democracy – is spelled out in the following question: to what extent can the government maintain effective intelligence services without threatening democracy itself?[6] To make their decisions, accountability holders can consider whether the means that are deployed – intelligence collection techniques, for example – are necessary and proportionate to the objectives of a mission (the scope and the nature of the security threat to be defused).

The primary mission of intelligence agencies is to further national security, particularly the physical security of the people and the political system in which they live. In a democracy, national security supports a political system – established through the apparatus of government – which the people consider worth living in and defending. The US government is characterised by an adherence to the liberal democratic values that are enshrined in the Constitution of 1789. These values are understood broadly as civil liberties including freedom of speech, freedom of assembly, protection against unreasonable seizures, government transparency, and the rule of law. Depending on the situation, decisions can favour liberties over security, security over liberties, affect the one but not the other, lower or further liberties and security at the same time. Liberal democratic values define the democratic order and are an essential part of national security in a modern democracy. Over time, democratic states cannot achieve legitimacy and stability unless they consistently respect fundamental freedoms and the rule of law. In the best cases, national security and respect for liberal democratic values reinforce each other.[7] Here, intelligence oversight helps maintain the integrity of intelligence agencies and contributes to their effectiveness by focusing security policies on vital and proportionate operations. In the 1990s, the CIA awarded the Agency Seal Medallion to Senator Daniel Patrick Moynihan (D-NY), a former chairman of the Senate Select Committee on Intelligence and vocal supporter of government transparency, for having demonstrated 'that effective oversight of intelligence can be realized in a democratic nation without risk to the intelligence process'.[8] Democratic oversight and government transparency should encourage government officials to develop sound intelligence policies and decisions. However, official decisions, including the award of government contracts, are driven by multiple factors beyond effectiveness and efficiency.

Countering security threats sometimes requires compromising some liberties. Secrecy and transparency inevitably clash as necessary intelligence actions, such as government surveillance, directly impinge upon the right to privacy. Policy-makers and intelligence professionals are under pressure to make the most effective use of their limited resources to ensure national security. Such a burden can foster a tendency to increase surveillance powers at all costs. Public support for security measures limiting civil liberties initially increased after the 9/11 attacks, and the government expanded its surveillance powers.[9] Particularly high levels of threats can encourage government officials to engage in domestic spying, even if they know many stakeholders will be concerned about infringement on civil liberties. The Palmer Raids carried out by the Bureau of Investigation in the early twentieth century, the domestic activities of the CIA in the early Cold War and, more recently, the NSA surveillance programme PRISM all attest to the persistence of the tension between national security imperatives and civil liberties, and the involvement of both government and private organisations in controversial programmes.[10]

The growth of government intelligence activities has generated concern over the effects of secrecy on democracy. Secrecy is an essential and a legitimate means of protecting intelligence sources and methods. However, government and corporate secrecy limits public access to information and public understanding of what intelligence services do on their behalf. Journalists like Dana Priest and William Arkin have argued that the growth of intelligence outsourcing in the twenty-first century hides a worrying expansion of secret intelligence activities.[11] In their work they correctly note that government secrecy spreads far beyond government to include hundreds of thousands of contractors who hold a security clearance. However, intelligence scholars Richard Aldrich and Christopher Moran find paradoxically that Western societies are entering a new era of transparency fostered by new technologies and the growth of intelligence workforces.[12] As these conflicting positions demonstrate, the extent to which intelligence outsourcing hides and reveals intelligence practices is unclear.

Although executive decisions, Congress, the press and whistleblowers can limit government secrecy, the tension between secrecy and transparency will not disappear. In many ways this tension defines intelligence practices in modern democracies. It is particularly obvious when intelligence officers and contractors leak sensitive government information.[13] At the individual level, deciding what constitutes the proper balance between secrecy and transparency, and by extension what constitutes proper accountability, is subjective. While former officer Thomas Drake and former contractor Edward Snowden consider that they blew the whistle on abusive NSA programmes, their critics point out that they failed to follow the proper channels to voice their concerns and, ultimately, their leaks damaged US national security.

In the worst cases, careless decision paths jeopardise the effectiveness of intelligence activities and threaten liberal democratic values. Such accountability problems result from the violation or the distortion of a delegation of public authority, from the people to the elected officials, from the elected officials to the bureaucracy and from the bureaucracy to the private sector. When political appointees impose their political preferences on intelligence analysts, they threaten the independence and the quality of the work produced by the intelligence community, and they undermine its core mission: speaking truth to power. An intelligence agency using extreme interrogation methods can both disregard human rights and threaten national security. Besides the fact that scientific research has cast doubt on the effectiveness of such collection techniques, public knowledge of their use – by government employees or contractors – can impact negatively on the battle for hearts and minds, which is often considered to be central to the success of counter-insurgency campaigns.[14]

Accountability holders' position on the trade-off between national security priorities and democratic values reflects their place in the system of intelligence accountability and their preference at a certain point in time. In some cases, legal standards may force them to take action; in other situations, discretion will give them more room to interpret political and moral standards. When Snowden leaked sensitive government information to journalists and flew to Russia, he used his discretion and decided to break the law. By contrast, Drake shared information with a journalist and decided to stay in the United States.[15] Once accountability holders have accessed relevant information and assessed the situation, they decide whether to implement standards. If they wish to do so, they can threaten to use or make use of their authority to rectify what they perceive to be a problematic situation. When one or more conditions of accountability – access to information, existence of adequate standards, and authority and willingness to use them – are not satisfied, a problem emerges and leaves a trail of evidence. Insiders can experience or witness problems first-hand, or learn about them from colleagues discussing an internal investigation. Sometimes, problems go unheeded for a while before somebody identifies them. Outsiders learn about problems when they become public either through operational failures or disclosures of information.

The literature on intelligence accountability often takes the emergence of a problem as a point of reference to make the distinction between anticipatory and reactive oversight. This distinction is derived from political scientists Mathew McCubbins and Thomas Schwartz's seminal study of congressional oversight, in which they emphasise the distinction between two ideal-typical forms of oversight: police-patrol and fire-alarm. Congressional overseers engage in police-patrol when, at their own initiative, they examine a sample of executive agency activities 'with the aim of detecting and remedying any violations of legislative goals and, by its surveillance, discouraging such violations'. Fire-alarm oversight relies on a system of rules, procedures and practices, or standards. The violation of a rule triggers a fire alarm and attracts the attention of key accountability holders who will seek to remedy the situation. McCubbins and Schwartz find that members of Congress prefer to act as fire-fighters because it suits their capabilities and purpose.[16] Intelligence scholars have made similar findings. Anticipatory oversight through periodic or improvised meetings, phone calls and other means of communication plays, at best, a limited role in the intelligence accountability process. This form of oversight is also difficult to trace for an outsider.[17] Significant accountability actions, such as internal investigations, congressional hearings and new regulations, are generally, not to say always, triggered by some form of stimulus. Thus, reactive oversight or firefighting is more visible to outsiders and has been more widely discussed in the literature.

The question of what stimuli trigger responses (the second step in my model of intelligence accountability) is crucial to understanding accountability holders' willingness to take responsibility. An accountability holder may be aware of a problem, but not willing to invest the capital necessary to get informed and take action. Accountability can also escalate from a limited, administrative level to a more intensive level, usually involving political actors and public decisions. The key difference between limited and more intensive accountability is the involvement of media and interest groups, which bring issues to the attention of society and into the political arena. At this political level, indicators such as press releases, news articles and public hearings all point to the existence of problems and can prompt responses from a variety of accountability holders. Of course, a problem can also remain unidentified, in which case nobody will seek to tackle it.

The recognition of a problem should provoke information sharing between accountability holders and holdees through meetings and reports. This initial step can help the responsible authorities develop viable policy options to palliate regulatory gaps and other issues revealed by the accountability problem. Depending on how strong accountability triggers are, and how well the conditions for accountability have been fulfilled, accountability holders will or will not make decisions to solve the problem that has been identified. Accountability holders can reward or punish holdees, for example by promoting or demoting them. They can also regulate on the problem and reform accountability procedures.[18] In the mid-1970s Congress investigated abusive intelligence practices and, in an under-regulated and highly political context, reformed the US system of intelligence accountability to establish permanent congressional intelligence committees. This reform was a turning point in the history of US intelligence that institutionalised a more democratic approach to intelligence affairs. In some cases, accountability holders might decide not to intervene, either because they do not have the authority to do so, or because they prefer not so do so at a specific point in time. In other words, what outsiders might perceive as a lack of punishment does not always signal an absence of oversight.

In the third and final step of the accountability model developed in this book, accountability responses lead to three types of outcomes. First, in the best scenario, appropriate decisions are implemented, and lead to a sustainable outcome – the problem is solved and the accountability process is successful. Given the variety of actors and issues involved in the intelligence accountability process, the possibility that an accountability holder takes some appropriate decisions but does not solve a problem completely is likely. This second type of outcome could, for example, involve decisions that provide better access to information but overlook the existence of inadequate standards and procedures, or decisions that only solve a problem temporarily. Third, in the worst-case scenario, the accountability holder completely fails to solve a problem or creates new problems, and the outcome of the accountability process is unsatisfactory. At any stage, accountability holders who are not satisfied with the outcome may want to reconsider the situation and push for change. The accountability process will start again.

An Institutional Overview of Intelligence Accountability in the United States

The conceptual model of accountability used in this book brings together multiple actors across the public-private divide. In the United States, the accountability relationship between the people and their government is diluted into a set of institutional relations between the three branches of government. Each branch checks and balances the others' powers and, when doing so, acts both as an accountability holder and holdee.[19] Most scholars approach intelligence accountability from this institutional perspective and emphasise the role and positions adopted by one or more branches of government.[20] Since government institutions are accountable to the people, who delegated sovereignty to them, the role of wider society including citizens and private organisations such as the news media and contractors is also crucial to understanding the accountability process.[21] In the US, public and private actors interact with each other in various ways to create one of the most elaborate systems of intelligence accountability in the world. This section provides a basic overview of the role played by each of these intelligence accountability holders based on existing literature, and indicates where contractors fit into the system.

The executive branch bears the primary responsibility for the scope and conduct of national security and dominates the US system of intelligence accountability.[22] The executive control of intelligence activities focuses on meeting national security requirements. At the highest level, the President sets national security priorities and communicates them through strategic documents and public announcements. He issues Executive Orders and Directives that structure and guide the national intelligence effort, *and* nominates intelligence leaders like the Director of National Intelligence (DNI) and the Director of the CIA, who set agendas reflecting his priorities once they are in office.[23]

When carrying out his responsibilities, the President is helped by a series of institutions. The National Security Council (NSC) plans policies, coordinates their implementation and monitors national security operations on behalf of the President.[24] The President's Intelligence Advisory Board (PIAB) offers expert advice to the President on intelligence matters, and has no line authority.[25] Within the PIAB, the Intelligence Oversight Board (IOB) 'oversees the Intelligence Community's compliance with the Constitution and all applicable laws, Executive Orders, and Presidential Directives'.[26] The Office of Management and Budget (OMB) national security staff helps the President allocate national resources and provides programmatic guidance to all relevant departments and agencies to implement his political agenda. Two of the OMB's most important tasks are the formulation and execution of the US intelligence budget, and the oversight of government agencies' performance.[27] When the President believes that ordinary procedures will not be sufficient to expose problems, he can use his authority to establish a temporary commission of enquiry. In 1975, President Ford set up the Commission on CIA Activities within the United States to investigate allegations that the agency had conducted illegal domestic activities.[28]

At a lower level, departments and agencies implement intelligence policies and their employees conduct key intelligence activities supposed to fulfil policy objectives. The executive branch is organised in a hierarchical fashion, which gives senior officials varying degrees of control over their employees' activities, whether they are civil servants or contractors. Senior officials benefit from a unique position from which they can set the conditions that lead to the achievement of the administration's policies.[29] They are regular consumers of intelligence products and the feedback they provide to public and private intelligence producers can be considered as a form of control that guides and, when necessary, redirects intelligence activities. Executive control primarily occurs through day-to-day management and administrative accountability in each intelligence agency. The significant number of organisations involved in the national intelligence effort, and the diversity of their missions, has given birth to a vast system of guidelines and directives. These regulations help to coordinate individuals' goals with those of their organisation.

At this internal level of accountability, informal and formal sanctions – ranging from verbal warnings about poor performance to suspension, demotion and removal – help superiors correct the behaviour of their supervisees. In the Department of Defense (DoD), for instance, the Under Secretary of Defense for Intelligence exercises oversight over the Defense Intelligence Agency (DIA), the National Geospatial-Intelligence Agency (NGA), the National Reconnaissance Office (NRO) and the NSA. This Under Secretary acts both as Director of Defense Intelligence and as the primary military intelligence advisor to the Director of National Intelligence. When regulatory violations occur, intelligence officers must identify, investigate and report them through their chain of command to the DoD Senior Intelligence Oversight Official.[30] Intelligence agencies rely on their general counsel, who works with the Department of Justice, to ensure the legality of the activities conducted by their employees.[31] Within each intelligence agency, an Inspector General (IG) investigates, inspects and audits programmes and operations to control their regularity and effectiveness.[32] IGs report to the head of their agency or department and to Congress. They are important actors in this accountability system because they have the authority to access sensitive information, the expertise necessary to understand it, a certain degree of autonomy within their agency, and the ability to trigger external oversight when they share information with Congress.[33]

The executive branch benefits from a positional authority associated with its role in the implementation of intelligence policies. Intelligence officials enjoy direct access to relevant information and considerable expertise. They can withhold information to protect sources and methods, and prevent external oversight or create apertures.[34] Intelligence agencies decide on people's access to information when they supervise declassification programmes and requests, vet both their own employees as well as congressional staffers and lawyers who require access to classified information.[35] However, intelligence officials and their political masters are not free to do as they wish; Congress and the courts can review their decisions and limit executive powers.

The legislative branch has a broad oversight mandate echoing the democratic legitimacy of its members. At the most general level, Congress has the power to legislate on intelligence matters and frame mandates, methods and structures. The legal framework established by Congress plays a crucial role in delimiting the capabilities of the intelligence community. Congress passed the National Security Act of 1947, which laid the foundation of the modern US national security apparatus, and amended this act multiple times to adapt intelligence structures and processes. The act now includes multiple references to contracts and the role of contractors in the intelligence community.[36] In 2004, legislators reformed the intelligence community to establish the ODNI.[37] As the representative of the taxpayers, Congress authorises (approves programmes and activities) and appropriates (allocates specific amounts of money to authorised programmes) funds for the intelligence budget on a yearly basis. The congressional power of the purse is the ultimate instrument of guidance and oversight. Congress uses this power to set personnel ceilings, orient key intelligence programmes and oversee their execution.[38] The Senate also has the power to confirm or reject the nomination of senior intelligence officials, which makes it partly responsible for these officials' policies.

When carrying its oversight functions, Congress relies on a pool of expertise provided by its staffers, investigative bodies such as the Government Accountability Office (GAO), the Congressional Research Service (CRS) and the Congressional Budget Office (CBO), as well as wider society. Congressional oversight is organised along committee lines. By restraining intelligence oversight to the work of a few committees, Congress acknowledges the need for secrecy and maintains some degree of democratic accountability. Since the mid-1970s, two committees are dedicated to the oversight of intelligence activities: the House Permanent Select Committee on Intelligence (HPSCI) and the Senate Select Committee on Intelligence (SSCI). At least a dozen additional committees oversee specific aspects of the government's intelligence activities. These committees' staffers investigate allegations of wrongdoing and abuse, the performance of intelligence agencies and any other matter of interest.

Members of the HPSCI and the SSCI benefit from subpoena powers, which give them full and current access to any piece of information deemed relevant to the course of their function.[39]

They can send ad hoc or more systematic requests for information to the executive branch, and summon intelligence officials and experts to testify at a hearing. A select group of congressional leaders receives prior notification of covert actions. Although these senior representatives cannot formally veto covert actions, they can use notifications as a lever against the executive branch and threaten to withdraw their support to other policies.[40] In exceptional circumstances, Congress can authorise the establishment of a commission of enquiry. For example, representatives established the National Commission on Terrorist Attacks Upon the United States (the 9/11 Commission) jointly with the President.[41] All of these powers can be used to access information, identify problems and solutions, set accountability standards and procedures, punish and reward intelligence officials.

Congress lies at the forefront of American political life, which grants it a capacity to focus public attention. Given its unique position and its strong democratic legitimacy, Congress carries some of the responsibility to explain national security to society and use public hearings, statements, reports, and outreach to the news media to make intelligence activities as transparent as possible. This capacity to investigate and disseminate information can foster other congressional actions or simply act as a mechanism of reputational accountability pushing the executive branch to take action. Occasionally, congressional investigations impact more clearly on the balance of powers within the government. In 1975, the investigations carried out by the United States Senate Select Committee to Study Governmental Operations with Respect to Intelligence Activities (also called the Church Committee, by the name of its chairman, Democrat Senator Frank Church of Idaho) shed light on a series of abuses of civil liberties committed by the FBI and the CIA in the early Cold War. In a context of crisis in government legitimacy following the Watergate scandal, the rise of the civil rights movement and the opposition to the Vietnam War, this committee's work paved the way for the institutionalisation of the congressional and judicial oversight of intelligence activities.[42]

These powers place Congress at the centre of the US system of intelligence accountability. Yet representatives often lack both time and expertise to devote to intelligence oversight. In 2016, the SSCI relied on forty-four staff members to help oversee seventeen intelligence agencies and a budget exceeding $50 billion.[43] Only a limited number of employees at the GAO, the CRS and the CBO specialise in national security and have the security clearance required to access sensitive information. Under these conditions, overseers have to be extremely selective and are often forced to react to problems instead of anticipating them. Congress is also limited by its dependence on the executive branch: it can only reliably conduct oversight if intelligence officials are able and willing to exert control and be overseen. Congressional overseers are outsiders, and this position limits their knowledge and hold on intelligence activities. If Congress is completely unaware of some intelligence activities, it cannot be expected to ask intelligence officials about them. If intelligence officials are unaware of a problem, they cannot be expected to alert their congressional overseers.[44] Even when congressional overseers learn about problems, they have limited recourse to change the behaviour of intelligence agencies. Legislators are generally reluctant to curtail funding for a programme or discuss it publicly because they feel bound by the secrecy that protects intelligence sources and methods. Criticising or punishing the intelligence community is politically risky and unlikely to generate the political capital representatives need for re-election.[45]

The judicial branch distinguishes itself from the other institutions of government by its strong reliance on the standard of legality. The courts guarantee the rights of litigants against abusive governmental actions and play a vital role in the reconciliation of liberty and national security, or individual rights and the acquisition of personal information by the intelligence community.[46] At the highest level, the Supreme Court has made a series of decisions interpreting the 'unreasonable search and seizure' clause of the Fourth Amendment to the Constitution.[47] Lower-level federal courts rely on a broad set of regulations to review the decisions made by intelligence officials and their partners. The vast legal regime applying to government agencies allows the courts to review intelligence matters in such diverse areas as classification, espionage convictions, surveillance and civil liberties, human rights and labour rights, as well as contracting.[48]

The power of the courts is limited because they can only adjudicate to the extent the executive branch grants them access to information. The courts provide some anticipatory oversight when intelligence officials submit informal requests for clarification or formal requests for surveillance warrants.[49] In the aftermath of the Watergate scandal and following revelations that government agencies had tapped the personal communications of US citizens, Congress passed the Foreign Intelligence Surveillance Act (FISA) of 1978. This act established the Foreign Intelligence Surveillance Court (FISC) and granted it 'jurisdiction to hear applications for and grant orders approving electronic surveillance anywhere within the United States'. The surveillance requests submitted to this court must target a foreign power or the agent of a foreign power.[50] Most of the academic research on the judicial oversight of intelligence has focused on the role played by the FISC and overlooks the role of more traditional courts. Critics emphasise the deference of the FISC to the executive branch. Studying intelligence outsourcing opens up a different and under-researched set of issues – such as waste, fraud and abuse – on which federal courts adjudicate. Overall, judicial review depends on the regulations enacted by the executive and legislative branches, and the ability and willingness of key individuals to invoke these rules.[51] Despite some limitations, the judiciary's ability to review executive and legislative decisions, and defend individual rights, make it an essential part of the US system of intelligence accountability.

In the US political system, citizens, think tanks, academia, interest groups and companies also contribute to intelligence accountability. Societal scrutiny of intelligence takes many forms. Citizens regularly hold their representatives in the executive and legislative branches to account through elections. However, intelligence affairs scarcely appear to have determined the outcome of presidential and congressional elections; if anything, there seems to be an electoral disconnection.[52] Despite this disconnection, democratic elections act as a deterrent and force policy-makers to maintain a minimum level of public consent with their policies. Though there is a lack of research on this topic, public opinion can be expected to impact on intelligence affairs, for example, by persuading representatives to take a more critical stance towards controversial intelligence programmes.[53]

Societal actors facilitate accountability actions but generally lack the authority to impose their positions and drive change. Coverage of the Snowden leaks by reputable newspapers like the *New York Times* demonstrated how the media can educate and mobilise public opinion, convey shifts in preferences and boost reputational accountability. Major newspapers have historically used their capacity to reach the US electorate to increase public pressure on the government by revealing abuses. The *New York Times*'s 1972 front page on CIA operations against American anti-war activists is a good example of an article that revealed executive abuses of power, eventually triggering congressional investigations that culminated in the creation of permanent intelligence oversight committees. In the long run, regular and balanced reporting of national security affairs fosters public awareness of intelligence issues.[54] Besides the news media, companies can limit the government's intelligence activities more directly by refusing to cooperate with federal agencies. When the administration of George W. Bush started a warrantless wiretap programme in the aftermath of the 9/11 attacks, some telecommunications companies preferred not to cooperate. Apparently, the legal and reputational risks of getting involved in the programme outweighed other rationales for cooperating with the government.[55] The roles companies and contractors can play as accountability holders will be explored at various points in this book to expand the traditional understanding of intelligence accountability in the United States.

Despite remarkable achievements, societal scrutiny of intelligence activities remains limited. Societal actors lack institutional assets and authorities to exert immediate and systematic effects on intelligence policies and activities.[56] Interest groups can directly litigate against the government or provide support to citizens pursuing litigations against the government. For example, the American Civil Liberties Union (ACLU) successfully litigated under the FOIA to gather and publicise a series of government documents on rendition, detention and interrogation during the presidency of George W. Bush.[57] Though the ACLU directly challenged the government's position on the trade-off between national security and government transparency, the judiciary branch had the final word and decided that releasing some of the requested documents was acceptable.[58]

The work of media and public interest groups can be biased, sensationalist and inaccurate due to their limited access to information and political agenda. Media coverage of intelligence outsourcing has largely pictured contractors as 'bad guys'. However, the history of US intelligence shows that government officials make mistakes and contractors can get it right. Accountability is a matter of perspective. While civil liberties advocates praised the Snowden leaks, intelligence officials strongly condemned them and the media coverage that followed.[59] Leaks can foster public debate, but at what cost? Besides the damage unauthorised disclosures of sensitive information can do to intelligence sources and methods, their impact on accountability is debatable. Public scrutiny through leaks is often confined to a reactive role of 'regulation by revelation'.[60] When relying on leaks of information, the public risk relying on an unrepresentative source of information, revealing only one part of a broader story. Though external and unofficial means of scrutiny foster participative democracy and a sense of accountability, they are not free from bias.

The academic literature on intelligence accountability does not address the place of contractors and the practice of outsourcing. Outsourcing creates a need to design procedures that allow government officials to gain access to information on contractors and incentivising contractors' behaviour to keep it in line with the public interest.[61] Executive control, legislative oversight, judicial and societal scrutiny offer multiple opportunities to hold contractors and their government sponsors to account, but the extent to which these accountability channels have been used is unclear.[62] Given the important role contractors play in the intelligence community, understanding how they fit into the US intelligence effort and system of democratic accountability is crucial. To develop a more robust understanding of the relationship between intelligence accountability and outsourcing, the next chapter explores the institutionalisation of US intelligence from the origins of the Republic to the end of the Cold War.

Notes

1. Gailmard, 'Accountability and Principal-Agent Theory'.
2. Bovens, 'Analysing and Assessing Accountability'.
3. Mugan, '"Accountability": An Ever-Expanding Concept?', pp. 555–7.
4. Behn, *Rethinking Democratic Accountability*, pp. 59–60; Grant and Keohane, 'Accountability and Abuses of Power in World Politics', p. 36; Owen E. Hughes, *Public Management and Administration*, pp. 194–5.
5. Romzek and Dubnick, 'Accountability in the Public Sector'; Weber, 'The Question of Accountability in Historical Perspective'; Lester, *When Should State Secrets Stay Secret?*, p. 32; Zegart, *Spying Blind*, p. 45.
6. Lustgarten and Leigh, *In from the Cold*, p. viii.
7. Powers, 'Introduction', p. 3; Dujmovic, 'Getting CIA History Right', p. 238.
8. Powers, 'Introduction', p. 3. Sceptics might note that the CIA might have awarded this medal to Moynihan to tame his severe criticism of the agency.
9. Trouteaud, 'Civil Liberties', p. 175; US Congress, Public Law 107–56, *Uniting and Strengthening America by Providing Appropriate Tools Required to Intercept and Obstruct Terrorism Act of 2001*, 107th Congress, 2nd session, 26 October 2001.
10. Jeffreys-Jones, *The CIA and American Democracy*; Jeffreys-Jones, *The FBI: A History*; editor, 'NSA Slides Explain the PRISM Data-Collection Program', *Washington Post*, 6 June 2013, available at <http://www.washingtonpost.com/wp-srv/special/politics/prism-collection-documents/> (accessed 28 May 2018).
11. Priest and Arkin, *Top Secret America*.
12. Aldrich and Moran, '"Delayed Disclosure"'.
13. On Drake, see Jane Mayer, 'The Secret Sharer: Is Thomas Drake an Enemy of the State?', *New Yorker*, 23 May 2011, pp. 46–56.
14. Nagl, *Learning to Eat Soup with a Knife*; Dickson, 'Counter-Insurgency and Human Rights in Northern Ireland'; Duke and Van Puyvelde, 'The Science of Interrogation'.
15. Between 1947 and 2015, the US government tried 177 US government employees and thirty contractors on espionage-related charges. See Herbig, *The Expanding Spectrum of Espionage by Americans*, p. 14.
16. McCubbins and Schwartz, 'Congressional Oversight Overlooked', pp. 165–6.

17. Johnson, 'Governing in the Absence of Angels'; Zegart, 'The Domestic Politics of Irrational Intelligence Oversight', p. 5.
18. Kingdon, *Agendas, Alternatives, and Public Policies*, 20; Durbin, *CIA and the Politics of US Intelligence Reform*, p. 36.
19. Neustadt, *Presidential Power and the Modern Presidents*, p. 29.
20. For examples of institutional approaches to intelligence accountability, see Johnson, *A Season of Inquiry*; Johnson, 'The Contemporary Presidency'; Born and Leigh, *Making Intelligence Accountable*.
21. Van Puyvelde, 'Intelligence Accountability and the Role of Public Interest Groups'; Hillebrand, 'The Role of News Media in Intelligence Oversight'.
22. Lester, *When Should State Secrets Stay Secret?*
23. Executive Order 12333, United States Intelligence Activities, 4 December 1981.
24. Jordan et al., *American National Security*, p. 81.
25. Ibid. p. 165.
26. White House, 'The President's Intelligence Advisory Board', available at <http://www.whitehouse.gov/administration/eop/piab> (accessed 28 May 2018).
27. White House, 'The Mission and Structure of the Office of Management and Budget', available at <http://www.whitehouse.gov/omb/organization_mission/> (accessed 28 May 2018).
28. Nelson A. Rockefeller et al., Commission on CIA Activities within the United States, *Report to the President*, 6 June 1975, available at <http://archive.org/stream/reporttopresiden01unit#page/n9/mode/2up> (accessed 28 May 2018). See also Hastedt, 'Foreign Policy by Commission'.
29. DCAF Intelligence Working Group, 'Intelligence Practice and Democratic Oversight – A Practitioner's View', *DCAF Occasional Papers no.* 3 (2003), p. 39.
30. US Department of Defense, 'About the Department of Defense Senior Intelligence Oversight Official', available at <http://dodsioo.defense.gov/About-DOD-SIOO/> (accessed 28 May 2018). This position was formerly named Assistant to the Secretary of Defense for Intelligence Oversight. See Lotz, 'The United States Department of Defense Intelligence Oversight Programme, p. 122.
31. Lowenthal, *Intelligence: From Secrets to Policy*, p. 284. For example see Radsan, '*Sed Quis Custodiet Ipsos Custodes*'.
32. Frederick M. Kaiser, *Statutory Offices of Inspector General: Past and Present*, Congressional Research Service Report for Congress, 25 September 2008.

33. Lester, *When Should State Secrets Stay Secret?*, pp. 56–60.
34. Ibid. p. 132; Johnson, 'Accountability and America's Secret Foreign Policy', pp. 113–14.
35. See for example Central Intelligence Agency, *Freedom of Information Act*, available at <http://www.foia.cia.gov/> (accessed 28 May 2018).
36. US Congress, Public Law 80–253, *National Security Act of 1947*, 80th Congress, 1st session, 16 July 1947; Office of the Director of National Intelligence, 'IC Legal Reference Book: 1947 National Security Act', available at <https://www.dni.gov/index.php/ic-legal-reference-book/national-security-act-of-1947> (accessed 28 May 2018).
37. US Congress, Public Law 108–458, *Intelligence Reform and Terrorism Prevention Act*, 108th Congress, 2nd session, 17 December 2004.
38. Lowenthal, *Intelligence: From Secrets to Policy*, pp. 287–91.
39. US Code, Title 50, Section 3091, *General Congressional Oversight Provisions* (2016).
40. Lester, *When Should State Secrets Stay Secret?*, pp. 126–39; Lowenthal, *Intelligence: From Secrets to Policy*, pp. 293–4.
41. Zelikow et al., *The 9/11 Commission Report*, p. xv; US Congress, Public Law 107–306, *Intelligence Authorization Act for Fiscal Year 2003*, 107th Congress, 2nd session, 27 November 2002.
42. US Senate, Select Committee to Study Governmental Operations with Respect to Intelligence Activities, Book II, *Intelligence Activities and the Rights of Americans*, 94th Congress, 2nd session, 26 April 1976; US Senate, Public Law 95–511, *Foreign Intelligence Surveillance Act*, 95th Congress, 2nd session, 25 October 1978. On the institutionalization of external oversight of intelligence, see Lester, *Why Should State Secrets Stay Secret?*, pp. 74–139, 159–82; Johnson, 'Intelligence Shocks, Media Coverage, and Congressional Accountability', pp. 3–4.
43. Office of the Director of National Intelligence, US Intelligence Community Budget, available at <https://www.dni.gov/index.php/intelligence-community/ic-policies-reports/ic-policies-2?highlight=WyJidWRnZXQiXQ==> (accessed 28 May 2018); Senate Select Committee on Intelligence Staff Directory, available at <http://congressional-staff.insidegov.com/d/a/Senate/Senate-Select-Committee-on-Intelligence> (accessed 28 May 2018).
44. Posner, *Uncertain Shield*, p. 201; Zegart and Quinn, 'Congressional Intelligence Oversight'.
45. Lester, *When Should State Secrets Stay Secret?*, p. 104.
46. Issacharoff, 'Political Safeguards in Democracies at War', pp. 207–12.
47. See US Supreme Court, Olmstead v. United States, 277 US 438 (1928); US Supreme Court, Katz v. United States, 389 US 347 (1967).

48. Office of the Director of National Intelligence, Office of General Counsel, *Intelligence Community Legal Reference Book* (Washington, DC: ODNI 2012).
49. Born and Leigh, 'Democratic Accountability of Intelligence Services', p. 15.
50. US Congress, Public Law 95–511, Foreign Intelligence Surveillance Act, 25 October 1978, Section 103; US Code, Title 50, Chapter 36, Section 1804, Application for Court Orders, and Section 1823, Application for Order (2016).
51. National security lawyer A, interview with author, 28 July 2011, Washington, DC; Manget, 'Intelligence and the Rise of Judicial Intervention', p. 44.
52. Zegart and Quinn, 'Congressional Intelligence Oversight', pp. 760–4.
53. For a similar point on public opinion and foreign policy see Stuart Soroka, 'Media, Public Opinion, and Foreign Policy'; Page and Shapiro, 'Effects of Public Opinion on Policy'.
54. Seymour Hersh, 'Huge CIA Operation Reported in US Against Anti-War Forces, Other Dissidents in Nixon Years', *New York Times*, 22 December 1974, A1; Lester, *When Should State Secrets Stay Secret?*, pp. 89–90; Johnson, 'A Shock Theory of Congressional Accountability for Intelligence', pp. 344–5. For a more general account of the role of the press in US democracy, see Overholser and Jamieson, *Institutions of American Democracy: The Press*.
55. Mark Hosenball and Evan Thomas, 'Hold the Phone: Big Brother Knows Whom You Call', *Newsweek*, 22 May 2006, pp. 22–3; Ellen Nakashima and Dan Eggen, 'Former CEO Says US Punished Phone Firm', *Washington Post*, 13 October 2007, A1.
56. Caparini, 'Controlling and Overseeing Intelligence Services in Democratic States'.
57. American Civil Liberties Union, 'The Torture Report', available at <http://www.thetorturereport.org/node/8> (accessed 28 May 2018).
58. Van Puyvelde, 'Intelligence Accountability', p. 152.
59. Van Puyvelde, 'Médias, responsabilité gouvernementale et secret d'Etat'; Editor, 'The Black Budget', *Washington Post*, 29 August 2013, available at <http://www.washingtonpost.com/wp-srv/special/national/black-budget/> (accessed 28 May 2018).
60. Aldrich, 'Regulation by Revelation?'; Bruce, 'Laws and Leak of Classified Intelligence'.
61. Forrer et al., *Governing Cross-Sector Collaboration*, p. 52.
62. Savas, *Privatization and Public-Private Partnerships*, p. 301.

2 A Shared History of Successes and Excesses

This chapter examines the opportunities and risks accompanying public-private intelligence collaboration from the early days of the US Republic to the end of the Cold War. The values underpinning the formation of the United States have constituted a particularly permissive environment in which the private sector assumed an increasingly formalised role in national security affairs. In the early days of the Republic, the federal government remained reluctant to engage in intelligence activities, which left space for companies like the Pinkerton Agency to play a substantial role in the provision of intelligence services. At the dawn of the twentieth century, the government augmented its efforts to institutionalise intelligence but the public perception of intelligence as a disreputable activity slowed this process. The Second World War pushed the federal government to affirm its role in national security affairs and fostered the development of a robust industrial base to support US national security.

Throughout the Cold War, companies expanded their presence in the market for intelligence and supported the government's efforts in a host of different domains such as research and development (R&D) and counterintelligence and security. Among other collaborations, the successful development of the U-2 spy plane demonstrated that, under the right conditions, contracting could foster national security successes. However, the growing role played by contractors also caused some public concern. Critics feared the close bonds between the public and private sectors would weaken executive control and legislative oversight of the industry, and threaten the efficiency of the federal government's national security effort. In the mid-1970s congressional investigations revealed a series of intelligence abuses to the public, and showed that contractors had become entangled in government programmes that threatened civil liberties, human rights and government transparency. The growing collaboration between the intelligence community and the private sector also generated concern about the ability of contractors to keep national security secrets. All these concerns emphasised the need for government accountability holders to find an appropriate balance between controlling contractors and providing them with enough flexibility to excel.

The Public-Private Divide in US Political Culture

The significance given to liberalism and individualism in US political culture has influenced the conception of the public-private divide and the development of national security institutions. When the colonies declared their independence in 1776, the Founding Fathers of the United States drew inspiration to build a new political system from the writings of the libertarian philosophy that was so prominent in the late eighteenth century. Following the importance given to individual rights in the writings of the Enlightenment, the nature and scope of the government were to be defined by the degree to which they could guarantee the natural rights of citizens. In this conception, liberty and individual rights are intertwined, and the Bill of Rights embodies 'the American belief that freedom preserved *by* the state must always be qualified by guarantees of freedom *from* the state'.[1] Since individuality is the basis of the social order, the public interest is conceived as an addition of individual interests.

The representation of various interests characterises the American conception of sovereignty that power is disaggregated between the institutions of government and the people. These interests freely compete in the market for ideas, and according to James Madison, their concurrence compensates for humanity's lack of virtue.[2] This model of government empowers society and allows any individual or group of individuals concerned with a political decision to voice their concern to the government. This conception of sovereignty has impacted the roles given to the public and private sectors in

American society. The US Constitution of 1787 – the most elementary fundament of the rule of law – enshrines the limits of the confidence the American people delegates to the government, its public agencies and employees. In the US conception, the rule of law protects the private realm 'against incursions from the public domain of government'.[3] Public law scholar Élisabeth Zoller notes that the US republican model initially rejected the detachment between the state and civil society and made no formal distinction between public and private law.[4] It is only later, in the nineteenth century, that this distinction took shape. While the market emerged as 'a central legitimating institution', legal thought strived to develop a separation between public law and 'the law of private transactions'. In this context, private law was considered as 'a neutral system facilitating voluntary market transactions and vindicating injuries to private rights'.[5]

The US conception of the public-private distinction leaves relatively little space for the public sector to govern. This perspective is best exemplified by the Jeffersonian aphorism that 'government is best which governs least'.[6] Laissez-faire ideas, which have been prominent in US political thought, identify the realm of the market with individual freedom and progress and the realm of the government with coercion. In this liberal system, the private sector needs the public sector and appropriate government regulations to develop itself and prosper. Conversely, the federal government relies on the legitimacy of the market and the expertise of the private sector to further the public interest.[7] This conception of the public-private distinction contrasts with a social democratic tradition that associates the public sector with the pursuit of the public interest. In this tradition, government employees are held to stricter legal standards, they strive to maintain public support, and symbolise due process, administrative fairness, and the protection of citizens' rights. In contrast, the private sector is characterised by its pursuit of private interests and profit, and cannot be trusted with the furtherance of sensitive national security activities that are too close to the public interest.[8]

The idea of the government as a proponent of the public interest is also encountered in the United States. A senior government official notes, for instance, that civil servants have a 'duty of loyalty to the collective best interest of all' that commercial companies are lacking.[9] In reality, and despite the rhetoric of free market capitalism, state interventionism has also marked the development of the United States.[10] However, the contribution of the private sector and its market logic to the government's legitimacy and power has been openly embraced, and the correlation of public organisations with public interest and private organisations with private interests is not so straightforward. In contemporary America, the word public is often associated with a rather negative experience in such terms as 'public schools', 'public housing', while the private sector 'gets things done'.[11] In many ways, the private sector is more respected and accepted as a symbol of freedom. This cultural trait partly explains why the development and legitimisation of the US national security state has been accompanied by the growth of private sector support networks. Vice versa, US industrial development has been tied to government acquisition, as military contracts spurred a myriad of inventions that spilled over into the civilian realm.[12]

The importance given to the private sector is visible at different levels within US society, including in the realm of national security. Following a liberal notion, the federal government was given limited power to coerce its citizens. The role of the people in maintaining their security is reflected in the Second Amendment to the Constitution, which draws a parallel between 'the security of a free State' and 'the right of the people to keep and bear Arms'. This amendment can also be related to the situation in the United States at the time, and particularly the fear of a professional army, the reliance on militias controlled by the individual states, and the subordination of the military to civilian control. Debates about the organisation of the military in a democratic society and the weight given to citizen soldiers and military professionals have been central throughout the history of American military policy.[13] Following the War of Independence (1775–83), the fear of federal despotism and standing armies combined to give considerable powers to individuals. Richard Morgan points to an 'antiexecutive element' in the American political tradition and traces its origins back to 'colonial resistance to royal governors'.[14] This fear of military establishments was expressed by President George Washington who, in his farewell address, deemed it crucial to 'avoid the necessity of those overgrown military establishments, which, under any form of government, are inauspicious to liberty, and which are to be regarded as particularly hostile to Republican Liberty'.[15] In the United States, individually armed citizens can freely gather in militias to ensure those in power respect their liberties and their political freedom. The American Revolution (1763–83) clearly demonstrated a preference for a 'citizen army motivated by duty and patriotism' opposing 'an old-style army that included the use of foreign mercenaries'.[16] Ever since the Revolution, citizens, militias and commercial companies have played a significant role in the provision of security to the US people and their allies.

Public and Private Intelligence in the Early Republic

In the early days of the US Republic, government decisions were decentralised and senior officials used a variety of ad hoc arrangements to harness the capabilities of societal actors. The history of US intelligence in this era is replete with examples of intelligence provided by non-governmental or private sources. Most of these services were provided in the context of wars since the establishment of a peacetime intelligence apparatus remained unacceptable. Before the War of Independence, Benjamin Franklin and the Continental Congress's Committee of Secret Correspondence relied on a series of agents who were paid to conduct specific missions. For example, in the late 1770s, Arthur Lee, a physician living in London, was tasked with finding out the position of foreign powers towards the Continental Congress. Lee met with a French agent to set up a trading firm called Roderigue Hortalez et Cie, which was a cover to arrange French financial support to the Continental Congress.[17] After the independence of the thirteen colonies in 1783, future President George Washington had his own experience in intelligence collection. Under his command, at the height of the American Revolutionary War, the Culper spy ring, a network of civilian auxiliaries, gathered information and led covert operations against the British army.[18]

Intelligence operations are bound to draw on the knowledge and cooperation of local agents to gather information on enemies and disrupt their plans. When these operations expand, leaders and governments tend to organise their intelligence efforts. At the start of his presidency, George Washington earmarked public funds to 'finance intelligence operations', but he did not establish a formal intelligence apparatus.[19] The lack of government intelligence structure pushed officials to rely on non-governmental actors. Intelligence remained decentralised and persons with relevant knowledge were enlisted when needed, as individuals or in groups, to carry out reconnaissance, as was the case in the Indian Wars.[20] The youth of public institutions and a shortage of public resources explain the US government's reliance on private networks in the late eighteenth and nineteenth centuries. State action relied on personalised contracts that delegated government authorities to private providers of supplies and services.[21] This reliance on non-governmental actors was not limited to intelligence, nor to the US case. From the sixteenth century onwards, the use of privateers – private warships authorised by a country's government to attack foreign shipping – allowed several Western countries to disrupt their adversaries' trade. Their use was common during the Revolutionary War, as they were entitled to attack enemy vessels in wartime.[22]

The public need for security, and the absence of a federal institution centralising the national security effort, left plenty of room for the private sector to expand its domain of activities. Among other organisations, the Pinkerton Agency became famous by providing security services to a wide range of clients, including the federal government. In many ways, the story of the Pinkerton Agency epitomises the role played by the private sector in the early history of US intelligence. Allan Pinkerton, a Scottish immigrant who had been a cooper, a deputy sheriff, and then a detective on the Chicago police force, established the agency in 1850. His agency was contracted by private railroad companies to protect their infrastructure in a time when lawlessness threatened many private interests. Pinkerton benefited from considerable exposure to elite networks in both the business and military realms, which allowed him to capture government contracts.[23]

During the Civil War (1861–5), the organisation of intelligence in the Union and the Confederacy was individualised and depended on commanders. When George B. McClellan became commander of the Union's Army of the Potomac, he hired Allan Pinkerton and his agents, whom he had contracted beforehand to secure his railroad company, to carry out intelligence functions as civilians.[24] The Pinkertons were not the only detective force involved in the Civil War. Lafayette Baker, another figure of the Civil War, carried out intelligence collection and counterintelligence for General Winfield Scott, the commander in chief of the US Army, and then for Secretary of State William Seward and Secretary of War Edwin M. Stanton. Baker later became a special agent for the War Department and was eventually promoted to the rank of Colonel in 1863. His trajectory and Pinkerton's show how, at an individual level, the boundaries between public and private sectors were already porous at the time.

Though Pinkerton and Baker played important roles in the war, they were never in charge of the entire intelligence apparatus. Pinkerton, for instance, was doing counter-espionage and interrogation of prisoners, but scouting and signals intelligence remained the domain of the division commander.[25] Besides these intelligence services, commercial companies provided much of the supplies that sustained the Civil War. The Union's reliance on private supplies was such that it overloaded the purchasing infrastructure of the government, leading to numerous cases of waste and fraud. The government lacked experienced officers to oversee its acquisitions and make sure that contractors respected their engagements. When the House of Representatives investigated government contracts during the Civil War, congressmen found that suppliers were 'irresponsible agents who sacrificed the public interests through lack of integrity'.[26]

Despite these concerns about the ascendancy of the public interest, private suppliers continued to play a crucial role in the provision of security. In the aftermath of the Civil War, Pinkerton was hired by Secretary of State Hamilton Fish to track American support to Cuban rebels. The Pinkertons also acted as an independent police force serving individuals, companies and the government; they conducted private investigations for firms such as Western

Union, combated international crime for other states, and set up the first US federal criminal database.[27] The role played by the Pinkerton agency in establishing the foundations of the Bureau of Investigation and the military intelligence services emphasises the federal government's inability or reluctance to engage in national security intelligence at the time. While the United States had yet to establish a permanent intelligence apparatus, private organisations offered a growing range of services to whoever was able and willing to pay.

The provision of security by the private sector was not restricted to the US experience. In the nineteenth century, private individuals as well as companies were acting as a police or detective force in France and Great Britain. However, the existence of a national police force and the historical monopoly of the public authority over means of coercion limited the expansion of private security in these two countries.[28] In the United States, where the state had not established a clear monopoly over national security functions, the private sector had an enduring influence. Towards the end of the nineteenth century, while the private detective industry was declining in France and Great Britain, private police and investigators became more potent in the United States.

Institutionalisation Attempts and Tensions

From the late nineteenth century onwards, the emergence of the public administration paradigm set a trend towards institutionalisation that laid the foundation of a more permanent US intelligence apparatus. The effort to institutionalise intelligence started in the late nineteenth century with the establishment of a series of organisations at the federal level. In 1863, the commander of the Army of the Potomac set up the Bureau of Military Information, which is generally regarded as the first professional intelligence agency in the United States. A series of intelligence agencies were then created in an attempt to streamline civilian and military intelligence. The Federal Secret Service of the Treasury Department was established in 1865, the Office of Naval Intelligence in 1882, the Military Intelligence Division in 1885, and the Bureau of Investigation in 1908 as a part of the Department of Justice. In 1896, Arthur Wagner, a US Army Major and military instructor, emphasised the importance of 'the services of a spy permanently attached to a command', and noted that these were 'likely to be much more valuable than those of one who is employed only for the single occasion, and whose efforts are not stimulated by a hope of profitable employment in the future'.[29] According to this view, the professionalisation of intelligence services would foster their continuity and reliability in the same way as for the US military in the first half of the nineteenth century. Perceptions were slowly evolving, but significant reticence persisted and new intelligence institutions remained limited in funding and capacities.[30]

The establishment of a handful of intelligence organisations demonstrated that the government was willing to exert some degree of control over the provision of intelligence, but it did not replace the role of the private sector. The overall utility of intelligence in peacetime remained disputed and the US government was reluctant to directly engage in intelligence activities. In his book on military doctrine, Wagner remarked: 'Spies may be primarily divided in two classes: military and civilian', and noted that the first ones are 'often men of the most exalted character and distinguished courage, and deserve a better fame, and a better fate if captured, than that usually accorded to spies'; while 'the second class consists of men who often deserve all the obloquy so freely cast upon spies in general'. The military instructor further recognised the necessity of espionage in wartime and considered that 'whatever their motives or individual characteristics, spies are indispensably necessary to a General'.[31] But centralisation and systematisation efforts through the development of doctrine and education were complicated by the absence of General Staff and War Colleges, and the widespread suspicion toward standing armies and associated phenomena.

At home, public fear of anything that could secretly threaten civil liberties continued to limit the institutionalisation of intelligence. In 1909, representatives considered that 'a general system of espionage was repugnant to our race'.[32] This rejection of intelligence as a dirty world fitted well with the idea Americans had of themselves as a righteous nation.[33] As a result, American intelligence capabilities remained relatively underdeveloped when compared to major powers such as Great Britain and France.[34]

In the absence of a well-established government apparatus, private organisations kept playing an important role in the provision of domestic security. Following the second industrial revolution (1870–1914), the maturation of capitalism and the market economy provided new opportunities for private security providers to expand their customer base beyond the government. Industries needed stability to prosper, and private agencies met their growing demand for security. The Thiel Detective Service Company and James R. Wood Detective Agency served both President McKinley and corporate managers. But private involvement in domestic security matters generated strains with public authorities. When the Pinkertons opened an office in New York in the 1890s, tensions emerged with the local police. Such problems became more frequent with the professionalisation and increasing centralisation of urban police during the Progressive Era, from the 1890s to the 1920s. The Pinkerton Agency, in particular, focused public attention on some of the most controversial activities carried out by the private security industry. Pinkerton employees allegedly infiltrated unions and incited them to carry out violent acts in order to provide evidence to arrest them. In 1892, Pinkerton agents violated the law when bearing weapons and opening fire against an angry crowd during the Homestead strikes in Pennsylvania. The 'massacre' that ensued seemed to confirm the charges of fabrication and class bias that were often held against the private agency. Public reactions to the 'massacre' expressed a growing feeling that 'protection [of property] should be rendered by the civil authorities'.[35] A series of states passed anti-Pinkerton laws, and Congress passed the Anti-Pinkerton Act of 1893 and a ban against services of quasi-military forces.

The diverse set of clients the Pinkerton agency served was another cause for concern. Trust in Pinkerton agents vanished as rumours suggested some of Pinkerton's employees were working for the Spanish government during the Spanish-American War of 1898. Prior to 1914, the Pinkertons had served foreign governments such as Britain, France, Russia, Canada and Germany, which posed a significant problem of reliability that discredited the commercial agency.[36] Public expectations regarding the provision of security were shifting in favour of public authorities. However, existing laws remained too narrow to restrict the development of the private security industry.[37] During President Wilson's first term (1913–17), the economic recession fostered increasing tensions between workers and their employers and private organisations continued to work for corporate managers to protect infrastructures, spy on labour movements and break strikes.[38]

The US government appeared less scrupulous to enlist the private sector in its intelligence collection efforts when the First World War approached. After the US entry into the war, Congress recognised the necessity of domestic surveillance and passed the controversial American Espionage Act of 1917. Fearing the rise of anarchism and communism following the October Revolution of 1917 in Russia, the Justice Department outsourced counter-revolutionary work to private detectives during the First World War. Apparently, the nascent Bureau of Investigation did not satisfy the government needs in this area. Most certainly, the Bureau did not have the national coverage and networks an agency such as Pinkerton's had at the time.[39] Public support for domestic surveillance grew after the end of the war and the creation of the Soviet Union in 1922.[40] However, counter-subversion efforts did not lead to the establishment of a government monopoly on domestic surveillance. The necessity of a more permanent intelligence capacity continued to conflict with the widely held view that espionage was immoral. Encroachments on the privacy of US citizens prompted an outcry from civil liberties groups concerned with freedom of speech.[41] Americans considered peacetime espionage as a 'corrupt outgrowth of Old World diplomacy, alien to the open and upright American way'.[42] While private organisations did not hesitate to spy at home and abroad, government leaders such as Presidents Wilson and Hoover continued to condemn intelligence activities. Secretary of State Henry Stimson decided to close down the State Department's cryptanalysis operations in 1929 and later explained that 'Gentlemen do not read each other's mail.' The moral standing of these public figures added to the US suspicion towards a big federal government, slowing the institutionalisation of intelligence and the formalisation of public-private intelligence collaboration.[43]

Similar concerns hindered the development of the US defence industry.[44] During the First World War, the government relied extensively on private supplies to feed the war effort. The War Department alone entered into thirty thousand contracts, forcing the government procurement scheme to evolve drastically.[45] This reliance on the industry caused significant concerns over the interlocking between the nation's war mechanism and its economic system. In the early 1930s, a special congressional committee reviewed the war mobilisation plan for the First World War and criticised the military-industrial alliance in peacetime. The committee was divided. One camp argued for more flexibility and discretion to facilitate public-private collaboration in support of future mobilisations, while the other advocated further government regulations over the industry. Popular books like *Merchants of Death* and *Blood, Iron and Profits* depicted the defence industry as a bunch of crooks who had engineered the US entry into the First World War.[46]

The rise of state interventionism to counter the effects of the Great Depression during the 1930s was an important step towards further institutionalisation at the federal level. President Roosevelt's New Deal reform programme (1933–8) put the government at the forefront of socio-economic policies. The New Deal was based upon the notion that the government could act as a centralising force for change, rallying public and private sectors in the interest of all in order to bring about economic recovery, wealth and security for the nation. The programme expanded the role of government and affected popular notions of this role. New Deal reforms, although they were waning from 1937 onwards, led to a rapprochement between the executive branch, Congress and the private sector.[47] This rapprochement would have long-standing effects on American political life, counteracting the American philosophy of laissez-faire. During Roosevelt's presidency (1933–45), the Federal Bureau of Investigation and its Director, J. Edgar Hoover, started to play a greater role in law enforcement, counterintelligence and security at the national level. In a symbolic shift from private to public authority, Hoover became the new Pinkerton. Remarkably, both Pinkerton and Hoover had a vested interest in hyping the threats they confronted to keep the money coming.[48]

While public attitudes toward the role of the federal government were evolving, private sector involvement in domestic security continued to generate public concern. The La Follette Civil Liberties Committee of the US Senate (1936–41) summoned representatives of the Pinkerton and Burns agencies to give testimony on their anti-labour activities.[49] The hearings led Majority Leader Robinson (D-AR) to put forward a resolution that held that 'the so-called industrial spy system breeds fear, suspicion and animosity, tends to cause strikes and industrial warfare and is contrary to sound public policy'.[50] Private companies were unpopular and increasingly relegated to the provision of industrial security services such as war plant protection. However, all these concerns were set aside as industries played a central role in implementing economic and military support to the government and its allies in the run-up to and throughout the Second World War.[51] When national security interests are at stake, public authorities rarely hesitate to harness private sector capabilities to augment national power.

An Era of Public–Private Expansion

The US entry into the Second World War was a turning point in intelligence history. The Japanese surprise attack on Pearl Harbor on 7 December 1941 acted as a catalyst, emphasising the importance of a more permanent intelligence apparatus able to gather, analyse and disseminate key information to senior decision-makers in a timely manner. The success of the Office of Strategic Services (OSS) during the war further demonstrated the importance of intelligence collection, analysis and covert operations. Even though the OSS was disbanded in 1945, public perceptions were shifting in favour of a more permanent intelligence apparatus.[52] The Second World War also cemented the relations between the government security apparatus and the private sector.[53] In order to wage total war, the United States used all possible means to enlist support from the industry and developed new forms and techniques of contracting. Many business executives served on government boards during the war and 'had come to accept, even expect, a degree of government intervention and control which they had deeply resented before the war'.[54] The public-private collaborations developed during the war spurred important innovations such as the development of the microwave radar, which significantly improved technical intelligence collection capabilities. The experience of the war convinced leaders on both side of the public-private divide that they should pursue their collaboration.[55]

In the aftermath of the war, increasing tension with the Soviet Union and the policy of containment of the Soviet Bloc aggravated the need for permanent intelligence organisations. Christopher Andrew considers that the real acceptance of intelligence gathering and covert operations – the two most controversial types of intelligence activity – in peacetime occurred during the presidency of Dwight D. Eisenhower (1953–61), who, even then, considered it to be a 'distasteful but vital necessity'.[56] In a nod to Stimson's famous phrase, Eisenhower's Director of Central Intelligence, DCI Allen Dulles, considered that 'when the fate of a nation and the lives of its soldiers are at stake, gentlemen do read each other's mail – if they can get their hands on it'.[57] In a period of fifteen years from 1946 to 1961, the federal government laid the foundations of the national security state. The National Security Act of 1947 established the DoD, the CIA and the National Security Council. Two years later the Central Intelligence Agency Act of 1949 clarified the powers of the CIA and formalised its ability to acquire goods and services from the private sector.[58] In 1952, President Truman signed a memorandum creating the NSA to 'provide an effective, unified organisation and control of the communications intelligence activities of the United States conducted against foreign governments'.[59] The establishment of the NRO and the DIA followed in the early 1960s.

This institutionalisation movement and a favourable economic context offered new opportunities to consolidate and formalise the ties between the intelligence community and the private sector. Large government expenditures in the domains of armament and welfare helped to overcome the pre-war depression years.[60] The arguments developed by scholars associated with the Chicago School of economics in the 1950s provided a rationale for economic liberalism and free markets, and partly inspired the government to privatise some of its functions. Proponents of privatisation argued that shifting the production of goods and services from the government to the private sector would foster competition, improve government performance and reduce expenditure.[61] These economic arguments were relatively well received by the US people, whose belief in self-government has historically been strong, and a series of government decisions set up the policy of contracting out commercial activities.[62] This policy facilitated the acquisition of increasingly sophisticated products and services from the defence industry. In turn, this industry thrived on the government's demand and cornered a growing part of the American economy.[63]

The contribution of the private sector to the national intelligence effort was particularly prominent in the domain of R&D. Companies generally benefit from a pool of research skills and knowledge that far exceeds government capabilities. The United States has traditionally put a great emphasis on the role of technology in waging war in order to achieve both material and information superiority. The Cold War and its arms race reinforced this American characteristic and brought R&D to the forefront of national security policies.[64] To overcome the isolation of communist societies, which were hard to infiltrate by human means, the intelligence community invested in technical means of intelligence collection.[65] The development of US overhead collection capabilities epitomises the nexuses between intelligence and technology and the public and private sectors. The origins of the RAND (for R and D) Corporation in 1946 as a project within the Douglas Aircraft plant in Santa Monica, CA, constitutes one of the most well-known examples of public-private cooperation in this context. The key figures involved in the launch of project RAND, such as Generals Henry 'Hap' Arnold and Curtis LeMay, were part of the military establishment and the defence industry. Their vision was to build a team of great minds to keep US technology ahead of the rest of the world. Project RAND's first report, released one year before Congress passed the National Security Act, made a strong case for government investment in overhead surveillance.[66] In the following years, many big defence companies saw a market opportunity and branched into R&D for the defence and intelligence communities, therefore diversifying the range of technologies and services available to government organisations.

The development of the U-2 spy plane – a cooperative project between the CIA, the Air Force, Lockheed Corporation and a series of sub-contractors – is a case in point. The CIA was the lead agency for this project and first signed a letter contract with Lockheed on 22 December 1954, providing a series of performance specifications. The agency was responsible for the airframes, cameras and life-support gear, and it arranged for security, contracting, film processing and access to foreign bases, while the Air Force oversaw the development of the engines and the selection of pilots. Lockheed took charge of the core technical aspects of the project, including the construction and testing of the aircraft. The CIA and Lockheed eventually signed a formal contract on 2 March 1955. This fixed-price contract included a provision for a review three-fourths of the way to determine if the costs were going to be on target. No review of the contract was necessary, and Lockheed delivered the aircraft on time, on 25 July 1955, and under budget.[67] The plane was tested in the following months and the first U-2 overflights of the Soviet Union took place the next summer. The spy plane served the US intelligence community for decades and is widely considered as one of the biggest intelligence-gathering successes in the history of US intelligence. U-2 overflights provided impressive amounts of information to decision-makers both at the strategic and tactical levels, and gave them an important window into Soviet capabilities and intentions.[68] To this day, the US Air Force continues to use follow-ons of the U-2 to conduct high-altitude reconnaissance.

Given the technical challenges posed by the development of this unique plane, the involvement of two government partners and a number of contractors and subcontractors, the success of this project is a remarkable achievement. This success can be explained by a variety of factors. Lockheed had the know-how and was well prepared to develop the U-2, not least because it had previously competed to develop similar technology for the Air Force. At the CIA, the project captured the attention of senior officials, including the DCI, who understood and emphasised the need for new technical means of collection.[69] The U-2 project was also set up to be self-sufficient and contract management, administration, logistics and security teams were all directly working on the project, which kept them committed. The CIA internal history of the programme points out that 'simplified covert procurement arrangements and the lack of detailed and restricting specifications' allowed creative designers to develop a 'state-of-the-art aircraft in record time'.[70] The story of the U-2 spy plane proves that when government managers balance the need for flexibility and control and key actors remain engaged throughout the procurement process, outsourcing can lead to national security successes.

The US intelligence community's interest in overhead reconnaissance continued to grow in the following decades to the point that technical means of intelligence collection gained primacy over human intelligence. A few years after the first U-2 flight, the CORONA programme led to the launch of the first US reconnaissance satellite, considerably extending the scope of photographic surveillance over the Soviet Union and China. This satellite programme received a significant boost when the Soviet Union shot down a U-2 spy plane flying over its territory in 1960. Using unmanned satellites orbiting outside of the stratosphere was less risky than flying reconnaissance planes, but more challenging from a technological point of view. The CIA and the Air Force once again provided the main impetus behind the development of the CORONA satellites, and the private aerospace sector helped them develop and manufacture key components. Although CORONA broke through a series of technological barriers, it encountered a series of problems. Delivery dates were repeatedly postponed, and costs rose significantly during its development following a series of technical failures. Such issues are difficult to avoid in the realm of technical intelligence, since R&D is bound to remain a hazardous process.[71] Despite these issues, the CIA history of the programme praises 'CORONA's contributions to US intelligence holdings on denied areas'.[72]

Technology acted as a vector, fostering the intelligence community's reliance on companies and developing intelligence officials' role in project management. The role played by contractors in government-sponsored R&D efforts prompted government officials to ponder the outsourcing process. In a 1962 report, White House officials asked: To what degree can contractors increase the government capabilities? What criteria can determine which functions contractors and the government should perform? How to select and supervise contractors?[73] Answering these questions would require further regulations and procedures. In the intelligence community, the emphasis on TECHINT was logically reflected at the organisational level with the establishment of new organisations like the Directorate of Science and Technology at the CIA in 1963.[74] The Church committee report emphasises the strong connections and personnel mobility between this directorate and private industry, and notes that 'all research and development for technical systems was done through contracting'.[75]

Another aspect of research and development in which private entities started to play an increasingly prominent role in the early Cold War is analysis and strategic advice. In the aftermath of the Second World War, the US government encouraged the emergence of independent entities able to advise the government on complex issues on which it felt it needed help. The RAND Corporation established itself as a leading defence and national security think tank, developing cutting-edge political research and analysis for the US Air Force, the DoD and the rest of government. RAND researchers wrote a number of influential studies on strategy and the balance of power that would define early thinking on international relations in the nuclear age.[76] They helped establish the field of Soviet studies with publications such as *The Operational Code of the Politburo* in 1951, and developed an array of methodological tools that would influence social scientific research far beyond the US government and the Cold War.[77]

Companies also played a role in counterintelligence and security, providing secrecy and deniability to the CIA. In the 1960s, the CIA Office of Security contracted out tasks such as document destruction, guard work, security clearance investigations, technical and physical support for surveillance.[78] The agency also created shell companies to provide cover to its officers and agents in those parts of the world where governmental covers were scarce. The intensification of covert operations against the Soviet bloc in the 1950s multiplied the use of business entities owned by the agency and conducting or appearing to conduct business independently. The real or pseudo-companies had directors, officers and even stockholders, and provided salaries and tax attribution for agency personnel working under their cover. Unlike traditional contractors, these corporate shells were under the control of the Agency, allowing its officers to conceal their involvement and hinder hostile access to information on their sources and methods. By acting covertly, the CIA was also able to work with third parties, including companies, without damaging their reputation.[79]

During the golden age of covert operations, in the early Cold War, the CIA used similar arrangements to acquire capabilities covertly. The Church committee report notes that in 1952, 3,142 overseas contract personnel worked for the Office of Policy Coordination, a semi-autonomous unit of the CIA responsible for covert action.[80] From 1950 onwards, Air America provided air support for CIA operations, transporting arms, ammunitions and personnel across Southeast Asia. Companies also provided CIA officers and their agents with access to real estate and helped channel funding for specific activities. A complex of investment and insurance companies handled contract agents' pension funds and insured them during dangerous operations. When the CIA did not need these private capabilities any more, or when companies were attracting too much attention, the Agency closed them down or sold them.[81] In the media and publishing sector, covertly funded companies acted as a conduit for CIA propaganda, a type of covert political action. The development of a public-private network in this area was central to American efforts to win hearts and minds during the Cold War. For example, the CIA established the Congress for Cultural Freedom in 1950 to sponsor numerous publications backing US policies worldwide such as *Encounter* in the United Kingdom, *Der Monat* in Germany, *Daily American* in Italy and *El Mercurio* in Chile. CIA funds established Radio Free Europe, which disseminated Western propaganda toward the Eastern bloc.

To maintain these cover stories, the CIA enlisted help from other federal government agencies such as the Internal Revenue Service and the State Department. The need for interagency cooperation contributed to the complexity and increasing formalisation of public-private collaboration in intelligence operations. For instance, the US Forest Service was asked to award a contract to a CIA proprietary to assist with a particular cover story, and the Department of

Labor was required to intervene when, for reasons of secrecy, proprietary contracts were not renegotiated.[82] Executive departments adapted to the agency's need for secrecy, providing some flexibility when it was needed. Despite the use of contracts, the reliance on proprietary companies bore little to no resemblance to contracting firms and government contracting practices. The main purpose of proprietary companies was to maintain cover stories and provide 'plausible deniability' for covert operations. While some scholars might argue that this is a type of service, there was no real market or independent offer for the provision of plausible deniability. The CIA created both the demand and the supply.

Public Concerns about the Intelligence–Industrial Complex

The close ties between the national security apparatus and the private sector continued to raise public concerns in the post-war era, mostly about the propriety and effectiveness of cross-sector collaboration. In 1961, President Eisenhower famously expressed his concern about the growth of the military industry in his farewell address when he observed:

> We have been compelled to create a permanent armaments industry of vast proportions. [. . .] We recognize the imperative need for this development. Yet we must not fail to comprehend its grave implications [. . .]. In the councils of government, we must guard against the acquisition of unwarranted influence, whether sought or unsought, by the military-industrial complex. The potential for the disastrous rise of misplaced power exists and will persist.[83]

The term military-industrial complex is often used pejoratively to describe the web of vested interests that developed between the federal bureaucracy (developing and implementing policies), Congress (controlling the purse) and the industry (providing services and goods). In this iron triangle, Representatives support employment in their constituencies through the military industry. The industry opens public affairs offices, hires retired senior officers, and maintains congressional liaisons to lobby in support of its business. Government agencies promote the industrial interests corresponding to their bureaucratic priorities and spend their budget on defence technologies. Networks of acquaintances that transcend the public-private divide and stem from a revolving door that shuffles between the industry and government offices reinforce this coalition of interests.[84]

The military-industrial complex is problematic because the existence of close ties between the public and private sectors raises questions about government officials' ability and willingness to control contractors and maintain the ascendancy of the public interest. These issues rose to prominence during the early Cold War, when demobilisation and public perceptions of the Soviet threat led Congress to what then Senator Proxmire (D-WI) described as a 'panicky and uncritical policy toward the Pentagon spending' which allowed the industry to grow without 'adequate controls on contracts'.[85] The requirement for secrecy, which is so common in national security affairs, posed particular accountability problems as it spread from the government to the industry and prevented established channels of oversight to operate effectively. The promotion of national security interests by public and private entities lacked transparency, which brought into question the legitimacy of the policies pursued by the government. Critics like Proxmire argued that this system allowed defence officials to keep huge cost overruns secret and avoid public scrutiny. Secrecy requirements also complicated, and sometimes prevented, company directors' duty to exercise great care and diligence in the management of their assets.[86]

The concept of the intelligence-industrial complex is an application of these criticisms to the realm of intelligence. Project IBEX, managed jointly by the CIA, the NSA and the SAVAK (the Iranian Organisation of Intelligence and National Security from 1957 to 1979) illustrates some of the problems caused by the intelligence-industrial complex. IBEX was a surveillance programme designed to provide American technology to the Shah of Iran to gather information on neighbouring countries. The programme was leaked in 1977 when three American employees of Rockwell International Corporation were shot to death in Tehran. At the time, journalist

Bob Woodward's article in the *Washington Post* drew attention to a number of practices used in this project. Woodward noted that, in the interest of secrecy, covert projects such as IBEX usually 'hide or insulate some of the payments that go out to US contractors'. In this case, checks to contractors 'were drawn following a series of complicated transactions involving the CIA and the Touche Ross Washington office', but also the Iranian government and Riggs National Bank. The system faced 'allegations of widespread corruption' and the whole project was criticised as a case of technological dumping for impractical US equipment and concepts.[87]

In the 1970s, the strength of the civil rights movement, anti-war protests, economic difficulties and a series of public scandals all combined to raise public pressure on US policy-makers to set limits to government intelligence activities. The year of intelligence, in 1975, marked the congressional willingness to exercise its constitutional responsibility and oversee the intelligence community. In the same way that Eisenhower's farewell address was central in raising public awareness about the influence of the military-industrial complex, congressional investigations led by Senator Frank Church and Representative Otis Pike examined the scope of the relationship between the intelligence community and its private support networks and the risks intelligence activities could pose to liberal democracy.[88] The Pike Committee focused its efforts on intelligence costs and procedures and its reports reveal the scope of contracting at the time. During a hearing held by the Pike committee in August 1975, Assistant Secretary of Defense for Intelligence Albert Hall indicated that the DIA contracted out approximately 16 per cent of its intelligence budget, the NSA 28 per cent, the Army 27 per cent, the Navy 37 per cent, and the Air Force 86 per cent.[89] In its appendix, the Pike committee report also included the policy and procedures used by the CIA for ensuring compliance with government contracting policies.[90] This report shows that intelligence contracting was already relatively common at the time and that an accountability regime was in place at the administrative level to govern such collaboration.

The Church committee investigations revealed how the CIA involved private partners in a series of activities that threatened human rights, civil liberties and government transparency. In the 1950s, the CIA's Scientific Division launched a project codenamed MKUltra, which sought to develop 'chemical, biological, and radiological materials capable of employment in clandestine operations to control human behavior'. The programme brought together 'specialists in universities, pharmaceutical houses, hospitals, state and federal institutions, and private research organizations'. In one shocking experiment, the CIA surreptitiously administered hard drugs to unwitting subjects. Despite the fact that this experience resulted in the death of a civilian employee of the Army in 1953, the illegal programme continued.[91] Congress also investigated the pitfalls of the proprietary system and found that proprietaries had limited visibility in the CIA budget – which made them more difficult to oversee.[92] This was worrying given their widespread use in some of the most sensitive CIA operations, both abroad and at home. In another project codenamed MERRIMAC, the CIA used a front company called Anderson Security to infiltrate legitimately formed anti-Vietnam War groups.[93] Though these abuses were concerning, it is worth noting that contractors and front companies played a secondary role in all of them. Companies were merely a means to implement or maintain controversial programmes under cover. The real issue in all these cases was not the role of private entities, but the expanding scope of government intelligence activities and the public perception that the CIA had become a 'rogue elephant'.[94] However, the CIA was not out of control; elements within the US administration instigated and allowed these programmes to exist.

The Church committee was concerned about the role of companies in the national intelligence effort and warned about the impact of the 'confluence of conflicting roles' between the public and the private sector in 'a free and open society'. In its final report, the committee remarked that 'in a totalitarian society, governmental and "private" enterprises are essentially one'. The key to avoiding such excesses was to ensure that decision-makers could maintain the 'delicate balance between governmental and private actions'.[95] As the intelligence community grew, government and private sector executives shared ideas, acquaintances, a similar sense of concern for national security and a pool of institutional knowledge that brought them ever closer. The porous boundaries between public and private sectors raised concern that national security would become captive to private interests. During the Pike Committee hearings, congressmen expressed concern about the close ties between the intelligence community and its contractors and considered the possibility that private interests could bias senior officials' decisions in favour of the industry.[96] In a book published in 1978, George O'Toole, a former CIA officer, exposed networks of influence that linked the intelligence community and the private sector. O'Toole found that the private industry's intelligence needs fuelled the recruitment of serving and retired intelligence officers.[97] Members of professional organisations like the National Military Intelligence Association, the Association of Retired Intelligence Officers and the Society of Former Special Agents of the Federal Bureau of Investigation held senior security executive positions with leading companies in most sectors of the US economy, from telecommunication to airline companies.[98]

The revolving door between the public and private sectors raised questions about possible conflicts of commitment and interests. Military historian Alex Roland argues that, during the Cold War, intelligence became politicised because the information it was providing supported both the industry and the government security policies.[99] For Roland, alarming information on Soviet capabilities and the tendency to assume worst-case Soviet intentions increased the governmental demand for intelligence and benefited intelligence producers in the public and private sectors. While government intelligence agencies and the industry had a common interest in boosting the threat perception to capture taxpayers' money, Roland sets the bar of politicisation too low and provides little evidence to support his claim. Close public-private interactions and networks do not prove politicisation, but raise legitimate concern about the impartiality of the decisions made by intelligence officials.

The year of intelligence and the subsequent establishment of congressional oversight opened a new era in the history of US intelligence, in which political actors and dynamics started playing an increasingly important role. Congressional investigations showed that the intelligence community and its private outriders needed to be watched carefully by external actors. This new era challenged intelligence officials and their political masters to find a balance between regulation and flexibility, respect for public service values and effective national security. At the CIA, 1975 was considered a year of turmoil: worldwide attention on the Agency concerned Director William Colby 'over the possibility of CIA contractors turning away from the Agency' to avoid disclosure of their involvement with the Agency.[100] From this perspective, revelations encroached upon the flexibility the CIA had benefited from since its establishment. At the administrative level, the relationship between the intelligence community and its contractors was also affected by a number of acquisition reforms in the mid-1970s, which established new structures and policies like the Federal Acquisition Regulations (FAR). However, this regulatory movement did little to improve the situation and, by the late 1970s, defence acquisition was still widely criticised for being riddled by waste, fraud and abuse.[101] In fact, the growing body of government regulations started to burden outsourcing with a 'sea of paperwork'.[102]

The election of President Reagan in 1980 and the nomination of William Casey as DCI ushered in a more aggressive posture towards communism that translated into the resurgence of covert actions. In this context, the Iran-Contra scandal demonstrated the persisting limits of the US system of intelligence accountability. After Congress outlawed a CIA operation to overthrow the Sandinista regime in Nicaragua in the early 1980s, a group of National Security Council staffers decided to overlook the amendment and pursue the operation. To circumvent the limits imposed by Congress, these officials relied on an extensive network of private assets – including air proprietaries, contract agents, freelance organisations, and holding companies – and foreign (Israeli) partners to provide support to the Contras in Nicaragua.[103] This unique incident shows how a group of senior officials can use private assets to obscure intelligence operations from legitimate accountability holders, but it does not prove that the use of private assets systematically weakens accountability. In this case, and indeed in all the controversial cases of public-private collaboration mentioned in this chapter so far, government officials originated the misuse of intelligence powers and the private sector assumed the position of a co-pilot.

One final type of risk emerging from the collaboration between the intelligence community and the private sector is the possibility that hostile organisations target contractors to collect intelligence on sensitive government activities. In 1953, a National Security Council decision established the Communications Security Board, bringing government and industry partners together to discuss and oversee communications security issues.[104] This concern persisted throughout the 1960s, as evidenced by the establishment of a DoD taskforce to study 'the risks introduced by the widespread use of resource-sharing information systems and to make recommendations to improve their security'. These recommendations were then codified by government organisations such as the National Institute of Standards and Technology, a public agency that works with the private sector to develop standards of conduct.[105] More than a decade later, information security concerns had reached the highest sphere of government. A 1976 National Security Council decision expressed the President's concern about:

> possible damage to the national security and the economy from continuing Soviet intercept of critical non-government communications, including government defence contractors and certain other key institutions in the private sector. The President has therefore decided that communication security should be extended to government defense contractors dealing in classified or sensitive information at the earliest possible time. He has also directed that planning be undertaken to meet the longer-term need to protect other key institutions in the private sector, and, ultimately, to provide a reasonable expectation of privacy for all users of public telecommunications.[106]

Since contractors played an increasingly prominent role in the development and maintenance of information technology to support intelligence systems, the information security risks they posed became more obvious. These risks were widely publicised with the release of Robert Lindsey's book *The Falcon and the Snowman: A True Story of Friendship and Espionage* and its subsequent adaptation into a movie by John Schlesinger. The fact-inspired story followed Christopher Boyce, a disillusioned employee working for an intelligence contractor, TRW, who decided to use his post in a secure communication facility to spy for the Soviet Union.

When Boyce was arrested for espionage in the late 1970s, TRW became infamous for its lax security protocols.[107] While Boyce and TRW attracted some public attention, government employees also compromised US secrets. In 1978, former CIA employee William Kampiles sold a top-secret spy satellite manual to the Soviets for $3,000. Kampiles bragged about conning the Soviets to a CIA friend and was subsequently convicted of espionage.[108] In subsequent years the government launched a series of initiatives to help American companies improve their information security, such as the President's National Security Telecommunications Advisory Committee, but this effort did not stop security breaches.[109] The release of the Mitrokhin archive, the collection of notes secretly made by Vasili Mitrokhin during his career as KGB archivist, later confirmed the government's concern was justified. Documents in the archive show that the Soviet Union successfully intercepted fax communications from major defence companies working with the US intelligence community such as Boeing, General Dynamics, Grumman, IBM and Lockheed. KGB residencies in the United States also ran a series of agents who were working for leading American defence contractors such as McDonnell Douglas and TRW.[110] These cases demonstrate that penetrating the US national security state through its contractors is a traditional method of infiltration used by hostile organisations. However, publicly available information suggests that contractors were not a more frequent source of compromise than their government counterparts. From 1949 to 1989, contractors initiated sixteen of the 133 (12 per cent) publicly known compromises to US national security.[111]

Overall, public concerns regarding the intelligence-industrial complex are legitimate. Contractors have compromised national security secrets and allowed some elements of the federal government to conduct activities that threatened civil liberties, human rights and government transparency. However, these risks are inherent to the conduct of intelligence and there is no evidence to suggest that they are inherently tied to the involvement of contractors in the national intelligence effort. Indeed, government agencies and officials have never needed the private sector to encroach upon civil liberties, threaten human rights or invest taxpayers' money in ineffective projects.

Conclusion

The ties between intelligence officials and the private sector can be traced back to the early days of the US Republic. The US government, like all non-communist governments, does not own major manufacturing assets and purchases most of the goods and support services it needs from the private sector. The ties between the public and private sectors became increasingly formalised as the government expanded its role in national security affairs throughout the twentieth century. The institutionalisation of intelligence accentuated the need for public accountability holders to find a balance between flexibility and control in the conduct of intelligence missions. Imminent threats to national security, during major wars and later in peacetime, encouraged the government to expand its intelligence capabilities and seek flexibility and expertise from the private sector. Periods of public-private expansion during the First World War and after the Second World War generated public concern over inefficiencies, conflicts of interest, abuses of power and information security, pushing the government to regulate and adapt its collaboration with the private sector.

The historical connections between the public and private sectors explain how contractors have contributed to a host of intelligence successes and excesses. Controversial government intelligence programmes have threatened core democratic values like human rights, civil liberties and transparency, and occasionally involved contractors. However, the presence of contractors has never been a necessary or sufficient condition for intelligence accountability problems to emerge. In the examples reviewed in this chapter, government officials' decisions in the face of severe national security threats and the inherent complexity and risks of national security projects best explain intelligence excesses, not the involvement of the private sector. In turn, these excesses, and societal change, shaped the public debate on the role of intelligence as a tool of government. This debate largely focused on the role of government agencies, not on contractors.

On the whole, government officials and their private partners share the responsibility for a number of intelligence successes and excesses throughout US history. But officials, unlike their private counterparts, have a duty to stir cross-sector collaboration to serve the public interest in national security. Since national security interests evolve, government accountability holders must strive to systematically balance the need for regulation and flexibility in the relationship between the intelligence community and its contractors. The next chapter will show how the redefinition of national security in the post-Cold War era challenged government accountability holders to maintain this balance.

Notes

1. Foley, *American Credo*, pp. 37–40; Becker, *The Declaration of Independence*, pp. 27–30, 72–3.
2. James Madison, 'The Federalist (51)', in Goldman, *The Federalist Papers*, p. 257; Wood, *The Creation of the American Republic*, p. 54; Zoller, *Introduction au Droit Public*, pp. 129, 143.
3. Foley, *American Credo*, p. 79.
4. Zoller, *Introduction au Droit Public*, p. 121; Stone, 'Corporate Vices and Corporate Virtues', pp. 1441–5.
5. Horwitz, 'The History of the Public/Private Distinction', p. 1424.
6. Savas, *Privatization and Public-Private Partnerships*, p. 5.
7. Henig, 'Privatization in the United States', p. 652; McKay, *American Politics and Society*, p. 39; Polanyi, *The Great Transformation*, p. 68.
8. Weber, 'Politics as Vocation', p. 78; Meyer, *The Theory of Social Democracy*, p. 91; Baber, 'Privatizing Public Management', p. 136; Donahue, *The Privatization Decision*, p. 216.
9. David M. Walker (Comptroller General of the United States), cited in Scott Shane and Ron Nixon, 'In Washington, Contractors Take on Biggest Role Ever', *New York Times*, 4 February 2007, A1.
10. Fine, *Laissez-faire and the General-Welfare State*; Jeffreys-Jones, *The American Left.*
11. Savas, *Privatization and Public-Private Partnerships*, p. 11; Singer, *Corporate Warriors*, p. 70.
12. Nagle, *A History of Government Contracting*, p. 2.
13. Shalhope, 'The Ideological Origins of the Second Amendment', p. 608; Weigley, *The American Way of War*, p. xx.
14. Morgan, *Domestic Intelligence. Monitoring Dissent in America*, p. 109. See also Alexander Hamilton, 'The Federalist, 8', in Goldman, *The Federalist Papers*, pp. 39–43; Alexander Hamilton, 'The Federalist, 26', in Goldman, *The Federalist Papers*, pp. 128–9.

15. George Washington, ‘Farewell Address to the Nation’, 19 September 1796, available at <http://gwpapers.virginia.edu/documents/farewell/transcript.html> (accessed 28 May 2018).
16. Percy, *Mercenaries*, pp. 123–4; Reinders, ‘Militia and Public Order in Nineteenth-Century America’, pp. 82–5.
17. Central Intelligence Agency, Center for the Study of Intelligence, ‘Intelligence in the War of Independence, Intelligence Operations’, available at <https://www.cia.gov/library/center-for-the-study-of-intelligence/csi-publications/books-and-monographs/intelligence/intellopos.html> (accessed 28 May 2018).
18. P. K. Rose, ‘The Founding Fathers of American Intelligence’, available at <https://www.cia.gov/library/center-for-the-study-of-intelligence/csi-publications/books-and-monographs/the-founding-fathers-of-american-intelligence/art-1.html> (accessed 28 May 2018); Voelz, ‘Contractors and Intelligence: The Private Sector in the Intelligence Community’, p. 588.
19. Andrew, *For the President’s Eyes Only*, p. 11; Bell, *Secretaries of War and Secretaries of the Army*, p. 10.
20. Permanent General Laws Relating to Indian Affairs – The Revised Statutes. Title XIV, Chapter 1, SEC.1112, in Charles J. Kappler (ed.), *Indian Affairs: Law and Treaties* (Washington: Government Printing Office, 1904), available at <http://digital.library.okstate.edu/kappler/Vol1/HTML_files/AFF0002A.html> (accessed 28 May 2018); Dunlay, *Wolves for the Blue Soldiers*, pp. 8–9.
21. Nagle, *A History of Government Contracting*, pp. 15–107.
22. Weigley, *The American Way of War*, pp. 51–3; Thomson, *Mercenaries, Pirates, and Sovereigns*, p. 10.
23. Hogg, ‘Public Reaction to Pinkertonism and the Labor Question’, p. 172; Jeffreys-Jones, *American Espionage*, p. 13; O’Toole, *The Private Sector*, pp. 21–2; Morn, *The Eye That Never Sleeps*, p. 46.
24. Central Intelligence Agency, ‘Intelligence in the Civil War’, p. 17, available at <https://www.cia.gov/library/publications/additional-publications/civil-war/Intel_in_the_CW1.pdf> (accessed 28 May 2018); Central Intelligence Agency, ‘Saving Mr Lincoln’, available at <https://www.cia.gov/library/publications/additional-publications/civil-war/SML.htm> (accessed 28 May 2018).
25. Finnegan, *Military Intelligence*, pp. 10–11; Andrew, *For the President’s Eyes Only*, p. 18; National Archives and Records Service: Case Files of Investigations by Levi C. Turner and Lafayette C. Baker, 1861–1866 (1970), pp. 2–3, available at <http://library.indstate.edu/about/units/rbsc/neff/PDFs/Turner_Baker_pamphlet.pdf>

(accessed 28 May 2018); Fishel, *The Secret War for The Union*, pp. 54–5.

26. Nagle, *A History of Government Contracting*, p. 202.
27. Morn, *The Eye That Never Sleeps*, p. 63; MacKay, *Allan Pinkerton: the Eye Who Never Slept*, pp. 11, 71–2, 78, 149–53, 183; Durie, *The Pinkerton Casebook*, pp. 1, 36, 176; Dempsey and Forst, *An Introduction to Policing*, p. 18; Sparks, *Inside Lincoln's Army*, pp. 260–1.
28. Morton, *The First Detective*, pp. 217, 222–3, 230; MacKay, *Allan Pinkerton*, p. 72; Morn, *The Eye That Never Sleeps*, pp. 68–9. On the history of French private police and its attempt to gain more legitimacy, see Kalifa, *Naissance de la Police Privée*, pp. 275–6; Forcade and Laurent, *Secrets d'Etat*, pp. 63–4. For the British case: TNA: MEPO 2/130: correspondence detailing the support Pollaky's Continental Inquiry Office offered to British police; C. R. Elrington (ed.), 'Paddington: Paddington Green', *A History of the County of Middlesex: Volume 9: Hampstead, Paddington* (1989), pp. 185–90, available at <http://www.british-history.ac.uk/report.aspx?compid=22663> (accessed 28 May 2018); Editor, 'Paddington Pollaky: A Detective Mentioned In Sullivan Opera', *Times*, 28 February 1918, 3F.
29. Wagner, *The Service of Security and Information*, p. 136.
30. Andrew, *For the President's Eyes Only*, pp. 22–8.
31. Wagner, *The Service of Security and Information*, pp. 135–6.
32. US House of Representatives, debate, *Congressional Record*, 60th Congress, 2nd session, 8 January 1909, p. 651, in Ken G. Robertson (ed.), *British and American Approaches to Intelligence* (Basingstoke: Macmillan, 1987), p. 254.
33. Marone, *Hellfire Nation*.
34. Andrew, *The Defence of the Realm*, pp. 3–213; Jeffery, *MI6: The History of the Secret Intelligence Service*, pp. 3–323; Laurent, *Politiques de l'ombre*, *passim*.
35. Hogg, 'Public Reactions to Pinkertonism and the Labor Question', pp. 176–9; Leon Wolff, *Lockout!*, p. 164; Jeffreys-Jones, *American Espionage*, pp. 18–19; O'Toole, *The Private Sector*, 27; Morn, *The Eye That Never Sleeps*, pp. 48, 104, 188–9.
36. Jeffreys-Jones, *American Espionage*, pp. 3, 16–21, 26, 37, 55.
37. US Congress, *Anti-Pinkerton Act*, 52nd Congress, 2nd session, 3 March 1893; Churchill, 'From the Pinkertons to the PATRIOT Act', pp. 24–5.
38. Jeffreys-Jones, *American Espionage*, p. 21.
39. Ibid; O'Toole, *The Private Sector*, p. 28.

40. Cohen, 'Putting a Human and Historical Face on Intelligence Contracting', pp. 243–4. Such societal support also existed in the United Kingdom; see McIvor, '"A Crusade for Capitalism": The Economic League, 1919–39'.
41. Stone, 'Judge Learned Hand and the Espionage Act of 1917: A Mystery Unravelled'.
42. Andrew, *For the President's Eyes Only*, pp. 29–30, 73.
43. Stimson, *On Active Services in Peace and War*, p. 188; Woodrow Wilson, Message to Congress, 8 January 1918, available at <http://wwi.lib.byu.edu/index.php/President_Wilson's_Fourteen_Points> (accessed 28 May 2018).
44. Koistinen, 'The "Industrial-Military Complex" in Historical Perspective: The InterWar Years', pp. 819, 830–1; Koistinen, 'The "Industrial-Military Complex" in Historical Perspective: World War I', p. 378; McNeill, *The Pursuit of Power*, p. 346.
45. Nagle, *A History of Government Contracting*, p. 297.
46. Engelbrecht and Hanighen, *Merchants of Death*; Seldes, *Iron, Blood and Profits*.
47. Polenberg, *The Era of Franklin D. Roosevelt*, pp. 14–24.
48. Morn, *The Eye That Never Sleeps*, 191; Rhodri Jeffreys-Jones, email correspondence with author, 10 December 2014.
49. US Senate, *Report of the Special Committee on Investigation of the Munitions Industry*, 74th Congress, 2nd session, 24 February 1936, pp. 3–13; John Edward Wiltz, 'The Nye Committee Revisited'; Jeffreys-Jones, *American Espionage*, p. 131.
50. Editor, 'Labor Draft is Expanded', *Reading Eagle*, 7 April 1937, available at <http://news.google.com/newspapers?nid=1955&dat=19370407&id=URoyAAAAIBAJ&sjid=jeIFAAAAIBAJ&pg=4906,1498632> (accessed 28 May 2018).
51. Churchill, 'From the Pinkertons to the PATRIOT Act', p. 39; Polenberg, *The Era of Franklin D. Roosevelt*, p. 24.
52. Kahn, 'The Intelligence Failure of Pearl Harbor', pp. 150–2; Central Intelligence Agency, Center for the Study of Intelligence, 'Historical Intelligence Documents: From COI to CIG', Document 2, available at <https://www.cia.gov/library/center-for-the-study-of-intelligence/kent-csi/vol37no3/html/v37i3a10p_0001.htm> (accessed 28 May 2018); Valero, '"We Need Our New OSS, Our New General Donovan, Now"', pp. 91–118.
53. Koistinen, 'The "Industrial-Military Complex" in Historical Perspective: The InterWar Years', p. 839; Bradley, 'Address at the Third National Industry Army Day conference', p. 13.

54. Nagle, *A History of Government Contracting*, p. 464.
55. Ibid. pp. 442, 463.
56. Andrew, *For the President's Eyes Only*, p. 248.
57. Dulles, *The Craft of Intelligence*, p. 71.
58. US Congress, Public Law 81–110, *Central Intelligence Agency Act*, 81st Congress, 1st session, 20 June 1949, Sec. 10.
59. Memorandum from President Harry S. Truman to the Secretary of State, the Secretary of Defense, Subject: Communications Intelligence Activities, 24 October 1952, p. 5.
60. McNeill, *The Pursuit of Power*, p. 365.
61. Tingle, 'Privatization and the Reagan Administration', p. 233; Donahue, *The Privatization Decision*, p. 216; Feigenbaum et al., *Shrinking the State*, pp. 5–11, 38–9.
62. Executive Office of the President, Bureau of the Budget, *Commercial-industrial activities of the government providing products or services for governmental use*, Bulletin No. 55–4, 15 January 1955.
63. Jones, *Arming the Eagle*, p. 329. On the development of private intelligence services for private individuals and companies after the Second World War, see Hougan, *Spooks*.
64. Mahnken, *Technology and the American Way of War since 1945*, p. 2; Lewis, *The American Culture of War*, p. 183; McNeill, *The Pursuit of Power*, pp. 368–96.
65. James Schlesinger, 'A Review of The Intelligence Community', 10 March 1971, p. 4, available at <http://www.gwu.edu/~nsarchiv/NSAEBB/NSAEBB144/document%204.pdf> (accessed 28 May 2018); Bukharin, 'US Atomic Energy Intelligence Against the Soviet Target, 1945–1970', p. 661.
66. Douglas Aircraft Company's Engineering Division, Preliminary Design of an Experimental World-Circling Spaceship (SM-11827), 2 May 1946, p. 1.
67. Pedlow and Welzenbach, *The CIA and the U-2 Program*, pp. 43–5, 60.
68. Ibid. pp. 315–20; Tenet, 'The U-2 Program: The DCI's Perspective', pp. 1–4; Pocock, *The U-2 Spyplane*.
69. Dulles, *The Craft of Intelligence*, pp. 65–8.
70. Pedlow and Welzenbach, *The CIA and the U-2 Program*, p. 320.
71. Central Intelligence Agency, 'Breaking through Technological Barriers', available at <https://www.cia.gov/library/center-for-the-study-of-intelligence/csi-publications/books-and-monographs/a-12/breaking-through-technological-barriers.html> (accessed 28 May 2018); Greer, 'Corona'; National Reconnaissance Office, 'Intelligence

at Considerable Risk (1955–1960)', at <http://www.nrojr.gov/teamre-con/res_his-ConsidRisk.html> (accessed 28 May 2018).
72. Ruffner, *CORONA: America's First Satellite Program*, p. 37.
73. Executive Office of the President, Bureau of the Budget, *Report to the President of the United States on Government Contracting For Research and Development* (Washington, DC: Government Printing Office, 1962).
74. Lewis, *Spy Capitalism*, p. 267; Jeffrey T. Richelson, 'Science, Technology and the CIA', 10 September 2001, available at <http://www.gwu.edu/~nsarchiv/NSAEBB/NSAEBB54/> (accessed 28 May 2018).
75. US Senate, Select Committee to Study Governmental Operations with Respect to Intelligence Activities, Supplementary Detailed Staff Reports on Foreign and Military Intelligence, Book IV, 23 April 1976, p. 78.
76. See for example Wohlstetter, *Delicate Balance of Terror*; Brodie, *Strategy in the Missile Age*; Kahn, *The Nature and Feasibility of War and Deterrence*; Kaplan, *the Wizards of Armageddon*, pp. 51–73.
77. Leites, *The Operational Code of the Politburo*. For more analyses of this type, see RAND, 'RAND Classics', available at <http://www.rand.org/pubs/classics.html> (accessed 30 May 2018); RAND Corporation, *Project Air Force, 1946–1996* (Santa Monica, CA: RAND), pp. 40–41, available at <https://www.rand.org/content/dam/rand/www/external/publications/PAFbook.pdf> (accessed 30 May 2018).
78. O'Toole, *The Private Sector*, pp. 160–6; US Senate, Select Committee to Study Governmental Operations with Respect to Intelligence Activities, Book I, *Foreign and Military Intelligence*, 94th Congress, 2nd session, 23 April 1976, pp. 210–12.
79. US Senate, Select Committee to Study Governmental Operations with Respect to Intelligence Activities, Book I, pp. 205–7, 234–5; Lewis, *Spy Capitalism*, p. 47; Prados, *Presidents' Secret Wars*, pp. 230–1, 277.
80. US Senate, Supplementary Detailed Staff Reports on Foreign and Military Intelligence, p. 31. On the Office of Policy Coordination, see Warner, 'The CIA's Office of Policy Coordination'.
81. Prados, *President's Secret Wars*, pp. 231–2, 267, 276–8, 456–5; US Senate, Select Committee to Study Governmental Operations with Respect to Intelligence Activities, Book I, p. 209.
82. Parmar, 'Conceptualising the State-Private Network in American Foreign Policy', p. 24; Turner, 'Covert Action: An Appraisal of the Effects of Secret Propaganda'; Jeffreys-Jones, *The CIA and American*

Democracy, pp. 60, 87, 133, 158; Prados, *President's Secret Wars*, p. 319; Tudda, *The Truth is Our Weapon*, p. 41; Wilford, *The Mighty Wurlitzer*, p. 10; US Senate, Select Committee to Study Governmental Operations with Respect to Intelligence Activities, Book I, pp. 223, 247–8.

83. Dwight Eisenhower, 'Farewell Address to the Nation', 17 January 1961, available at <http://mcadams.posc.mu.edu/ike.htm> (accessed 28 May 2018); Ledbetter, *Unwarranted Influence: Dwight D. Eisenhower and the Military Industrial Complex.*
84. Adams, *The Politics of Defense Contracting*; Craig and Logevall, *America's Cold War*, p. 362; Lavallee, 'Globalizing the Iron Triangle'; Roland, *The Military-Industrial Complex*, pp. 28, 32, 49.
85. Proxmire, *Report from Wasteland*, pp. 4, 19, 109.
86. Lewis, *Spy Capitalism*, pp. 108–9, 116–18, 121–3.
87. Bob Woodward, 'IBEX: Deadly Symbol of US Arms Sales Problems', *Washington Post*, January 2, 1977, A1.
88. US House of Representatives, Select Committee on Intelligence, 'US Intelligence Agencies and Activities: Intelligence Costs and Fiscal Procedures', 31 July, 1, 4, 5, 6, 7, 8 August 1975, Part I, pp. 163–4, 204.
89. US House of Representatives, Select Committee on Intelligence, 'US Intelligence Agencies and Activities: Intelligence Costs and Fiscal Procedures', 5 August 1975, Part I, p. 204.
90. Ibid. pp. 552–6.
91. US Senate, Select Committee to Study Governmental Operations with Respect to Intelligence Activities, Book I, pp. 389, 394–403, 422; US Senate, Select Committee on Intelligence, Joint Hearing before the Select Committee on Intelligence and the Subcommittee on Health and Scientific Research of the Committee on Human Resources, *Project MKUltra, the CIA's Program of Research in Behavioral Modification*, 95th Congress, 1st session, 3 August 1977.
92. US Senate, Select Committee to Study Governmental Operations with Respect to Intelligence Activities, Book I, pp. 250–1.
93. Snider, 'Recollections from the Church Committee's Investigation of NSA'; US Senate, Select Committee to Study Governmental Operations with Respect to Intelligence Activities, Book I, pp. 223–4.
94. Haines, 'The Pike Committee Investigations and the CIA', pp. 81–92; Mistry, 'Narrating Covert Action', p. 118.
95. US Senate, Select Committee to Study Governmental Operations with Respect to Intelligence Activities, Book I, p. 206.

96. US House of Representatives, Select Committee on Intelligence, 'US Intelligence Agencies and Activities: Intelligence Costs and Fiscal Procedures', Part I, pp. 66–9.
97. Examples can be found in the papers of former NSA Director Samuel Philips. Library of Congress, Washington, DC, Manuscript Division: Papers of Samuel C. Phillips, Box 137/2: T. A. Wilson (Boeing), letter to Samuel C. Phillips, 30 September 1975.
98. O'Toole, *The Private Sector*, pp. 118–50. See also: US Senate, Select Committee to Study Governmental Operations with Respect to Intelligence Activities, Book I, p. 239; National Archives and Records Administration, CIA Records Search Tool, Maryland: President of the Security Affairs Support Association, letter to Mr John McMahon, Deputy Director, Central Intelligence Agency, 1 March 1983.
99. Roland, *The Military-Industrial Complex*, pp. 31–2.
100. National Archives and Records Administration, CIA Records Search Tool, Maryland: James H. McDonald, Director of Logistics, Analysis of CIA Competitive Procurement Actions – FY 1975, MBO OL-D-01-76, Memorandum for Deputy Director for Administration, 28 May 1976.
101. US Congress, Public Law 93–400, Office of Federal Procurement Policy Act, 93rd Congress, 2nd session, 30 August 1974; Fox, *Defense Acquisition Reform, 1960–2009: An Elusive Goal*, p. 9; Jones, *Arming the Eagle*, pp. 355, 398–402; Roland, *The Military-Industrial Complex*, pp. 22–9.
102. Nagle, *A History of Government Contracting*, p. 505. See for example: National Archives and Records Administration, CIA Records Search Tool, Maryland: Stanley Sporking, General Counsel, Briefing Paper – CIA Contracting Safeguards, Memorandum for the Director of Central Intelligence, OGC 82-00846.
103. Jeffreys-Jones, *The CIA and American Democracy*, pp. 245–6; Prados, *Presidents' Secret Wars*, pp. 408–63; Scott and Rosate, 'Such Other Functions and Duties'.
104. National Security Council, Decision 168, Communications Security, 20 October 1953.
105. Anderson and Choobineh, 'Enterprise Information Security Strategies', p. 23; Willis H. Ware, Security Controls for Computer Systems: Report of Defense Science Board Task Force on Computer Security – RAND Report R-609-1, Reissued October 1979, p. xi.
106. Brent Scowcroft, National Security Council, National Security Decision Memorandum 338, *Further Improvements in Telecommunications Security (TS)*, 1 September 1976, p. 1, available

at <http://www.fas.org/irp/offdocs/nsdm-ford/nsdm-338.pdf> (accessed 28 May 2018).

107. Lindsey, *The Falcon and the Snowman*; Sulick, *American Spies*, pp. 62–3.
108. Richelson, *A Century of Spies*, pp. 346–7.
109. Executive Order 12382, President's National Security Telecommunications Advisory Committee, 13 September 1982.
110. Andrew and Mitrokhin, *The Mitrokhin Archive*, pp. 280–1, 454.
111. Katherine L. Herbig and Martin F. Wiskoff, *Espionage Against the United States by American Citizens 1947–2001*, Technical Report 02–5, July 2002; PERSEREC, *Espionage and Other Compromises to National Security 1975–2008*, 2 November 2009.

3 The Growth of Intelligence Contracting in the Post-Cold War Era

The relationship between the intelligence community and its contractors deepened and diversified in the post-Cold War era. On the domestic front, a privatisation movement, initially championed by President Reagan in the 1980s, reduced the scope of government and increased its reliance on the private sector. Significant budget and personnel cuts affected the intelligence community in the 1990s and set the conditions for further contracting out at the turn of the twentieth century. The 'new world order' that followed the collapse of the Soviet Union forced the community to rethink its missions and focus on a broader array of state and non-state threats.[1] In this context, contractors became increasingly essential to the intelligence community's effort to address 'new' threats. This rapprochement was reinforced by an IT revolution, which provided further opportunities for cross-sector collaboration and posed increasingly complex accountability challenges.

When America was hit by a series of coordinated terrorist attacks on 11 September 2001, these trends were catalysed and intelligence outsourcing boomed. In the time of crisis that followed the attacks, policy-makers and senior intelligence officials decided that capability gaps needed to be filled rapidly. Vast amounts of money were appropriated to the intelligence community and intelligence managers relied on contractors to augment not only support but also core intelligence capabilities. Government officials have justified the post-9/11 boom in the outsourcing of intelligence labour by presenting it as a necessity resulting from the requirements that were faced by the community at the time. This explanation is convincing, but 'new' threats, the IT revolution and the growing demand for intelligence in the global war on terrorism were not the only factors behind the intelligence community's growing reliance on contractors. Government decisions to cut down the intelligence community during the 1990s laid the foundation for the growth of intelligence contracting in the early twenty-first century. From this perspective, the boom in intelligence outsourcing was a self-created necessity.

From 9/11 onwards, intelligence outsourcing proliferated and diversified, and the market for national security intelligence thrived. A snapshot of intelligence contracting in the global war on terrorism emphasises its use across a large spectrum of activities, from the most banal kind of administrative support to core functions like intelligence operations and analysis. The post-9/11 boom in intelligence contracting raises important questions about the respective roles of the public and private sectors in the national intelligence effort. A closer look at the organisation of cross-sector interactions reveals a complex reality in which public and private incentives are not always well aligned. A variety of private entities relate to the intelligence community in ways that are not always harmonious and economically viable. While relying on contractors allowed the government to ramp up its intelligence effort, the influx of contractors in the intelligence community challenged US intelligence accountability holders' ability to maintain the primacy of the public interest.

The Domestic Context: Privatisation Policies

Privatisation policies gained increasing appeal and expanded to the realm of national security throughout the second half of the twentieth century. The end of the Cold War prompted the prominence of a capitalist ideology and economic arguments that consider privatisation as a positive solution to the shortfall of government resources, capabilities and performance. President Reagan pushed privatisation to the forefront of the national agenda in the 1980s in a deliberate effort to reduce the scope of government and change the balance between public and private sectors in a search for more efficiency. In his inaugural address, Reagan assumed an ideological stance, arguing that 'government is not the solution to our problem; government is the problem'.[2] His administration outsourced a considerable amount of government activities, including military logistical support services.[3]

The Clinton administration and Congress streamlined privatisation across multiple areas. In 1993, Vice-President Al Gore initiated a national performance review to determine how to transform the government bureaucracy in an 'entrepreneurial government' and guarantee better public performance levels.[4] Capitalism and privatisation, it was expected, would reinvent the government. Deregulation was deemed to guarantee better public performance levels by focusing government officials on mission-essential activities. A series of legislation modernised government procurement and partly redefined inherently governmental functions.[5] On the White House website, Gore drew a list of achievements resulting from this initiative and announced that 'with 377,000 fewer employees, the federal government is now the smallest it has been since President Eisenhower'.[6] As a part of this initiative, Congress mandated a 55 per cent reduction of the federal acquisition workforce, which reduced internal oversight of government contractors and stretched the government's procurement system to its limits.[7]

In the absence of a clear threat posed by the Soviet Union, national security issues waned in importance and the downsizing of government soon spilled over to the defence and intelligence communities. Former DCI Tenet recalls that 'the conventional wisdom was that we had won the Cold War and it was time to reap the peace dividend'.[8] According to a senior intelligence official, the intelligence community was 'decimated' in the 1990s and some agencies lost as much as 40 per cent of their capability.[9] Meanwhile, the defence and intelligence communities were encouraged to rely more extensively on contractors' supplies and services to support their missions.[10] Companies like ManTech provided support services to Army intelligence during the First Gulf War (1991), and then in Bosnia (1995) and Kosovo (1998–9). These wars confirmed the importance, but also the difficulty, of managing a growing number of contractors at a time when government policies reduced the DoD acquisition workforce by 50 per cent.[11]

Public–Private Intelligence Collaboration and the 'New World Order'

The threats facing the United States in the post-Cold War era called for a disaggregation of its security strategy and an increasing reliance on non-state actors. With the disintegration of the Soviet Union, President George H. W. Bush announced a 'new world order' in which the United States would continue to play a prominent role as a superpower. US intelligence agencies were faced with a diversified set of new challenges while their workforce was downsized. In 1993, DCI James Woolsey famously underlined this shift when he told Congress: 'we have slain a large dragon, but we live now in a jungle filled with a bewildering variety of poisonous snakes. And in many ways the dragon was easier to keep track of.'[12] In the words of a former intelligence officer, when the Soviet enemy collapsed, the intelligence community had to focus on 'literally the entire world, all of the peoples, all of the cultures, all of the languages'.[13]

The end of bipolarity paved the way for the emergence of 'new' conflicts where security professionals faced adversaries such as insurgents that cross the traditional nation-state boundaries and work in conjunction with criminal organisations.[14] The rise of non-state threat actors, particularly the terrorist threat, in the 1990s encouraged a rapprochement between the intelligence community and the private sector. Terrorists' ability to penetrate open societies and their indiscriminate targeting of civilians called for greater cooperation between the civilian entities that might be targeted – such as transportation and communication networks, energy circuits and US businesses at home and abroad – and government agencies. These security trends reoriented intelligence collection toward individuals and networks. The growing number of intelligence targets across the United States and beyond meant that the government could hardly bear sole responsibility for national security. This new world disorder called for a new division of labour between the intelligence community and the private sector.

One of the common wisdoms that emerged from security circles in the 1990s was that *it takes networks to fight networks*.[15] In the world of national security intelligence, the so-called open source revolution generated enthusiasm for the development of networks of experts bridging the public-private divide. In an article published in 1993, Robert Steele, an early advocate of open source intelligence, imagined 'an extended network of citizen analysts, competitive intelligence analysts in the private sector and government intelligence analysts, each able to access one another, share unclassified files, rapidly establish bulletin boards on topics of mutual interest'.[16] Public-private collaboration could broaden not only the producers, but also the consumer base for intelligence. The open source intelligence movement was livening up a basic truth of intelligence: society constitutes a pool of knowledge, global reach, experience and skills that government intelligence agencies cannot overlook. From this perspective, it is logical for the community to rely on, and share information with, the private sector to augment its capabilities.[17] This focus on networks, coupled with the IT revolution, solicited a deeper alliance between the intelligence community and the private sector, and fostered an environment in which intelligence contracting thrived.

Harnessing the IT revolution: In-Q-Tel

The IT revolution that started in the late 1980s pushed the intelligence community to meet its requirements through technology solutions developed by commercial vendors. The private sector was setting the pace of innovation, developing superior, more diverse and cheaper solutions and attracting the most talented experts.[18] The government was no longer the technology leader it had been when it initiated and oversaw the development of the U-2 spy plane and the CORONA satellite programme in the early Cold War. The private sector was now playing the leading role in this domain and became an essential partner for the intelligence community. Specialised companies like Planning Research Corporation captured multi-million-dollar contracts from the Department of Defense in the mid-1980s to develop intelligence systems that could process data and support government intelligence analysts.[19] Well-established defence companies, such as

DynCorp and Raytheon, jumped on the bandwagon and developed their IT offer to capture more government contracts.

To harness the IT revolution, some federal agencies sought to develop new ways of collaborating with contractors. The growth of government acquisition regulations in the second half of the twentieth century progressively complicated the procurement process and scared innovative companies away from the government. Increasingly risk-averse government agencies struggled to keep up with the rate of technological innovation.[20] The intelligence community was starting to be overwhelmed by the exponential growth of the volume of information available to its employees, and senior intelligence officials realised that the capabilities gap between the private sector and the intelligence community was growing wider. To maintain its leadership, the community would have to reconsider its relationship to the private sector and develop more effective ways to influence and tap into commercial capabilities.[21] Under the leadership of DCI Tenet, the CIA fostered the creation of In-Q-Tel, a private sector not-for-profit corporation established by Gilman Louie, a former Lockheed CEO. In March 1999, the CIA awarded a contract to In-Q-Tel and became its first and only client.[22] The young company was charged with identifying and investing in promising firms seeking to develop cutting-edge technology that could serve US national security interests. In-Q-Tel would leverage market forces to help the CIA solve some of its most critical IT problems and stay ahead of the technology curve. The establishment of In-Q-Tel was a pivotal moment in the history of the relationship between the intelligence community and its contractors, which demonstrates how contracting out can be wielded in innovative ways to tap into the private sector's potential.

In-Q-Tel was established as a hybrid organisation incorporating aspects of a private sector venture capital firm and the traditional government procurement model.[23] Based on its contract with the CIA, the company receives an annual disbursement of taxpayers' money – typically over $25 million a year – to run its operations and invest in promising technology companies. Unlike traditional venture capitalist firms, In-Q-Tel judges success based on the ability to transfer new and useful technologies to the intelligence community, rather than solely on the financial gains it can make from its investments. This approach has prompted In-Q-Tel to invest in companies that would otherwise be difficult for the government to identify, and that have the potential to develop technologies relevant to both the government and private sectors. This focus on convergent technologies facilitates co-investments with venture capitalist firms, minimises the risks posed by investments in R&D, and keeps costs lower than if services and products were designed for the government alone. When the CIA signed its first contract with In-Q-Tel, it established a centre to manage its relationship with the company and oversee the technical potential of the projects identified by In-Q-Tel. The In-Q-Tel Interface Center (QIC) brings together over a dozen experienced CIA employees who identify and communicate an unclassified set of problems to In-Q-Tel every year. This problem set provides basic guidance for In-Q-Tel to look for promising companies in relevant domains such as information security, knowledge management and data analytics. The QIC has an observer role on In-Q-Tel's board, which gives it direct access to all the company's decisions. However, In-Q-Tel is autonomous and can decide not to take the QIC's observations into account.

In-Q-Tel employees rely on their expertise in venture capital and IT to actively scout the market for relevant solutions and evaluate the integrity and compatibility of potential investees. When In-Q-Tel finds a unique technology or concept that is economically viable and useful, it decides on its own to invest in a company and develops a work plan for technology transfer to the CIA. In exchange, the technology developer receives financial and technical support from In-Q-Tel to build a robust business plan and refine its technology concepts. Deals with emerging companies are structured as development agreements based on performance milestones. When some of these milestones are not reached, In-Q-Tel can simply withdraw and recoup part of its investment.[24] Each In-Q-Tel investment is reported to CIA officers who work at the QIC and reach out to their colleagues within the intelligence community to find end users. When everything goes well, a prototype – a data analytics software, for example – is shared and tested by CIA employees in real-life situations. If the prototype is promising but not effective, In-Q-Tel can provide further guidance to the emerging company. If the prototype works well, the agency decides whether or not it wants to purchase the product incubated by In-Q-Tel. At any stage in this process, the CIA can turn down the product put forward by In-Q-Tel and look for other offers on the market.

When the CIA decided to outsource its technology incubation efforts to In-Q-Tel, it shifted away from the traditional model of government acquisition in which public agencies remain in charge. At the time, the notion that a private company would make equity investments in private companies using taxpayers' money encountered some reluctance in Congress, at the CIA and across the industry.[25] More than a decade later, In-Q-Tel is widely regarded as a success story, praised by senior intelligence officials like DCI Tenet and D/CIA Petraeus.[26] Publicly available evidence supports the notion that In-Q-Tel is a success. From 1999 to 2009, In-Q-Tel invested in some 120 companies, delivered over 100 technology pilots to the CIA, and made between twelve and twenty successful exits.[27] Since its inception, In-Q-Tel attracted more than $9 in venture capital for every $1 it invested.[28] Importantly, many of the companies In-Q-Tel discovered would not otherwise have considered contracting with the government.[29] This success has even spilled over into the civilian world as In-Q-Tel invested in companies that developed widely used applications like Google Earth, or became leaders in their market, like the cybersecurity companies Palantir Technologies and FireEye. The In-Q-Tel model has also generated interest from the DoD, the National Aeronautics and Space Administration, and the US Army, which have all sought to replicate this success. In the last decade, the company attracted more investments from the federal government and expanded its customer base within the intelligence community to include the DIA and the NGA.[30]

The success of this model can be explained by its departure from more traditional modes of acquisition and accountability. This bears relevance to the central question that drives this book because it shows that outsourcing can, under the right conditions, successfully complement traditional modes of intelligence accountability. In-Q-Tel has first benefited from a favourable context in which senior officials maintained their support of the company, and experienced employees staffed key positions at the interface between the public and private sectors. The In-Q-Tel model itself presents a number of features that explain its effectiveness. One of the main strengths of the In-Q-Tel arrangement is that it eases information sharing between the intelligence community and the IT market. As a company, In-Q-Tel is ideally positioned to offer the CIA a wider window into new technologies and expand its prospective supplier base beyond the traditional defence industry partners. The QIC and In-Q-Tel keep the CIA informed and involved in the incubation process before contracts are awarded. The CIA has an indirect observer position on the board of the companies In-Q-Tel invests in.[31] This position allows CIA officials to identify and address potential problems early on, rather than react to them at a later stage. The In-Q-Tel model also offers advantages to technology developers. From their perspective, working with the government adds prestige to their brand. At a more practical level, the guidance provided by In-Q-Tel experts gives them a window into the intelligence community's needs and helps them improve their business plans and products.[32]

In-Q-Tel leverages the marketplace to help the CIA acquire relevant technologies early and at a lower cost.[33] The company adopts a proactive stance and reaches out to firms with interesting technologies, instead of merely issuing solicitations.[34] In-Q-Tel invests in convergent technologies that can be sold to the government and in the traditional marketplace. This increases the potential customer base for the technology developers, helps attract other investors and ultimately reduces the cost of the products, which are not developed for a unique user. To make this possible, the CIA guarantees that In-Q-Tel and its technology developers will 'retain title to the innovations created and freely negotiate the allocation of IP derived revenues'.[35] The rationale is that companies which have a broad client base and own their innovations are more likely to stay in business and continue innovating after an initial investment. They have a greater chance to prosper, thereby increasing the possibility of a financial return on investment for In-Q-Tel.

The autonomous status of In-Q-Tel is essential to the success of this model. In-Q-Tel has its own board of directors and it chooses its CEO who, in turn, decides who gets hired. The CIA cannot veto investment decisions, hire or fire, promote or demote In-Q-Tel employees. This autonomy insulates technology incubation from political influences and operational pressures, which can sometimes push decision-makers to 'short-change' long-term investments and devote more resources to current needs.[36] Nevertheless, the government exerts some pressure on In-Q-Tel as its sole customer, and though officials might not be able to veto the company's decisions, they can voice their displeasure and orient strategic priorities. In-Q-Tel's autonomy places it in a solid position to maximise its commercial status, culture and networks. The company does not simply invest in technology developers; it helps them refine their plans and concepts. When doing so, it fosters a continuous relationship with private companies rather than the set of one-time transactions which often characterises government procurement. When engaging with technology developers the company is not bound by government procurement regulations or civil service policies and procedures. In-Q-Tel can lure talent, encourage and discipline its employees through compensations. The company offers competitive salaries to its employees, and though these compensations are not as high as those offered in Silicon Valley, they are still higher than those offered in government. Employees can receive performance bonuses, which help align their incentives to the organisation's objectives. To be sure, there are some limits to the In-Q-Tel model. While federal acquisition regulations do not apply to In-Q-Tel's relationship to the market, the company remains subject to a number of other legal restrictions regarding public disclosures, compensations and labour laws that do not apply to government agencies.[37] From this perspective, outsourcing does not free technology incubation from all regulations, but subjects it to another accountability regime that can be more suited to the modern reality of R&D.

The example of In-Q-Tel stands out as a success, but it is not a panacea that can solve all the problems of intelligence procurement. A host of specific factors can explain its success, including the unique status of the CIA and the statutory flexibility from which it has long benefited. This success might be difficult to replicate in other agencies, which have different cultures and operate under different legal standards. While the relationship between In-Q-Tel and the CIA thrived, other agencies like the FBI and the NSA continued to experience severe management issues with their procurement process. These issues will be explored in the next chapter to shed light on some of the main accountability problems that have affected the relationship between the intelligence community and its contractors in the early twenty-first century.[38]

Explaining the Post-9/11 Boom in Intelligence Contracting

The impact of the 9/11 attacks on the United States and its intelligence community cannot be overstated. The attacks acted as a catalyst that reinforced pre-existing trends and focused the national intelligence effort on the terrorist threat. The intelligence community significantly expanded to support the global war on terrorism, and so did intelligence outsourcing. Spending on intelligence contracts roughly doubled from 1996 to 2006, to reach $28 billion.[39] Some of the factors behind this growth emerged before the advent of the global war on terrorism and simply kept affecting the conduct of national security intelligence. New IT needs increased procurement spending across the community, especially in technical agencies like the NSA where procurement spending doubled from 2000 to 2004 and was forecast to double again in the following decade.[40] At the political level, the administration maintained a political environment that remained supportive of privatisation, advocating market-based performance and the outsourcing of products and services that were not 'inherently governmental'.[41] The administration's policies led to an overall increase in federal spending on service contracts, which doubled from $164 billion in 2000 to $343 billion in 2010.[42]

Beyond these contextual factors, a series of more specific, short-term rationales best explain the post-9/11 boom in intelligence contracting. The growth of intelligence outsourcing in the global war on terrorism can be traced to the structural conditions under which an overwhelming increase in the demand for national security intelligence occurred. The 9/11 attacks legitimised the role of the government in securing the nation and the growth of the intelligence community instigated further cross-sector collaboration. In other words, the growth of the intelligence budget – which roughly doubled from the 1990s to the 2000s, peaking at more than $80 billion in 2010 – generated an increase of the intelligence community's reliance on the private sector in absolute terms. The community's reliance on private labour also increased in relative terms, when compared to the pool of government employees. To justify this relative growth, senior intelligence officials have repeatedly invoked the structural conditions that constrained the US intelligence community in the early 2000s.

Following 9/11, the requirements for intelligence products and services dramatically increased as senior officials were expected to provide a rapid and effective answer to the crisis. However, the scarcity of resources and loss of institutional knowledge caused by the downsizing of the 1990s meant that new challenges could hardly be met by government personnel alone.[43] Hiring freezes and attrition had left the intelligence community severely understaffed. A former senior military intelligence officer working for an intelligence contractor in the early days of the global war on terrorism put it simply: 'We've got more mission than we've got people'.[44] To support the surge in intelligence requirements, senior policy-makers decided to augment the capabilities of the intelligence community. According to the ODNI, 'more than 50% of the Intelligence Community workforce was hired after 9/11'.[45] From this perspective, the intelligence contracting boom of the early twenty-first century stems, at least in part, from the government's lack of strategic planning in the area of human capital, and the way in which the intelligence community reduced its workforce in the 1990s.[46] By letting employees leave and retire without renewing their positions, the community effectively lost capabilities. The human capital shopping spree that characterised the early days of the global war on terrorism was also based on the debatable conclusion that the US 'intelligence agencies on 9/11 just didn't have enough people to do the job'.[47] With hindsight, some commentators have criticised the decision to comfort the 'bureaucratic instinct that bigger is always better'.[48] Yet this move was effectively sanctioned by Congress, which appropriated a vast amount of money to the intelligence community. In an emergency situation and with the support of elected officials, the intelligence community expanded swiftly.

To augment its capabilities rapidly the government relied on commercial companies providing the services of former government employees. An unclassified document released by the ODNI notes that the 'dramatic surge required people with the institutional knowledge and tradecraft to fill skill gaps and train new hires. Much of that expertise existed among our retired ranks, who answered the post-9/11 call to duty as a de facto intelligence reserve corps'.[49] Michael Hayden, a former director of the CIA, similarly notes that the intelligence community was not experiencing a new growth but was simply 'buying back capacity, buying back capability, buying back resources and personnel that we had lost in the decade of the 1990s following the collapse of the Soviet Union'.[50] In this view, outsourcing intelligence allowed the government to keep experienced professionals in the community.

The alternative was to hire entry-level government employees. But recruiting new government employees takes time, a resource policy-makers lacked following the 9/11 attacks. Michael Chertoff, a former Secretary of Homeland Security turned chief principal at a firm focused on security and risk management, notes that the intelligence community needed the flexibility and the responsiveness of the private sector.[51] Contractors were expected to fill intelligence capability gaps temporarily, until the government could catch up and scale back its operations in the multiple theatres of the global war on terrorism. In some cases, they provided unique but perishable skills – allowing the community to improve its understanding of particular ethnic groups in Afghanistan, for instance. Contractors were also essential to help newly established government agencies such as ODNI and DHS to get their intelligence capability up and running.

The government could not have directly augmented its number of full-time employees because it is a very slow bureaucratic process. In an interview he gave me in his office at the Chertoff Group – the firm led by Michael Chertoff – in Washington, DC,

Michael Hayden explained that new government employees need to be vetted and trained in order to acquire the necessary experience and work efficiently, and this takes years. Outsourcing government activities to former employees who have the skills, the experience and the security clearance typically proceeds faster, often taking only a few weeks or months.[52] One of the reasons why this experienced workforce was not brought back into government at the time is because, absent some special dispensations, a retiree who was reemployed by the government had to give up part of his or her pension. For example, a retired officer with a pension of $100,000 a year, taking a new government position paid $150,000 a year, would have had to relinquish the pension he or she earned to the Treasury. This salary offset could be avoided by contracting out the services of former intelligence officers instead of hiring them as civil servants.[53]

Budgetary constraints also explain the latest boom in intelligence outsourcing. Once an activity is outsourced, a commercial company can get started quickly, direct important sums of money towards a product or service and absorb early expenses in the following years. This capability was particularly suited to the surge in intelligence requirements that marked the beginning of the global war on terrorism. In contrast, bureaucratic constraints force the government to spend its money in a more linear fashion, based on annual budgets, authorisations and appropriations. As a result, intelligence agencies find it difficult to spend vast amounts of money on unforeseen tasks and in a short period of time.[54] Much of the global war on terrorism was funded through supplemental appropriations and overseas contingency operations funding, which Congress renewed on a yearly basis. According to then DNI James Clapper, this budgetary situation complicated the hiring of government employees, who are 'very difficult to hire one year at a time'.[55] When funding is uncertain, hiring more civil servants is risky. Outsourcing offers more flexibility because it binds the government for the length of contracts, generally for a few months or years.

Intelligence managers were also limited by the congressional ceiling imposed on each agency's personnel. Although Congress can move these ceilings, it was reluctant to do so in the early

2000s. In an interview, Michael Hayden noted that 'money was always easier to get increased than it was to get end strength . . . because [raising the end strength] has an air of permanence about it, whereas money appropriated for this fiscal year, that's a good idea'.[56] Intelligence agencies were left with little option but to use supplemental appropriations to hire contractors and augment their capabilities temporarily. In this way, the workforce grew without being limited by congressional ceilings. These budgetary and political issues explain why the use of contractors was sometimes 'driven by factors unrelated to mission', as the government would later find out.[57]

From a managerial perspective, the use of contractors can alleviate problems of resource allocation by focusing government employees on key tasks and orienting contractors towards support tasks. This rationale for outsourcing requires the government to clearly define its core functions and support tasks. However, when intelligence contracting boomed after 9/11, the government had not clarified the distinction between core government and support functions, or the division of labour between the public and private sectors. Contractors were used as a temporary fix to palliate some of the capabilities gaps caused by the uncertain variation of intelligence requirements. At the height of the campaigns in Iraq and Afghanistan, the US government needed vast numbers of experts who could talk and understand the Arab world, but some of this expertise became surplus skills when the United States began to withdraw its troops. This flexibility made outsourcing a useful managerial tool, but political and bureaucratic impediments to the growth of the intelligence workforce were established for good reason. Working with limited resources forces officials to prioritise and adapt to the threat environment. When policy-makers raise the limits, managers can afford to be less careful about resource allocation.

The federal government's intention to use contractors as a temporary fix explains the lack of planning behind the community's increasing reliance on contractors. The former chief human capital officer of the ODNI confirmed this explanation for the growth of outsourcing in the post-9/11 era when he told me: 'I wish I could tell you it's by design. But I think it's been by default, there was no other choice but to turn to contractors.'[58] This argument presents the outsourcing of intelligence in apolitical and pragmatic terms as an aggregation of ad hoc managerial adjustments aiming at restoring or maintaining security. This narrative explains why, as we will see in the following chapter, intelligence leaders did not keep a close eye on the growth of the contractor community in the years following the attacks. In sum, the growth of intelligence contracting was necessary given the conditions that prevailed at the time.

Some commentators have suggested that intelligence officials have occasionally turned to the private sector to circumvent regular channels of accountability by shifting decisions from the public to the private sector.[59] While executive aspirations to operate without constraints provide a plausible intent, a careful examination of the events following the 9/11 attacks weakens the argument that outsourcing intelligence reduces political costs. Decision-makers do not need to rely on contractors to circumvent traditional intelligence processes or gain more power. Experienced officials can use the bureaucracy to their own ends. In the early days of the global war on terrorism, for example, Secretary of Defense Rumsfeld established an Office of Special Plans within the Department of Defense to sidestep traditional intelligence structures and processes and feed him tailored intelligence products.[60] Given the public attention security and intelligence contractors have drawn, at least since the Abu Ghraib prison scandal broke in 2004, the continuing government reliance on contractors despite the political and bureaucratic headache such arrangements have sometimes caused, suggests that the intelligence community had more significant reasons to augment its reliance on contractors.

Critics have argued that outsourced activities are less transparent than political and bureaucratic structures. Dana Priest, an investigative journalist for *The Washington Post*, holds that outsourcing masked 'the fact that the government was growing in response to the 9/11 attacks'.[61] Priest may be right, but intelligence agencies have never been controlled by completely overt bureaucratic and political structures and processes. Key intelligence accountability holders like the congressional intelligence committees and inspectors general work in secret most of the time and specific information about the size and budget of the intelligence community has long been kept secret. The government does not need the private sector to mask the growth of the intelligence community. Moreover, if outsourcing obscures intelligence practices and weakens intelligence accountability – a claim that still needs to be verified – it does not mean that decision-makers intended to use it to this end.

A third criticism is based on the notion of the intelligence-industrial complex, and considers outsourcing as a strategy policy-makers and intelligence officials use to further their own interest, and the interest of their former colleagues who have moved to the private sector. This strategy can be opportunist in an electoralist and nepotistic sense if the decision-maker intends to reward political allies. Allegations of cronyism have been widespread in the intelligence-industrial complex and are supported by at least two phenomena: the revolving door, or the flow of individuals moving from the public to the private sector and vice versa, and the American system of political funding. The first phenomenon feeds allegations that some government employees developed strong ties with commercial companies, and awarded them government contracts in order to obtain a job with one of these companies when leaving government. Although this sequence of events may actually not breach the law, the revolving door creates an incentive for senior policy-makers to make favours to commercial companies for which they have worked, or those that are willing to hire them in the future. The second phenomenon that feeds allegations of personal interest is the funding of political campaigns and the use of bribes by some of the companies that are involved with the intelligence community.[62] It is reasonable to suppose that companies that lobby or bribe public officials expect favours in exchange for their money. In at least two cases – those of former Republican congressman Randy Cunningham (R-CA) and former Executive Director of the CIA Kyle Foggo – public officials abused their government position to award intelligence contracts in exchange for personal gain. These cases, which will be examined in the next chapter, provide a thin evidence base to claim that intelligence outsourcing was a systematic effort by government officials to escape accountability and further their personal interests. When such questionable rationales played a role in the latest wave of intelligence contracting, their role was marginal.

Most of the evidence suggests that the post-9/11 outsourcing boom occurred as a result of the surge in intelligence requirements that followed the worst terrorist attacks on the United States in living memory. There is strong evidence that the intelligence community's reliance on the private sector was driven by a logic of capacity that sought to guarantee US national security. If anything, the history of intelligence teaches us that the government's intelligence apparatus cannot function without the private sector. The fiercest opponents of the intelligence community's reliance on the private sector, those who argue that intelligence (as a whole) should not be outsourced, overlook the fact that government bureaucracy is unable to provide all the innovation, flexibility and critical knowledge necessary for the craft of intelligence.[63] In the United States as well as in most modern democracies from France to South Africa and Australia, cross-sector collaboration is essential to intelligence because the government needs the expertise of the private sector to serve the public interest in national security.[64]

The Market for Government Intelligence

'It's nothing but a growth industry.' This is the catchphrase retired Major General James Marks, the former senior intelligence officer for all US land forces during combat operations in Iraq, used to describe the intelligence business in 2005.[65] Marks, who had then transitioned to a position as senior manager at McNeil Technologies, was right. The strengthening of the rationales for outsourcing generated a significant proliferation and diversification of intelligence contracting throughout the 2000s.

Publicly available information is indicative of the vast scope of intelligence outsourcing at the time. The NSA executed some 43,000 contracts in 2003, and used as many as 2,690 businesses to conduct its mission in 2004. In 2006, 70 per cent of the US intelligence budget ($28 billion) was spent on contracts.[66] This aggregate budget figure has worried a number of observers, who wonder who is driving the national intelligence effort. However, it is worth noting that this figure conflates the provision of services and supplies, including the development and acquisition of expensive collection platforms, which are likely to constitute the lion's share of the $28 billion spent on private contracts. In 2006, for instance, the NGA outsourced over $1.4 billion.[67] The following year, the DIA announced that it was preparing to pay contractors up to $1 billion to conduct intelligence collection and analysis over a five-year period.[68] That same year, contractors constituted around 35 per cent of the DIA workforce (nearly twice as much as in 1975). According to a former intelligence officer, over half of the workforce in the most sensitive division of the CIA, the National Clandestine Service (now the Directorate of Operations), was made up of contractors. One commentator explains that the wars in Afghanistan and Iraq overstretched the clandestine service and its global response staff.[69] A few months after he retired from his position as CIA director in 2009, General Hayden estimated that about 30 per cent of CIA employees were contractors. Similar figures reportedly applied to the NGA.[70] All this evidence confirms that contractors played a significant part in the national intelligence effort of the mid-2000s.

The government's demand for intelligence services and products fostered the development of a multi-billion-dollar market. Investigative journalist Tim Shorrock estimates that the value of the companies populating this market exploded from $980.5 million in 2001 to $8.3 billion in 2006.[71] This booming industry involved a growing range of actors. While little information is available about individual contractors, companies – whose structure is more permanent – are more visible and have therefore attracted more attention. Reporter Jeremy Scahill wrote an entire book about the rise of the private security company Blackwater, and Erik Prince's memoirs describe his experience as CEO of Blackwater.[72] Following the involvement of Blackwater employees in a number of controversies, the company was renamed Xe Services in 2009, and Academi in 2011.

The companies populating the market for intelligence vary immensely in size along a continuum that stems from well-established defence industry giants to small start-ups developing state-of-the-art technology, and body shops or 'rent-a-spies' relying on their Rolodex to supply intelligence agencies with contractors. Some of these companies have relied on government intelligence contracts and outside investment to expand their revenue from multiple millions to multiple billions of dollars. Their growth can be traced in the trade press, which periodically reports the multi-million-dollar contracts they sign with undisclosed government intelligence agencies. CACI International, a company based in Arlington, VA, which describes itself as 'a government contractor specializing in technology services and intelligence analysis', is a case in point. The company grew from a small IT business in the 1960s to a major intelligence contractor in the 2000s. Following the acquisition of a dozen other IT companies in the last decade, CACI reported that 43 per cent of its multi-billion dollar revenue came from its growing intelligence business in 2012.[73] The biggest companies in this market, such as Lockheed Martin, Raytheon and Booz Allen Hamilton, employ thousands of cleared personnel and have been serving the national security community for decades. They are so extensively involved with the government that they have arguably become semi-public organisations.

To provide complex technological products and services to the government, these prime contractors heavily rely on smaller, more specialised companies to which they subcontract their work. At this second level, the government relies on a contractual relation between two or more contractors to obtain intelligence supplies and services. This practice adds a layer in the accountability chain between the government and the individuals who implement its intelligence functions. As a result, a range of smaller companies, focusing more exclusively on specific activities, also emerged in the market for intelligence. Since the 1990s, companies that were not historically related to the intelligence community realised the tremendous business opportunity in this domain and developed their offer in the intelligence business. Companies like Google and AT&T, which are known for their IT achievements, have profited from greater government demand for intelligence.[74] The intelligence business has also expanded beyond the United States, and well-established defence contractors have signed intelligence contracts with foreign governments such as the United Kingdom and Afghanistan.[75]

The Scope of Intelligence Contracting

A snapshot of intelligence contractors' involvement in the global war on terrorism demonstrates the tremendous scope of their activities and raises questions about their growing role in the national intelligence effort. Since the beginning of the war on terrorism, intelligence contractors have been involved in a wide variety of core intelligence activities such as collection, covert action, analysis, dissemination, and counterintelligence and security. When carrying out these tasks, they have worked from places ranging from offices in the Washington, DC area to the frontlines of the wars in Afghanistan (2001–14) and Iraq (2003–11).

Contractors have been involved in all types of intelligence collection, from the most mundane to the most sensitive tasks. Companies have long contributed to the collection of signals (SIGINT), imagery (IMINT) and measurement and signature intelligence (MASINT) when they develop and build satellites, and more recently drones. Drones have been remotely controlled by contractors sitting in a control room in the United States or abroad, providing geospatial intelligence (GEOINT) and 24-hour surveillance of sensitive areas in faraway countries like Yemen and Pakistan, but also along the United States-Mexico border. Contractors worked in the National Counter Terrorism Center to collect data and update its terrorist databases. Following the 9/11 attacks, the government's emphasis on surveillance in the homeland fostered the emergence of commercial companies specialised in collecting and providing open source intelligence (OSINT) to the intelligence community. Some companies specialise in the aggregation of data on other companies' customers; others gather data on people's behaviour on the Internet, for example. The involvement of companies in government-sponsored data gathering and mining programmes has raised concern among civil liberties groups, which decry the growth of a new 'surveillance-industrial complex'.[76]

Contractors have also worked closer to the field. The US Army Intelligence and Security Command used contractors to conduct HUMINT operations in support of the coalition forces in Iraq and Afghanistan. In Afghanistan, contractors gathered intelligence to help locate militants and insurgent camps.[77] Contracted linguists worked directly in the interrogation room, while other contractors devised sets of techniques to interview detainees and some even interrogated them.[78] In the CIA Iraq station, contractors reportedly worked as case officers, recruited informants and supervised government agents supporting combat units.[79]

Contractors have contributed to some of the most offensive intelligence activities led by the US government in the global war on terrorism. The use of contractors for paramilitary operations was indirectly confirmed by the CIA in a press release stating that two contractors 'died while tracking terrorists near Shkin, Afghanistan, on October 25, 2003'.[80] Commercial companies have also been an essential part of the drone war in which remotely controlled unmanned aerial vehicles have allowed the CIA to conduct targeted killings. Contractors developed, built, maintained, loaded and operated drones. Reportedly, 'management and training responsibility for CIA's "targeted killing" efforts' was handed to Blackwater.[81] Contractors have been in charge of selecting targets and flying armed drones; however, according to journalists Dana Priest and William Arkin, 'they had to hand the joystick controls over to a federal employee – either a CIA officer or someone in uniform – once the vehicle got inside the kill box, meaning within the range of launching its missiles'. This ensured that a government employee representing the national interest would 'push the launch button'.[82] The involvement of contractors in such operations, even when they do not pull the trigger, raises important questions about the scope of their participation in sensitive government operations and the government's ability to conduct these operations independently.

Contractors have also been extensively involved in intelligence processing, analysis and dissemination. Companies developed data analytics software to process, manipulate and visualise increasingly vast amounts of diverse data and facilitate the work of intelligence analysts.[83] The DIA outsourced a number of major all-source intelligence reports.[84] A company named Aegis developed battlefield threat assessments for DoD personnel – researching, analysing and mapping the activities of foreign intelligence services, terrorist organisations, militias and criminal gangs in specific regions of Iraq.[85] Contractors at Science Applications International Corporation (SAIC) have analysed drone footage to track insurgents in Afghanistan and inform US military airstrikes. In one case, a contractor's analysis misinformed the decision of an Army captain to order an airstrike on 'a convoy that turned out to be carrying innocent civilians' in central Afghanistan.[86] This example highlights the tremendous implications of contractors' activities when they are involved in intelligence analysis that informs battlefield decisions.

Contracted analysts briefed senior intelligence officials and policy-makers, a significantly sensitive task given the influence experts can have in government.[87] Commercial companies even provided the US government with report officers who acted as 'liaisons between officers in the field and analysts back at headquarters'.[88] Contractors have also helped the government disseminate intelligence in more systematic ways. Raytheon Corporation designed and built the Distributed Common Ground System, which allowed the US military to fuse 'tactical intelligence from military units with signals intelligence and imagery from the national collection agencies'.[89] In this domain, critics of intelligence outsourcing have expressed concern but lacked evidence to prove that private incentives could bias the analysis and dissemination efforts of contractors and skew national security decisions.

The private sector has provided all sorts of management and support services to the intelligence community. These tasks are not core intelligence activities but they are, nonetheless, essential to the intelligence process. A number of companies provided specialised training to intelligence officials. For example, a company called Antheon trained instructors at the Army's intelligence school in Fort Huachuca, Arizona.[90] Commercial companies like CACI and non-profit organisations like BENS advised intelligence agencies on the efficiency of their structure, financial management system and workforce management practices.[91] In the field of procurement, Northrop Grumman subcontractors managed the system used by the DIA for 'processing bids and awarding contracts' and various sources have confirmed the involvement of commercial companies in drafting government agencies budgets, and writing statements of work which describe agencies' needs and requirements.[92] Outsourcing procurement services can be controversial because involving contractors in the selection and assessment of other actors can foster conflicts of interest and leave the impression that public officials are relinquishing control. In practice, the law requires government officials to make the final decisions in contracting.

At the CIA, companies acted as travel agents and planned international trips for the Agency's employees. Outsourcing travel services becomes more contentious when these trips include individuals who have been kidnapped. According to Jane Mayer, a journalist at the *New Yorker*, the CIA used front companies to operate extraordinary rendition flights for high-value detainees, and a subsidiary of Boeing was also involved 'to handle many of the logistical and navigational details for these trips, including flight plans, clearance to fly over other countries, hotel reservations, and ground-crew arrangements'.[93] These examples show that the boundaries between proprietary arrangements designed to maintain operations under cover, and the outsourcing of services to independent companies are blurred. Outsiders' confusion about these two types of practices has limited the debate on intelligence outsourcing.

Finally, companies have provided services in the area of counterintelligence and security, protecting intelligence sources and methods against enemy intrusions. Abraxas Corporation devised nonofficial covers for case officers overseas. Contractors have compartmentalised secret information and made sure intelligence producers and consumers accessed information on a need-to-know basis. They have investigated and vetted intelligence agency employees and their contractors before the government granted them security clearance.[94] Other companies physically protected and stored secret documents, and developed and maintained classified computer networks.[95] According to James Bamford, private contractors also acted as counterintelligence officers, overseeing clandestine meetings between agency officers and the agents they recruit.[96] Blackwater employees provided physical protection to personnel in and around some of the most dangerous CIA stations in the world and, more controversially, during CIA field officers' missions. According to one commentator, this security role expanded to the point that experienced special forces veterans working for Blackwater on CIA contracts 'became closely involved in both mission planning and execution', taking part in 'snatch and grab missions'.[97]

Contractors' involvement in all these intelligence activities raises a number of questions pertaining to accountability. Critics have asked whether contractors can be trusted with state secrets and sensitive missions to the same extent as government employees. The vast scope of intelligence contracting in the post-9/11 era poses further questions about the limits of modern government and officials' ability to control thousands of contracts and contractors across multiple domains of activity. Should contractors ever be involved in particularly sensitive intelligence collection programmes, covert actions and counterintelligence operations? Who is responsible for contractors' mistakes? How should a variety of intelligence activities, ranging from the simplest to the most complex, be outsourced? While simple goods and services like catering or guarding facilities in the United States can often be acquired with little ambiguity, outsourcing more demanding functions, like intelligence operations, analysis and management, is riskier and requires intricate contractual arrangements, as well as close supervision to ensure the behaviour of contractors remains aligned with the public interest. The extent to which the US system of intelligence accountability has been able to keep public and private interests aligned remains unclear. This situation is particularly concerning given the imperfections that characterise the market for intelligence.

An Imperfect Market

There is no fully free market for intelligence in the United States. A number of market imperfections cast doubt on the notion that outsourcing intelligence can generate new efficiencies. On the demand side, the US government dominates the market both as a buyer and a regulator. While the government has an interest in being efficient to save taxpayers' money, officials have to contend with other imperatives including a public oversight regime that limits free market.[98] On the supply side, the situation depends on the type of product or service the government seeks to acquire. Complex products like reconnaissance satellites and related services can often only be realistically provided by well-established prime contractors.[99] These big companies dominate the market and develop a diversified offer to satisfy one main customer: the government. In some cases, like In-Q-Tel, companies provide services that are so unique that there is little to no competition. This lack of competition limits the government's choices, and reinforces the need to plan and monitor the government's collaboration with the private sector carefully.[100]

When contracting out intelligence, the government faces a number of costs, most of which can be attributed to its oversight duties. Government employees need to administer the contracting process, that is to say identify and assess suitable contractors, and then negotiate and write contracts. Management costs, such as monitoring agreements, sanctioning vendors and negotiating contract changes, are also involved, especially when acquiring complex products and services like intelligence collection platforms. Government agencies often face difficulties in determining accurate costs and anticipating contractors' performance because of the unpredictable nature of intelligence activities such as surveillance, and support services such as personnel security abroad and R&D.[101] This uncertainty can prompt government officials to change contract requirements multiple times after the initial bid, a situation called spiral development. That is why the government often relies on specific types of contracts, such as cost-reimbursement contracts, that provide greater flexibility to the contractors. However, these contracts force the government 'to assume financial risk' and decrease the incentive for the vendor 'to perform its work on or under budget'.[102] When contractors are given enough room to change their initial offer, competition is based on promises rather than actual performance, and this can lead to sub-optimal outcomes. If vendors fail to deliver, the government needs to hold them to account. Monitoring contractors – before, during and after a contract is signed – is resource-consuming, and can undermine the economic rationale for outsourcing.

Secrecy requirements also impede on the market logic. The business of intelligence has developed under the veil of secrecy that pervades the US national security apparatus. Commercial companies, wary about their proprietary information, have embraced their own information security policies. Secrecy acts as a structural limit on the market. Following the federal acquisition regulations, full and open competition, including the advertisement of contracting actions, can be avoided for national security reasons. The CIA, for example, can conduct 'negotiated procurement without advertising' to protect its sources and methods.[103] In order to preserve secrecy and speed up procurement, contract officers often use no-bid, or sole-source, contracts according to which only one company can satisfy the government's demand. When so doing, the government supports the absence of competition in order to maintain secrecy. This reality conflicts with good business practices, which hold that competition is *the* key ingredient for successful privatisation.[104] Secrecy can also foster unnecessary competition and lead agencies like the CIA to bid up the cost of contracts 'because different pockets of the agency [are] trying to buy the same services'.[105] In this compartmentalised world, intelligence organisations do not systematically share information on the performance of their contractors, and this limits the government's ability to buy smartly.

The compartmentalisation of sensitive information also creates information asymmetries between private competitors. Security clearances, which are granted by the government, constitute a significant barrier to entry for would-be competitors. To access the sensitive knowledge and capabilities necessary to obtain government contracts, companies hire former officials with a security clearance and access to government information and networks. In some cases, companies bid individuals who work on other classified contracts, hoping to replace them with new individuals waiting for their clearance to be processed. This commodification of security clearances has had negative consequences on the market for intelligence. According to a former contract writer, 'if two candidates are competing for a job with a contractor, and one has deep relevant experience but no clearance, she will most likely lose to a candidate with less relevant experience but a current and active security clearance'.[106] In such situations, government requirements truncate the market logic, and the government misses out on new perspectives and young and motivated individuals with no clearance or waiting to get one. Well-established companies with a large number of cleared employees and the secured facilities to work on sensitive programmes are in a better position to obtain contracts than newcomers. Their continuing reliance on the government's demand allows them to maintain a pool of cleared employees, develop the necessary infrastructure, and further their knowledge of the complex set of procurement regulations that apply to the intelligence community. This situation creates an incentive for smaller and newer companies to associate with well-established prime contractors.

In sum, the market for intelligence is not a free market and is unlikely to become so considering the nature of its goods and services, the environment in which they are traded and, in particular, the central role of the government in national security affairs. These imperfect market conditions complicate intelligence acquisition and can explain the recurrence of delays and cost overruns. In 2006, the HPSCI found that major contracts signed by technical agencies like the NRO, the NSA and the NGA 'have cost taxpayers billions of dollars in cost overruns and schedule delays'.[107] With hindsight, the economic rationale behind the privatisation of intelligence is not very convincing. This does not mean that contractors have no place in the intelligence community, but it emphasises the need for careful and effective oversight of contractors to defend the public interest in national security.

Aligning Incentives

Aligning public and private incentives is the main challenge posed by outsourcing. Intelligence officials and their private sector counterparts often conceive of their relationship as a partnership.[108]

According to Tony Bovaird, a professor of public management, the notion of partnership supposes a level of mutual commitment that goes 'over and above that implied in any contract'. In a partnership, public and private actors share certain aspects of the production of goods and the provision of services, including risks, more so than in a simple contractual relationship.[109] The rhetoric of partnership reinforces the idea that the intelligence community encompasses the contractors augmenting US intelligence capabilities. Phenomena such as the revolving door between government and industry positions further contribute to this rapprochement. A former senior CIA officer recalls 'a very brotherly relationship' with the company Blackwater, which he felt was 'an extension of the Agency'. This brotherly relationship was certainly facilitated by Blackwater's hiring of former senior CIA officers such as Coffer Black and Robert Richer.[110] In May 2004, at its annual memorial ceremony, the CIA demonstrated this sense of community when it honoured the ultimate sacrifice of two civilian contractors working for its Directorate of Operations, who lost their life in an ambush in Afghanistan. More stars would be added in subsequent years to honour other contractors.[111]

However, the rhetoric of partnership and the notion that public and private interests converge around national security do not convince everybody.[112] The public-private distinction places individuals and organisations in two camps and assumes their incentives differ. The public sector is often defined by its capacity for disinterested judgement and decision-making, while the private sector is assumed to pursue private interests. On the public side, the intelligence community's main organisational incentive is national security, a public end that is embedded in the intelligence bureaucracy, at least since the passage of the National Security Act of 1947. In practice, government agencies sometimes distrust companies working for them, and refuse to share sensitive information with their contractors to protect the public interest.[113] Yet, public officials and agencies do not always stand for the public interest. They sometimes pursue organisational interests. Scholars have argued, for instance, that bureaucratic incentives led US Air Force intelligence to inflate the Soviet threat to attract greater government investment. Intelligence decisions can also be constrained by personal and political interests that do not necessarily align with the public interest in national security.[114]

The private sector is traditionally characterised by a search for profit that is most obvious at the organisational level, where it is embedded in the structure and culture of companies. In the market for intelligence, as in most other markets, public, private, small and large firms share an incentive structure that primarily aims to fulfil their owners' main interest: profit. Companies sometimes hesitate or even refuse to cooperate with the government for fear it may impact on their reputation and create proprietary and legal risks for them. The emergence of great multi-national firms in the security sector fosters a globalisation ethos that may eventually overtake the idea of national interest. Public companies, for instance, have a fiduciary responsibility to protect their brand on an international scale, which might contradict US government policies. Vice versa, companies whose incentives are well aligned with those of the government, like In-Q-Tel for instance, can take initiatives that contribute to the public interest in national security. However, companies are unlikely to invest in security if the results of their cost-benefit analysis are unfavourable to their bottom line. In privatisation theory, companies' search for profit can be controlled and harnessed to provide best value goods and services to the government. In other words, profit incentives and the behaviour of contractors are not problematic as long as government officials effectively monitor contractors' behaviour to ensure – usually through regulation and oversight – that the market logic does not threaten but serves the public interest in national security.

At the individual level, though profit can be expected to play a role in determining contractors' behaviour, it is not the sole incentive. As a former CIA analyst put it: 'exchanging an official blue badge for the contractor's green one does not automatically divest someone of a sense of professional dedication'.[115] There is no doubt that most of the public and private employees of the intelligence community are primarily driven by their national security mission, patriotism and self-reward. However, in some situations, economic interests prevail more clearly. This is the case of those early- to mid-career employees who left their agency on a Friday to come back as contractors with a higher pay check on the following Monday. But a number of intelligence professionals also started their career in the private sector before transitioning to a government position. At this individual level, the lines between public and private sectors and interests are often blurred and evidence needs to be analysed on a case-by-case basis. Overall, the extent to which government accountability holders have been able to keep contractors' behaviour aligned with the public interest is unclear. This important issue deserves further scrutiny.

Conclusion

This chapter has explained the growth of intelligence contracting in the post-Cold War era as the outcome of changing intelligence requirements. The demand for intelligence diversified after the fall of the Soviet Union and forced government agencies to engage with a wider array of complex threats, partners and processes. The IT revolution pushed the intelligence community to modernise its infrastructure and reach out to the private sector to harness its ability to innovate. New initiatives like In-Q-Tel emphasised the potential of outsourcing when public and private incentives are well aligned and government accountability holders achieve a balance between flexibility and control.

US intelligence priorities shifted dramatically following the 9/11 attacks and forced the community to concentrate its resources on counter-terrorism. In a context of crisis and following significant personnel and budget cuts during the 1990s, the intelligence community struggled to satisfy the growing number of requirements it was confronted with, and had little choice but to increase its reliance on contractors to fill a gap in core capabilities. The market for intelligence expanded to meet this demand, but it also remained deeply imperfect. In a domain where performance is barely quantifiable and competition is hardly free, contracting out is a complex process that must be carefully implemented. However, the need to ramp up following the 9/11 attacks clearly took over the longer-term logic of improving government efficiency, and the boom in intelligence contracting was not carefully planned.

The post-9/11 spike in intelligence contracting raises important questions about the nature of modern government, the relevance of the public-private distinction and its potential impact on the conduct of intelligence. Outsourcing intelligence reconfigures government boundaries, but it does not necessarily lead to a transfer of competence and authorities from the public to the private sector. The government keeps bearing significant responsibilities when intelligence activities are contracted out, but the means through which officials control contractors are not well understood and often assumed to be insufficient. The next chapter fills this knowledge gap and assesses the extent to which government accountability holders have been able to keep contractors' behaviour aligned with the public interest.

Notes

1. Carver, 'Intelligence in the Age of Glasnost', p. 156.
2. Ronald Reagan, 'Inaugural Address', 20 January 1981, Washington, DC, available at <http://www.presidency.ucsb.edu/ws/index.php?pid=43130> (accessed 28 May 2018); Executive Office of the President, Office of Management and Budget, *Circular No. A-76*, 4 August 1983.
3. Savas, *Privatization and Public-Private Partnerships*, p. 15; US Department of the Army, Logistics Civil Augmentation Program, Army Regulation 700–137, 16 December 1985.
4. Clinton and Gore, *Putting People First*, p. 1.
5. US Congress, Public Law 103–355, *The Federal Acquisition Streamlining Act*, 103th Congress, 2nd session, 13 October 1994; US Congress, Public Law 104–106, *The Federal Acquisition Reform Act*, 104th Congress, 2nd session, 10 February 1996; US Congress, Public Law 105–270, *The Federal Activities Inventory Reform Act*, 105th Congress, 2nd session, 19 October 1998.
6. Al Gore, 'Reinventing Government', National Archives and Records Administration website, available at <http://clinton4.nara.gov/WH/EOP/OVP/initiatives/reinventing_government.html> (accessed 28 May 2018).

7. Schooner, 'Fear of Oversight', pp. 629–30.
8. Tenet, *At the Center of the Storm*, p. 14.
9. Ronald Sanders, Office of the Director of National Intelligence, media conference call, 14 January 2010, p. 6.
10. Mark M. Lowenthal, statement before the US Senate Committee on Homeland Security and Governmental Affairs, Subcommittee on Oversight of Government Management, the Federal Workforce, and the District of Columbia, *Intelligence Community Contractors: Are We Striking the Right Balance?*, hearing, 112th Congress, 2nd session, 20 September 2011, p. 5; Stephanie O'Sullivan, Principal Deputy Director of National Intelligence, statement for the record, US Senate, Committee on Homeland Security and Governmental Affairs, hearing: 'The Intelligence Community: Keeping Watch Overt Its Contractor Workforce', 18 June 2014, p. 1.
11. Shorrock, *Spies for Hire*, pp. 102–3; Philip A. Odeen, Defense Science Board, Memorandum for Chairman, Defense Science Board, Final Report of the Defense Science Board Task Force on Outsourcing and Privatization, 27 August 1996, p. 2; Singer, *Corporate Warriors*, pp. 5–18; US Department of Defense, Inspector General, Audit Report On Civilian Contractor Overseas Support During Hostilities, Report No.91-105, 26 June 1991; Government Accounting Office, Defense Outsourcing: Challenges Facing DOD as It Attempts to Save Billions in Infrastructure Costs, GAO/T-NSIAD-97-110, 12 March 1997.
12. R. James Woolsey, testimony before the Select Committee on Intelligence of the United States Senate, *Nomination of R. James Woolsey to be Director of Central Intelligence*, 103rd Congress, 1st session, 2–3 February 1993, p. 76.
13. Ronald Sanders, interview with Mr Andrew Pourinski, Federal News Radio, 'Ask the Chief Human Capital Officer', 2 August 2007, p. 2, available at <http://www.dni.gov/interviews/20070802_interview.pdf> (accessed 28 May 2018).
14. Avant, *The Market for Force*, pp. 32–6.
15. Arquilla and Ronfeldt, *Networks and Netwars*.
16. Steele, 'National Security and National Competitiveness', p. 21.
17. Margetts, *Information Technology in Government* (London: Routledge, 2003), p. 125; Charles E. Allen, statement before the US Senate Committee on Homeland Security and Governmental Affairs, Subcommittee on Oversight of Government Management, the Federal Workforce, and the District of Columbia, *Intelligence Community*

Contractors: Are We Striking the Right Balance?, hearing, 112th Congress, 1st session, 20 September 2011, p. 2.

18. Bryan Bender, 'New Intelligence Policy Gives Private Sector Larger Role', *Defense Daily* 196/57 (1997), p. 1; Mara, *Maximizing the Returns of Government Venture Capital Programs*, p. 1.
19. *Business Wire*, 'Planning-Research; Wins $4.4 Million Intelligence Contract', 15 October 1985.
20. Wall and Covault, 'Trouble at NRO', *Aviation Week & Space Technology* 159/7, 18 August 2003, p. 25; Josh Lerner et al., 'In-Q-Tel', *Harvard Business Review*, 25 May 2005, p. 3.
21. US House of Representatives, Permanent Select Committee on Intelligence, *IC21: The Intelligence Community in the 21st Century*, VI. IMINT, 104th Congress, 5 June 1996, available at <http://www.gpo.gov/fdsys/pkg/GPO-IC21/html/GPO-IC21-6.html> (accessed 28 May 2018).
22. Yannuzzi, 'In-Q-Tel: A New Partnership', p. 33.
23. Molzahn, 'The CIA's In-Q-Tel Model. Its Applicability', p. 48; BENS, *Accelerating the Acquisition and Implementation of New Technologies for Intelligence: The Report of the Independent Panel on the Central Intelligence Agency In-Q-Tel Venture*, June 2001, p. 17.
24. Lerner et al., 'In-Q-Tel', p. 9; BENS, *Accelerating the Acquisition and Implementation of New Technologies for Intelligence*, p. 44.
25. Yannuzzi, 'In-Q-Tel: A New Partnership', p. 36.
26. Lerner et al., 'In-Q-Tel', p. 5; BENS, *Accelerating the Acquisition and Implementation of New Technologies for Intelligence*, pp. 10–11; Tenet, *At the Center of the Storm*, p. 26; David Petraeus, 'Remarks at the In-Q-Tel CEO Summit', 1 March 2012, available at <https://www.cia.gov/news-information/speeches-testimony/2012-speeches-testimony/in-q-tel-summit-remarks.html> (accessed 28 May 2018).
27. Mashhadi et al., 'In-Q-Tel as an Early Stage Investment Model', p. 5; In-Q-Tel, 'Portfolio', available at <https://www.iqt.org/portfolio/> (accessed 28 May 2018); Mara, *Maximizing the Returns of Government Venture Capital Programs*, p. 7.
28. Petraeus, 'Remarks at the In-Q-Tel CEO Summit'.
29. Belko, *Government Venture Capital*, p. 79.
30. In-Q-Tel, 'About IQT – Partners', available at <https://www.iqt.org/about-iqt/> (accessed 28 May 2018).
31. Editor, 'Inside In-Q-Tel: Exclusive Interview', *KMWorld*, July/August 2004, p. 28.

32. Molzahn, 'The CIA's In-Q-Tel Model. Its Applicability', p. 56.
33. Mara, *Maximizing the Returns of Government Venture Capital Programs*, p. 2.
34. Molzahn, 'The CIA's In-Q-Tel Model. Its Applicability', p. 52.
35. Yannuzzi, 'In-Q-Tel: A New Partnership', p. 33.
36. Michaels, 'The (Willingly) Fettered Executive', p. 830; Lerner et al., 'In-Q-Tel', p. 8.
37. Michaels, 'The (Willingly) Fettered Executive', pp. 803, 816.
38. Department of Justice, Office of the Inspector General, Audit Division, Federal Bureau of Investigation's Management of Information Technology Investments, December 2002, pp. 4–5; Michael V. Hayden, statement for the record before the Joint Inquiry of the Senate Select Committee on Intelligence and the House Permanent Select Committee on Intelligence, 17 October 2002, p. 8; Aid, *The Secret Sentry*, pp. 207–9.
39. Terri Everett, Office of the Director of National Intelligence, 'Procuring the Future: 21st Century Acquisition', presentation given at conference organised by the DIA, Boulder, Colorado, 14 May 2007, available at <http://www.fas.org/irp/dni/everett.ppt> (accessed 28 May 2018). The figure of $28 billion is based on the 2006 budget for the National Intelligence Program.
40. George Cahlink, 'Security Agency Doubled Procurement Spending in Four Years', *Government Executive*, 1 June 2004.
41. Executive Office of the President, Office of Management and Budget, *The President's Management Agenda*, 2002, p. 17.
42. David Berteau et al., 'DoD Workforce Cost Realism Assessment', p. 1.
43. Ronald Sanders, *Results of the Fiscal Year 2007 US Intelligence Community Inventory of Core Contractor Personnel*, 27 August 2008, p. 2.
44. Harris, 'Intelligence Incorporated', p. 46.
45. Office of the Director of National Intelligence, *Key Facts about Contractors*, p. 2, available at <https://www.fas.org/irp/news/2010/07/ic-contract.pdf> (accessed 28 May 2018).
46. Johnson, 'A Conversation with James R. Clapper, Jr., The Director of National Intelligence in the United States', p. 21.
47. Sanders, interview with Mr Andrew Pourinski, p. 2.
48. Priest and Arkin, *Top Secret America*, p. 85; US Senate, *Intelligence Authorization Act for Fiscal Year 2007*, Report 109–259, 109th Congress, 2nd session, 25 May 2006, p. 40; US Senate, Select Committee on Intelligence, *Nomination of Lieutenant General James Clapper, Jr., USAF, Ret., to be Director of National Intelligence*, 111th Congress, 2nd session, 20 July 2010, p. 2.

49. Office of the Director of National Intelligence, *Key Facts about Contractors*, p. 2.
50. Michael Hayden, interview with *Frontline*, 19 August 2010, available at <http://www.pbs.org/wgbh/pages/frontline/are-we-safer/interviews/michael-hayden.html> (accessed 28 May 2018).
51. Michael Chertoff, in video: C-SPAN, *Privatization of US Intelligence*, 20 August 2009, available at <http://www.c-spanvideo.org/program/288482-1> (accessed 28 May 2018).
52. Michael Hayden, interview with author, 8 August 2011, Washington, DC.
53. Ron Sanders, interview with author, McLean, VA, 6 April 2015.
54. Hayden, interview with author; US Senate, Select Committee on Intelligence, *Authorizing Appropriations for Fiscal Year 2004 for Intelligence and Intelligence-related Activities of the United States Government, the Community Management Account, and the Central Intelligence Agency Retirement and Disability System, and for Other Purposes*, Report 108–044, 108th Congress, 1st session, 8 May 2003, p. 19; Max Boot, 'Afterword: The CIA and Erik Prince', in Prince with Coburn, *Civilian Warriors*, pp. 347–8.
55. James Clapper, cited in US Senate, Select Committee on Intelligence, *Nomination of Lieutenant General James Clapper, Jr., USAF, Ret., to be Director of National Intelligence*, p. 11; US Senate, Post-Hearing Questions for the Record Submitted to Paula Roberts From Senator Daniel Akaka, *Intelligence Community Contractors: Are We Striking the Right Balance?*, 20 September 2011, p. 72.
56. Hayden, interview with *Frontline*.
57. Office of the Director of National Intelligence, *The US Intelligence Community's Five Year Strategic Human Capital Plan: An annex to the US National Intelligence Strategy*, 22 June 2006, p. 14; Paula J. Roberts, US Senate, Committee on Homeland Security and Governmental Affairs, Subcommittee on Oversight of Government Management, the Federal Workforce, and the District of Columbia, *Intelligence Community Contractors: Are We Striking the Right Balance?*, hearing, 112th Congress, 1st session, 20 September 2011, p. 36.
58. Sanders, interview with author.
59. Chesterman, *One Nation Under Surveillance*, pp. 117–18, 129; Hoogenboom, 'Grey Intelligence', p. 377; Michaels, 'All the President's Spies'; Singer, *Corporate Warriors*, pp. 216–17; Joshua Chaffin, 'Contract Interrogators Hired to Avoid Supervision', *Financial Times*, 22 May 2004, p. 6.

60. Seymour M. Hersh, 'Selective Intelligence: Donald Rumsfeld Has His Own Special Sources. Are They Reliable?' *New Yorker* 79/11, 12 May 2003, p. 44. On the broader context, see Pillar, 'Intelligence, Policy, and the War in Iraq', pp. 15–27.
61. Dana Priest, 'America's Security Overload', *The Daily Beast*, 21 September 2011.
62. Shorrock, *Spies for Hire*, pp. 375–8.
63. For categorical rejections of intelligence contracting see Caldwell, 'Privatized Information Gathering: Just War Theory and Morality'; Roper, 'Using Private Corporations'.
64. French Parliament, Rapport no. 201 (2014–15) de MM. Jean-Jacques Urvoas, député et Jean-Pierre Raffarin, sénateur, fait au nom de la délégation parlementaire au renseignement, Activité de la délégation parlementaire au renseignement pour l'année 2014, 18 December 2014; Tim Lhoman, 'Privatising Intelligence Gathering', *ZDNet*, 6 August 2013; Butt, *Outsourcing Intelligence*, pp. 44–50.
65. Harris, 'Spider and the Flies'.
66. Everett, 'Procuring the Future'; Office of the Director of National Intelligence, *Key Facts about Contractors*, p. 1.
67. Crampton et al., 'The New Political Economy of Geographical Intelligence', p. 6.
68. Pincus, 'Defense Agency Proposes Outsourcing More Spying; Contractors Worth $1 Billion Would Set Record', *Washington Post*, 19 August 2007, A3.
69. Boot, 'Afterword: The CIA and Erik Prince', p. 338.
70. Raelynn J. Hillhouse, ''The Achilles' Heel of the US War Effort', 4 October 2007, available at <http://www.thespywhobilledme.com/the_spy_who_billed_me/2007/10/the-achilles-he.html> (accessed 28 May 2018); Robert Baer, 'Just Who Does the CIA's Work?', *Time*, 20 April 2007; US Senate, Select Committee on Intelligence, *Nomination of Lieutenant General James Clapper, Jr., USAF, Ret., to be Director of National Intelligence*, p. 17; Michael D. Maples, 'Consolidating Our Intelligence Contracts', *Washington Post*, A14; Cahlink, 'Security Agency Doubled Procurement Spending in Four Years'; Walter Pincus, 'Reports Revive Debate on Contractor Use', *Washington Post*, 22 August 2009, A2.
71. Shorrock, *Spies for Hire*, pp. 23–5, 264–9.
72. Scahill, *Blackwater*; Prince, *Civilian Warriors*.
73. On the growth of CACI, see Harris, 'Intelligence Incorporated', p. 46; Zachary A. Goldfarb, 'CACI to Expand High-Security Force;

Purchase of Athena Innovative Adds Many Top-Secret Workers', *Washington Post*, 25 September 2007, D5; *Business Wire*, 'CACI Awarded $189 Million in Previously Unannounced Intelligence Contracts', 24 January 2012.

74. Verne Kopytoff, 'Google Has Lots to Do with Intelligence', *San Francisco Chronicle*, 30 March 2008.
75. See for example *Business Wire*, 'L-3 Selected as Prime Contract for UK Intelligence Contract', 28 February 2008; Walter Pincus, 'Afghan Intelligence Contracts Apply Some Limits', *Washington Post*, 27 July 2010, A15.
76. John Markoff, 'Chief Takes Over at Agency to Thwart Attacks on US', *New York Times*, 13 February 2002, p. 27, A1; Adam Mayle and Alex Knott, 'Outsourcing Big Brother: Office of Total Information Awareness Relies on Private Sector to Track Americans', 17 December 2002, available at <http://fidonet.ozzmosis.com/echomail.php/edge_online/9704b94534dfb3fd.html> (accessed 28 May 2018); Stanley, 'The Surveillance-Industrial Complex', pp. 25–7; Robert O'Harrow, Jr., 'In Age of Security, Firm Mines Wealth of Personal Data', *Washington Post*, 20 January 2005, A1.
77. Dexter Filkins and Mark Mazzetti, 'Contractors Tied to Effort to Track and Kill Militants', *New York Times*, 14 March 2010, A1.
78. Keith B. Alexander, Army Deputy Chief of Staff for Intelligence, statement before the Committee on Armed Services, Subcommittee on Strategic Forces, Fiscal Year 2005 Joint Military Intelligence Program (JMIP) and Army Tactical Intelligence and Related Activities (TIARA), hearing, 108th Congress, 2nd session, 7 April 2004, pp. 9, 13; Gale, 'Intelligence Outsourcing in the US Department of Defense', p. 74; Shorrock, *Spies for Hire*, pp. 11, 16; Chatterjee, *Outsourcing Intelligence in Iraq*, pp. 6–22; Jane Mayer, 'The Black Sites', *New Yorker* 83/23, 13 August 2007, p. 46; Katherine Eban, 'The Psychologists Who Taught the CIA How to Torture (and Charged $180 Million)', *Vanity Fair*, 10 December 2014.
79. Hayden, interview with *Frontline*; Baer, 'Just Who Does the CIA's Work?'; Miller, 'Spy Agencies Outsourcing to Fill Key Jobs'; US House of Representatives, Permanent Select Committee on Intelligence, *Annual Worldwide Threat Assessment*, 110th Congress, 2nd session, 5 February 2008, p. 26; Mark Mazzetti, Ashley Parker, Jane Perlez and Eric Schmitt, 'American Held in Pakistan Worked With CIA', *New York Times*, 21 February 2011, A1.

80. Central Intelligence Agency, 'Killed in Line of Duty', 21 May 2004, available at <https://www.cia.gov/news-information/press-releases-statements/press-release-archive-2004/pr05212004.html> (accessed 28 May 2018); James Risen and Mark Mazetti, 'Blackwater Guards Tied to Secret Raids by the CIA', *New York Times*, 11 December 2009, A1; Joby Warrick and R. Jeffrey Smith, 'Sources Say CIA Hired Blackwater for Assassin Program', *Washington Post*, 20 August 2009.
81. Jane Mayer, 'The Predator War', *New Yorker* 85/34, 26 October 2009, p. 36; James Risen and Mark Mazzetti, 'CIA Said to Use Outsiders to Put Bombs on Drones', *New York Times*, 21 August 2009, A1; R. Jeffrey Smith and Joby Warrick, 'Disclosure of "Targeted Killing" Program Comes at Bad Time for CIA', *Washington Post*, 21 August 2009.
82. Priest and Arkin, *Top Secret America*, p. 210; Joshua Foust, statement before the US Senate Committee on Homeland Security and Governmental Affairs, Subcommittee on Oversight of Government Management, the Federal Workforce, and the District of Columbia, *Intelligence Community Contractors: Are We Striking the Right Balance?*, hearing, 112th Congress, 1st session, 20 September 2011, p. 18.
83. For example: *Business Wire*, 'Insightful Wins Intelligence Contracts for Text Analysis', 23 May 2005. On the role of big data analytics in intelligence see Van Puyvelde et al., 'Beyond the Buzzword'.
84. Pincus, 'Defense Agency Proposes Outsourcing More Spying'.
85. Fainaru and Klein, 'In Iraq, a Private Realm of Intelligence-Gathering'.
86. David S. Cloud, 'Civilian Contractors Playing Key Roles in US Drone Operations', *Los Angeles Times*, 29 December 2011.
87. Former contractor, interview with author, Washington, DC, June 2011; Michael Hayden, C-SPAN, 'Privatization of US Intelligence', 20 August 2009, available at <http://www.c-spanvideo.org/program/288482-1> (accessed 28 May 2018).
88. James Bamford, 'This Spy for Rent', *New York Times*, 13 June 2004, A13.
89. Shorrock, *Spies for Hire*, pp. 12, 155, 253.
90. Ibid. pp. 5, 267.
91. Intelligence and National Security Alliance, *Critical Issues for Intelligence Acquisition Reform*, 2008; Business Executive for National Security, 'Pay for Performance at the CIA: Restoring Equity, Transparency and Accountability', January 2004; Senator Daniel Akaka (D-HI), US Senate, Committee on Homeland Security

and Governmental Affairs, Oversight of Government Management, the Federal Workforce, and the District of Columbia Subcommittee, *Government-wide Intelligence Community Management Reforms*, hearing, 110th Congress, 2nd session, 29 February 2008, pp. 22; PR Newswire US, 'CACI Awarded $89 Million in Previously Unannounced Contracts to Support National Security and Intelligence', 26 July 2005.

92. Foust, statement before the US Senate Committee on Homeland Security and Governmental Affairs, pp. 3–4; Department of Homeland Security, Office of Inspector General, Better Oversight Needed of Support Services Contractors in Secure Border Initiative Programs (OIG-09-80), June 2009, p. 4; Government Accountability Office, Improved Assessment and Oversight Needed to Manage Risk of Contracting for Selected Services, GAO-07-990, September 2007, p. 11; Shorrock, *Spies for Hire*, pp. 12, 175.
93. Jane Mayer, 'The CIA's Travel Agent', *New Yorker* 82/35, 30 October 2006, p. 34; Priest, 'Jet Is an Open Secret in Terror War', A1. A court case against this subsidiary was dismissed to protect state secrets. See Peter Finn, 'Suit Dismissed Against Firm in CIA Rendition Case', *Washington Post*, 9 September 2010, A2.
94. Greg Miller, 'Spy Agencies Outsourcing to Fill Key Jobs'; Greg Miller, 'A Bold Upstart With CIA Roots', *Los Angeles Times*, 17 September 2006; Priest and Arkin, *Top Secret America*, pp. 172–3; Shorrock, *Spies for Hire*, pp. 12, 179–80; Pelton, *Licensed to Kill: Hired Guns in the War on Terror*, p. 37; US Senate, Select Committee on Intelligence, *Intelligence Authorization Act for Fiscal Year 2007*, Report 110–2, 110th Congress, 2nd session, 24 January 2007, p. 34; US House of Representatives, Committee on Oversight and Government Reform, Rep. Elijah E. Cummings, *Contracting Out Security Clearance Investigations: The Role of USIS and Allegations of Systemic Fraud*, 113th Congress, 11 February 2014, p. 3.
95. Government contractor, interview with author, 28 July 2011, Washington, DC.
96. Bamford, 'This Spy for Rent', A13.
97. Boot, 'Afterword: The CIA and Erik Prince', p. 342.
98. Schooner, 'Fear of Oversight', p. 721.
99. Federal Procurement Data System, Top 100 Contractors Report. Fiscal Year 2015, available at <https://www.fpds.gov/fpdsng_cms/index.php/en/reports/62-top-100-contractors-report3.html> (accessed 28 May 2018).

100. Office of the Director of National Intelligence, *Intelligence Community Directive Number 801, Acquisition*, 15 August 2006; Office of the Director of National Intelligence, *Intelligence Community Policy guidance Number 801.1, Acquisition*, 12 July 2007; Office of the Director of National Intelligence, *Intelligence Community Policy guidance Number 801.2, Contracting and Procurement Policy*, 20 September 2008; Driessnac and King, 'An Initial Look at Technology and Institutions on Defense Industry Consolidation', pp. 65–6; Szajnfarber et al., 'Implications of DoD Acquisition Policy for Innovation', pp. 3–4.
101. Michaels, 'Beyond Accountability', p. 1100; Barthélemy, 'The Seven Deadly Sins of Outsourcing', p. 93.
102. Gale, 'Intelligence Outsourcing in the US Department of Defense', p. 41; Fox, *Defense Acquisition Reform*, p. 13.
103. US Congress, Public Law 81–110, *Central Intelligence Agency Act*, 81st Congress, 1st session, 20 June 1949, Section 2 (c)(6); Wright, 'Procurement Authorities of the CIA', p. 1229; Code of Federal Regulations, 48 CFR 6.302-6 – National security; Kate M. Manuel, *Competition in Federal Contracting: An Overview of the Legal Requirements*, Congressional Research Service Report for Congress, 30 June 2011, pp. 11, 13, 28.
104. Savas, *Privatization and Public-Private Partnerships*, p. 122.
105. Hayden, interview with *Frontline*.
106. Foust, statement before the US Senate Committee on Homeland Security and Governmental Affairs, p. 4; Intelligence and National Security Alliance, *Improving Security While Managing Risk*, October 2007, p. 9.
107. US House of Representatives, Permanent Select Committee on Intelligence, Subcommittee on Oversight, *Initial Assessment on the Implementation of the Intelligence Reform and Terrorism Prevention Act of 2004*, 108th Congress, 2nd session, 27 July 2006, p. 14.
108. Intelligence and National Security alliance, 'About Us;' Ewen MacAskill, 'NSA Paid Millions to Cover Prism Compliance Costs for Tech Companies', *Guardian*, 23 August 2013, p. 2; Robert S. Mueller, 'Remarks to the US Chamber of Commerce', 19 January 2006, available at <http://www2.fbi.gov/pressrel/speeches/mueller011906.htm> (accessed 28 May 2018).
109. Bovaird, 'Public-Private Partnerships', p. 200.
110. Prince, *Civilian Warriors*, pp. 100–2; Scahill, *Blackwater*, pp. 327–63.

111. Central Intelligence Agency, 'CIA Remembers Employees Killed in the Line of Duty', 21 May 2004, available at <https://www.cia.gov/news-information/press-releases-statements/press-release-archive-2004/pr05212004.html> (accessed 28 May 2018); Douglas Jehl, 'Two CIA Operatives Killed in an Ambush in Afghanistan', *New York Times*, 29 October 2003, A1; Risen and Mazetti, 'Blackwater Guards Tied to Secret Raids by the CIA'; Boot, 'Afterword. The CIA and Erik Prince', p. 342.
112. See Petersen, 'Terrorism: When Risk Meets Security', p. 183.
113. Gilman Louie, *The Ethos and Profession of Intelligence*, Panel: *Intelligence and the Private Sector*, transcript of a conference held at Georgetown University, 11 June 2014, Washington, DC, p. 12; Shorrock, *Spies for Hire*, pp. 309, 323; Video: C-SPAN, *Privatization of US Intelligence*; Strachan-Morris, 'The Future of Civil-Military Intelligence Cooperation', p. 259.
114. Rovner, *Fixing the Facts*, pp. 10–17; Philip H. J. Davies, 'Intelligence and the Machinery of Government: Conceptualizing the Intelligence Community', *Public Policy and Administration* 25/1 (2010), pp. 38–40.
115. Schwab, 'We're In It for the Money', p. 203.

4 The Accountability Regime for Contractors during the Global War on Terrorism

This chapter examines the accountability regime for intelligence contractors in the aftermath of the 9/11 attacks. The first section situates contractors within the US system of intelligence accountability, and examines government access to information on its private partners, the existence of accountability standards regulating the outsourcing process, and their application. From a procedural point of view, government accountability holders theoretically had access to all of the information they requested about intelligence contractors, but the lack of attention and planning behind the outsourcing of intelligence complicated their access to relevant information. The regulatory framework for contractors and the broader system of intelligence accountability allowed a number of officials to monitor and, when necessary, punish contractors' wrongdoing. However, their work did not prevent the emergence of a series of accountability problems. The second part of the chapter explores six examples of accountability failure to analyse the imperfection of the accountability regime for intelligence contractors in the global war on terrorism. These examples suggest that contractors were involved in three main types of intelligence accountability issues in the early 2000s, relating to inefficiencies, human rights abuses and conflicts of interest. The examples further illustrate two of the main findings of this book: the existence of significant government deficiencies in the management of contractors, and the shared responsibility behind the shortfalls of public-private collaboration.

The post-9/11 outsourcing boom visibly challenged the intelligence accountability process. While government accountability holders maintained their ability to access information, refer to existing accountability standards to form judgements, and penalise wrongdoing, they struggled to effectively manage the risks posed by the growth of intelligence outsourcing. In sum, the accountability regime for contractors engaged in the global war on terrrorism was not inexistent, but imperfect.

Contractors and the US System of Intelligence Accountability

This section uses the model of accountability presented in Chapter 1 to explain how the federal government held intelligence contractors to account during the global war on terrorism. Various government officials were able to access information about intelligence contractors, refer to existing standards and apply them to regulate contractors' conduct. However, government accountability holders often reacted to problems more than they anticipated them, and the accountability regime for contractors was initially undermined by a lack of political interest in the risks posed by intelligence outsourcing.

Access to Information on Contractors

Government officials' ability to access information on contractors is essential to establish accountability. Outsourcing intelligence complicates but does not prevent government accountability holders from accessing the information that provides a factual basis for their assessments. Common wisdom suggests that contracting out generates an institutional shift that deteriorates accountability holders' access to relevant information. However, the situation is more complex because accountability holders have unequal access to information on contractors. Within US society, there is a disparity of access to information between the companies that are contracted by the government and can access specific information on intelligence requirements and budgets, and the taxpayers, who are left out of the loop because they do not have the necessary 'need to know'. In some ways, US law protects corporate secrecy more than public secrecy. The FOIA, one of the main tools used by national security researchers to gather information on government activities, does not apply to companies and individual contractors, but only to executive agencies' records. Private companies' billings are not disclosed to taxpayers because contractors and the government consider them to be confidential. Publicly traded contractors also have the right to exclude certain material events from their public findings with the Securities Exchange Commission, including the signing of contracts with agencies like the CIA and the NSA.[1]

Specific information on intelligence contractors and their performance is very hard to come by for outsiders. While some information about government contracts for intelligence services like analysis are discoverable on federal government websites, contract requirements, contracts and performance reviews are not publicly available. This lack of transparency is not unique to public-private intelligence collaboration. Ordinary citizens do not have access to information on specific intelligence requirements, budgetary information about intelligence activities and information relating to intelligence sources and methods, regardless of the public or private status of the entities involved in the intelligence process. Secrecy is necessary for the intelligence community to preserve an edge over its adversaries, but it also limits the public debate on intelligence, and, by extension, on intelligence outsourcing.

Since the public cannot access much information about the intelligence community and its contractors, the executive and legislative branches play a central role, representing and defending the public interest. These key accountability holders have benefited from relatively good access to information on private intelligence providers. The executive branch initiates contractual relations with the private sector and select officials have direct access to essential information about the private conduct of government intelligence activities. In 2007, most of the core contract personnel (73 per cent) involved in the National Intelligence Program worked on government agencies' premises.[2] This layout theoretically allowed government officials to access basic information on the contractors working next to them. Access has been more complicated in the case of overseas contracts. Although government contracting officers have legal responsibility for contracts, their knowledge and understanding of a particular contract may be limited, and they may actually work 'at substantial remove from the contract's locale'.[3] That is why officers usually rely on a technical representative to monitor contractors' performance and ensure compliance with the government instructions on the ground. This system, though it does not always work perfectly, ensures the government maintains some degree of control over contractors' behaviour.

At higher levels, the distance between the senior executive service and daily intelligence activities means that experienced officials can hardly keep an attentive eye on the involvement of contractors in specific projects. Michael Hayden, the former Director of the CIA, recognised that despite his responsibility 'for everything done in the agency's name', his 'ability to control' got 'weaker with each layer or class of actor' ranging from agency employees, government contractors, to liaison services and sources acting on behalf of the US government.[4] For a long time, senior officials also neglected to think strategically about the growing role of contractors within the overall intelligence workforce, that is to say civilian, military and contractor personnel. Consequently, relevant information on the scope of outsourcing was not gathered, processed and analysed until the mid-2000s. This lack of strategic planning is an important factor that will be discussed in more detail in the next chapter.

Congress is another key player in the US system of intelligence accountability. Congressional intelligence committees have, according to two national security experts, had 'full access' to information on intelligence contractors.[5] In practice, this access was sometimes more complicated than when government employees carry out intelligence activities alone. The government's reliance on contractors adds organisational layers and, as a result, it can take more time and effort for congressional accountability holders to access key pieces of information. Contractors are not required to publish personnel directories or organisation charts, and this can complicate the establishment of the channels of communication that are necessary to conduct oversight.[6] An expert I interviewed pointed out that the intelligence committees took 'two or three years to know how many contractors there were' in the intelligence community, as the committees waited for information that had not been compiled and processed by the executive branch.[7] Congressional access to information is also limited to the activities congressmen, congresswomen and staffers ask about. In other words, committees do not always get the full picture.

The reliance on sub-contractors, who are not directly accountable to the government but to the companies contracting with the government, can complicate and sometimes prevent congressional access to information about intelligence activities. In the most extreme cases, subcontracting runs several layers deep and leads to a strong decentralisation of intelligence, which complicates the government's access to relevant information.[8] The supervision of the informal ties and influence between the intelligence community and the private sector is equally problematic because they do not leave a contractual paper trail and are therefore less visible to outsiders, including congressional overseers. These difficulties partly explain why Congress is often reacting to accountability problems more than it anticipates them.

Regulatory Standards

The second key condition for accountability to occur is the existence of appropriate standards. At the administrative level, a robust set of regulations governs intelligence outsourcing. Federal regulations set up a multi-layered system of oversight covering the entirety of the outsourcing process, from the preparation of bid specifications to the award and subsequent monitoring of contracts. At the start of this process, sourcing decisions are typically made at the unit level by a manager who considers intelligence requirements and identifies a need. The decision to outsource an activity must be justified by the government sponsor and the legal authority to do so is verified internally. Some functions, called inherently governmental functions, are 'so intimately related to the public interest as to require performance by Federal Government employees'. The Federal Activities Inventory Reform (FAIR) Act of 1998 notes that such functions might include decisions binding the US government, contract management, activities that would significantly affect the life, liberty or property interests of private persons, appointing, directing or controlling officers or employees of the United States, and exerting ultimate control over the acquisition, use or disposition of the property of the United States.[9] US law also specifies that 'gathering information for or providing advice, opinions, recommendations, or ideas to federal officials' – in essence, intelligence collection and analysis – do not qualify as inherently governmental functions.

When current regulations do not prohibit outsourcing, a legal concurrence is provided to a contracting officer who, in coordination with his or her subordinates, conducts market research, develops requirements documents, determines the scope of the project to be outsourced, provides cost estimates and assesses related risks. When a contract vehicle has been decided upon, the vendors' proposals are evaluated, government officials determine acceptable costs and select a source. A contract is awarded and subsequently managed by the contracting officer technical representative who provides oversight and technical direction, jointly with the contracting officer. The Federal Acquisition Regulations, a body of regulations that has formally existed since 1983, require government agencies to 'develop and apply efficient procedures for performing government contract quality assistance' and 'perform all actions necessary to verify whether the supplies or services conform to contract quality requirements'.[10]

Procurement policies developed by the Office of Management and Budget (OMB) and its Office of Federal Procurement Policy (OFPP) require government agencies to provide a greater degree of scrutiny when contracting services can affect the government's decision-making authority. Many intelligence activities that have been outsourced in the global war on terrorism could qualify as such, including some forms of intelligence analysis and management functions. This policy implicitly recognises that different incentives drive public and private actors, and seeks to limit the possibility of contractors skewing the public interest in their favour. A number of regulations specify procedures to implement these requirements, such as the use of quality assurance surveillance plans for performance-based contracts.[11] At the bottom of the accountability chain, the COTRs are often the government's principal point of contact with contractors, and ensure the latter 'provide exactly those products and services the government needs'.[12] They verify time and attendance, receive the contractors' invoices, monitor deliverables and report all of this information to the executive management of their agency. Companies that provide the contracted services also perform some supervision of their contractors.

When private providers default a contract or violate regulations, government agencies can rely on a host of sanctions to punish them. Standard government contracts include measures such as termination for default, withholding of award and incentive fees.[13] Federal regulations also authorise public officials to suspend and debar contracts. All these measures allow government authorities to punish contractors for their failure to perform. They remain post-event remedies and are sometimes ill suited to the needs of senior government officials operating in complex and fast-paced environments. These punishments have also been criticised for their lack of credibility. They have not prevented defaulting contractors from getting contracts with other agencies and repeating their mistakes.[14] Contractors come and go and, as a result, their mistakes may not have the same repercussions on them – for example, in terms of their reputation and career advancement – that they would have on government employees' careers.

Further guidance on the control of contractors exists at the department or agency level.[15] Consequently, the situation of intelligence contractors varies between and within each intelligence agency, and the overall regulatory regime for intelligence contractors is too complex to be covered exhaustively in this book. The CIA, for instance, benefits from exemptions to the federal acquisition regulations to protect its sources and methods.[16] The Agency has developed a lengthy contracting manual, and a contract law division within its Office of General Counsel ensures that procurement respects mandated legal standards. Mark Lowenthal, a former senior intelligence analyst at the CIA, recalls some of the red lines he had to contend with, when he notes that it was very clear that the contractors working with his staff could not be involved in acquisition or monitor other contractors.[17]

Specific laws also apply to intelligence contractors working abroad, especially in conflict zones.[18] The Military Extraterritorial Jurisdiction Act (MEJA) applies to contractors if they 'commit acts abroad that would qualify as federal crimes'.[19] Since 2004, this statute applies not only to contractors working directly for the Department of Defense but also to entities supporting a DoD mission, which could include agencies like the CIA and some of their operators.[20] Other federal statutes that apply to intelligence contractors working for the DoD include the War Crimes Act and the Uniform Code of Military Justice (UCMJ).[21] Despite the existence of these laws, the legal basis for punishing contractors' wrongdoing in the theatres of the global war on terrorism has sometimes been unclear. In 2010, a legislative attorney working for the Congressional Research Service concluded that 'contractor personnel who commit crimes might not fall within the statutory definitions'. This lack of legal clarity can create uncertainty regarding the courts' interpretation and, in the words of this attorney, 'discourage prosecution'.[22]

The federal government has long established regulations to control and manage intelligence contractors, but the mere existence of a legal framework does not ensure that contractors are effectively controlled. In practice, determining contractors' responsibilities can prove challenging because the lines of authority are more confused in a blended workforce, where government and contractor personnel interact on a daily basis. A government expert notes that 'a lot of contracts are bundled . . . that means there are a number of separate private firms that are operating within, under a certain contract. That means further decentralisation and difficulty in actually identifying or pinpointing who is responsible for what part of the contract.'[23] In some cases, contractors supervise not only other contractors but also government employees. This fragmentation of the government's authority can weaken the enforcement of existing statutes.[24] Further obstacles appear when contractors operate abroad, especially if they are involved in covert operations. In such cases, gathering a satisfying degree of evidence becomes practically impossible because substantive judicial review supposes very high costs to cover transporting evidence or relocating the court on the field, securing witnesses and so on.[25] These and many other obstacles complicate the implementation of existing standards when intelligence contractors work abroad and close to the field.

Applying Standards: A Mixed Record

An overview of the application of existing regulatory standards in the early years of the global war on terrorism reveals a mixed record. Available evidence suggests that government accountability holders were generally able to hold contractors to account at the administrative level, but seemed to react to problems more than they anticipated them. This is not unique to the case of contractors; scholars of intelligence accountability have pointed out the reactive nature of intelligence accountability and tied it to the politics of national security, which are often driven by problems and scandals.[26] The reactive nature of accountability was reinforced in the aftermath of 9/11 by a policy environment that was strongly oriented towards national security objectives. Following the attacks, policy-makers and senior intelligence officials were under enormous pressure to deliver on their promises to restore safety and security. In his 2002 State of the Union Address, President Bush made his priority clear when he said that 'the price of freedom and security is never too high'.[27] This resolute defence of freedom and security impacted on the conduct of intelligence. General Michael Hayden, the former director of the NSA and the CIA, recognised that during his tenure the intelligence community was 'effective' but not 'efficient', and explained, 'there's no way we could have done it [expanding intelligence capabilities] that quickly, that rapidly, that expansively, and had done it well, had done it efficiently'.[28] In other words, the administration prioritised national security results over cost-effectiveness. Senior officials used the impetus provided by the attacks to expand and reorganise the national intelligence effort, and oversight bodies were generally challenged to keep up with rapid changes.

Contract management was, understandably, not a priority in the years following 9/11. However, this does not justify why senior officials overlooked thinking strategically about the growing role contractors played in the national intelligence effort. This oversight was most evident in the government's absence of investment in its acquisition workforce, a decision that limited its ability to oversee contractors. In order to spot abuses and apply adequate sanctions, the government needs a contract management workforce that is able to implement existing regulations and maintain control over those intelligence activities that have been outsourced. After 9/11, this specialised workforce faced significant challenges. It had been significantly downsized in the 1990s, while rapid technological development further complicated intelligence acquisition. These evolutions required government expertise and workforce adaptation, but while outsourcing boomed, the contract management workforce did not keep pace with the growing list of requirements it confronted.[29]

Congress initially did not pay much attention to intelligence contracting either. This lack of interest can be related to Congress's position as an outsider, which does not control the conduct of intelligence but oversees the activities of the intelligence community. The congressional power of the purse, through budgetary oversight, was also limited because contractors did not figure in the intelligence budget. As a result, the outsourcing boom was not particularly visible to the legislature.[30] Congress could have legislated to prohibit the outsourcing of a particular type of activity or bar outsourcing to a particular company, just as it did with the Federal Activities Inventory Reform Act of 1998 and the Anti-Pinkerton Act of 1893, but it did not directly do so. In one notable case – which will be examined later in this chapter – Congress took some procurement responsibilities away from the NSA because the SIGINT agency had mismanaged a major acquisition programme. However, by and large, outsourcing remained an administrative issue to be tackled by executive branch officials.

While the post-9/11 political environment was not particularly supportive of intelligence oversight, some accountability holders continued to play their role at the administrative level. The activities of the Office of the Inspector General at the CIA, to focus on a specific example on which some information is publicly available, demonstrate a continuous awareness and evident efforts to tackle accountability problems involving contractors. This office is particularly relevant since the IG has 'full and direct access to all Agency information relevant to the performance of its duties'.[31] During his nomination hearing, John L. Helgerson, the IG between 2002 and 2008, mentioned that he intended 'to concentrate on the CIA procurement acquisition process for information technology and information systems', an area that he considered to be 'ripe for waste, fraud and abuse'.[32] Declassified reports from the Office of the Inspector General at the CIA reveal continuous scrutiny over intelligence contractors between 2001 and 2008. Among various tasks, the IG conducted recurrent investigations into allegations of contract fraud. Figure 4.1 shows that the sheer number of investigations concerning procurement problems remained relatively constant during this period.

Beside procurement fraud, investigations, audits or reviews dwelled on many other aspects including the mischarging and overpayment of contracts, wasteful or improper contract practices, and ethics improprieties – such as the acceptance of gratuities from agency contractors, or an improper relationship between a contracting officer's technical representative and an agency contractor. In at least two cases, the IG reports mention potential counterintelligence concerns about information security and background investigations involving contractors.[33] Specific information about

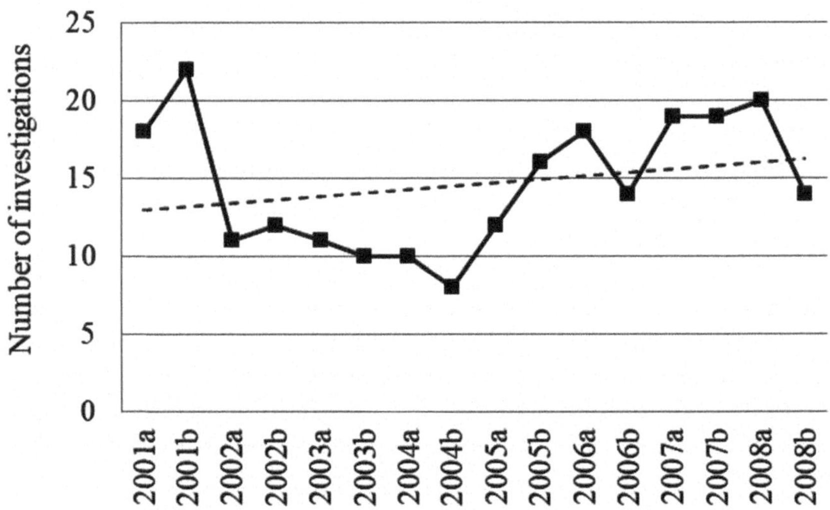

Figure 4.1 CIA IG investigations concerning procurement fraud, 2001–08. Source: Central Intelligence Agency, Office of the Inspector General, reports accessed on the website of the Electronic Frontier Foundation, available at <https://www.eff.org/cases/intelligence-agencies-misconduct-reports> (accessed 5 June 2018).

these cases remains classified. The Office of the Inspector General also played a more active role in furthering employees' awareness of these problems and, when necessary, referred cases to other accountability holders. Accountability at this level takes the form of ordinary bureaucratic tasks that are essential to the executive control of intelligence. In early 2001, in order to minimise problems regarding contract and procurement fraud, investigation staff representatives provided 'awareness briefings to contracting officers concerning common types of fraud indicators' and 'organized a fraud focus group to gather and share information'.[34]

The staff also issued employees bulletins on labour mischarging and other types of fraud. These measures eased government employees' access to important information regarding the proper conduct of public-private collaboration. They also show how accountability holders working at the administrative level can seek to be proactive and conduct anticipatory oversight. Overall, the CIA IG's position at the crossroads between the executive and the legislative branches allowed its staff to access information on contractors' behaviour, assess this information based on their expertise and keep Congress informed about cross-sector collaboration. This case might be relatively unique, since IGs at multiple DoD agencies like the NRO, the DIA, the NSA and the NGA 'lack the explicit statutory authorisation to access information relevant to their audits or investigations, or to compel the production of such information via subpoena'.[35]

In addition to the CIA IG, the courts also played an essential accountability role, examining the legality of government employees and contractors' activities in a host of areas. When intelligence officials have a reasonable belief that violations of federal law have been committed, matters are normally referred to the Department of Justice, which can then decide to prosecute government officials and contractors for their wrongdoing. For example, a series of staff investigations by the CIA OIG resulted in contractors' guilty pleas and monetary restitutions to the agency. In one case, an agency employee was 'convicted of conspiracy to accept gratuities in exchange for giving preferential treatment to an Agency contractor'.[36] Labour mischarging by intelligence contractors and subcontractors working for the NSA similarly led to a series of cases in the

US District Court for the District of Maryland. In one case of mis-charging, the judge sentenced a contractor to six months of home detention, three years of probation, the restitution of the monetary expenditures and a fine.[37] In another case, the District Court of Virginia convicted a civilian employee and a contractor working for the US Army's Intelligence and Security Command Headquarters (INSCOM) of committing honest-services wire fraud and bribery. The two individuals engineered the award of a multi-million-dollar government contract to a company they created, and proved unable to provide the required services.[38] These court cases prove that some intelligence contractors have been punished for their wrongdoing, and directly challenge the notion that contractors are not accountable. They also demonstrate that the courts play a role in regulating intelligence practices beyond the well-known case of the Foreign Intelligence Surveillance Court.

Procurement regulations have also allowed contractors to hold government officials to account and challenge allegedly misguided awards. Contractors can protest against the formation or award of government contracts, and dispute issues arising during the performance of a contract. Depending on the situation, companies can voice their concern to contracting officers, administrative boards of contract appeals, the comptroller general of the United States and federal courts. These procedures allow contractors to force the government to respect its own regulations and maintain some impartiality.[39] They do not prevent government officials from making poor and corrupt decisions but, in the words of law scholar Jon D. Michaels, they 'keep avarice and indifference to a minimum'.[40]

Though information on intelligence-related cases is rare, publicly available documents show that contractors have made use of these mechanisms throughout the 2000s. In one case, SOS Interpreting, Ltd. protested against a decision made by the DEA following the award of a contract for translation, transcription, interception and monitoring support services to another company. The GAO General Counsel heard the appeal and denied most of the charges made by the SOS Interpreting, which asserted that the DEA's decision to award the contract was inconsistent with its stated evaluation approach. However, the General Counsel recommended the DEA clarify its evaluation scheme. Interestingly, the decision corroborated the agency's concerns with the ability of SOS Interpreting to deliver the requested services, based on the fact that one of the company's contracts had been terminated for default within the last three years. This shows that, when they are able to do so, government authorities do take past performance into account in contract award decisions.[41] In another case, the Armed Services Board of Contracts Appeal (ABSCA) examined a dispute from Cubic Defense Applications, Inc. The Space and Naval Warfare Systems Command had awarded a contract to this company in 2003 to design develop, manufacture and test a communication system allowing Navy ships to exchange intelligence with military aircraft. Following the award of this contract, Cubic Defense Applications requested an increase in the contract price and appealed to contest the absence of timely decision on this request by its contracting officer. In its decision, the ABSCA dismissed the company's appeal as premature and used this opportunity to clarify the deadline for the contracting officers' decision.[42]

These ordinary cases never caught the headlines but they show that intelligence agencies and their contractors were subjected to the rule of law, and accountability was therefore not inexistent. They also demonstrate that contractors can play a role of accountability holder and, as such, deserve a place in academic models of intelligence accountability. While these examples demonstrate the existence of an accountability regime for intelligence contractors, a series of scandals publicly exposed some of the limits of this accountability regime in the global war on terrorism. These high-profile incidents crystallised accountability holders' attention around three main issues – inefficiencies, human rights abuses and conflicts of interest – that will now be explored through six examples of excess.

Inefficiency at the FBI: The Virtual Case File

At the turn of the twenty-first century, the FBI and the NSA initiated major acquisition efforts to modernise their IT capabilities. These initiatives exposed important problems within the agencies' procurement systems – most notably, a tendency to underestimate the planning and management efforts necessary for major acquisitions to be successful.[43] In September 2000, the FBI initiated the Trilogy project to modernise its IT infrastructure, provide a high-speed and secure network linking FBI offices and develop a user application to improve FBI employees' ability to search, analyse and disseminate information. Given its lack of expertise in the IT domain, the agency contracted out the first two objectives to Dyncorp and the third to SAIC, two well-established defence contractors. The first two components of the Trilogy project were completed by April 2004 but the third one, a user application named the Virtual Case File (VCF), ran into major trouble, ultimately forcing the FBI to terminate its contract after spending an estimated $170 million. The FBI's trouble with this IT modernisation project caught the attention of several accountability holders within the Department of Justice and beyond, leading to a host of reports and hearings.[44] These reports provide a rare window into the risks posed by the outsourcing of IT services in the leading domestic intelligence and security service of the United States.

From the onset of the VCF project, the FBI did not develop a coherent and stable view of its mission and operational needs in the IT domain. When the initial contract with SAIC was signed in June 2001, the FBI did not have a complete set of defined requirements for the VCF. As a result, the initial contract that was awarded yielded a lot of control to SAIC for developing technical requirements.[45] In the absence of precise guidance, the contractor took a role that became too important in the basic design of the bureau's IT architecture.[46] This is problematic since, as two leading experts point out, the development of a coherent view on the FBI mission and operational needs is a core function that 'cannot be delegated' to contractors, but must be established by the agency's leadership.[47]

After the VCF contract was awarded, the needs of the bureau continued to evolve in function of shifting security priorities. Reviews of the 1995 Oklahoma City bombing, the Robert Hanssen espionage case and the 9/11 attacks highlighted a variety of issues at the FBI including information security weaknesses, the untimely production of information and difficulties with sharing information.[48] In the aftermath of Al Qaeda's attacks on the US homeland, the FBI's priorities shifted towards the prevention of terrorism and its domestic intelligence responsibilities expanded. These developments impacted on the bureau's IT needs, encouraging FBI officials to expand the Trilogy contracts and accelerate their planned completion. Despite the well-known risks such changes implied – including cost overruns, delivery delays and diminished product quality – the FBI modified the VCF contract thirty-six times in three years.[49]

Throughout the life of the Trilogy project, FBI project management was inadequate, lacking in specifications and costs and schedule controls. Under the terms of the Trilogy contracts, vendors would be paid 'regardless of whether they met schedules or were even technically capable of completing such a challenging project'.[50] The contracts did not determine a clear roadmap for the projects, and lacked completion milestones, which could have helped government authorities to assess the contractors' progress and keep costs from growing.[51] The contract for the VCF application did not allow adequate time for testing a prototype and gathering feedback from end-users. Government officials presumed that everything would work fine, and this ultimately led to unrealistic scheduling of completion dates for various tasks.[52] As one expert report concludes: 'under these circumstances, effective program and contract management is essentially impossible'.[53] When the VCF project ran into cost overruns and delays, SAIC did not suffer penalties; instead, FBI employees stood in to compensate.[54]

On the whole, the FBI lacked the in-house expertise in project integration and contract management to successfully develop and implement such a complex IT modernisation effort.[55] While the bureau had the authority to hire more adequate personnel, it initially did not do so. This lack of expertise at the FBI was aggravated by high staff turnover. From late 2001 to early 2005, five chief information officers and ten project managers for various parts of Trilogy were involved in the project. Poor control over the development and implementation of the Trilogy project led to significant problems. An internal report found, in 2004, that the FBI's management system 'did not capture detailed Trilogy-related expenditures'.[56] The GAO later discovered that 'weak controls over the Trilogy Project led to payment of questionable contractor costs and missing assets' and noted that the FBI's 'overreliance on contractors diminished its ability to properly account for Trilogy Assets'.[57]

When SAIC eventually developed clear schedules for completion, the FBI was not able to assess whether they were reasonable because it continued to lack the necessary expertise. Given its lack of expertise, the FBI was 'overly dependent on outside contractors to undertake essential tasks, such as identifying key operational processes, defining the FBI's IT concept of operations, and making decisions about the major tradeoffs that are inevitably required'.[58] For instance, a company named Miretek was hired to assist the FBI with programme and contract management, fiscal and budgetary oversight, cost estimating, acquisition and source selection, and requirement definition. The involvement of contractors at multiple key posts in the development of this project limited the government's ability to control its contractors and created an environment that was ripe for conflicts of interest. In one case, 'an individual functioning in an advisory role to the FBI for increasing funding of the various contracts associated with Trilogy worked for a contractor that provided IT services on Trilogy'.[59]

When the FBI finally received the VCF application from SAIC in December 2003, it identified a number of deficiencies that made it unusable. Hundreds of additional problems were soon discovered, and this forced the bureau to develop a new plan for the VCF.[60] The project was scaled back, then determined to be unfeasible and ultimately terminated. At the time, this failure was particularly concerning because it hampered 'FBI agents and analysts from adequately searching and sharing information from investigative files'.[61] The bureau subsequently released a solicitation for proposals to develop a 'new electronic information management system' which also ran into trouble, thus highlighting systemic problems with the bureau's IT acquisition process.[62]

The Trilogy project highlights some of the main issues that affected the procurement of intelligence systems at the dawn of the twenty-first century. Contracting out complex projects when a government agency lacks expertise, is undergoing a significant movement of reform and is attracting a lot of political attention, is a risky endeavour. On the whole, both the FBI and its contractors are responsible for the failures of Trilogy. In a testimony before the Senate Appropriations Committee, then FBI Director Mueller recognised the responsibility of the bureau for not exercising adequate control over the Trilogy project. The government agency lacked the expertise and the personnel to plan and manage Trilogy and, as a result, the accountability regime for the contractors working on this project was lax. The leadership's desire to move quickly with the project and the decision to sign a contract without insisting upon the establishment of clear requirements, milestones and potential penalties for poor performance were all significant mistakes. Without an adequate incentive framework, cost overruns and delays were all the more likely.[63] SAIC also shares some responsibility for the failure of the VCF. According to a former SAIC senior official, 'the company knew the FBI's plans were going awry but did not insist on changes because the bureau continued to pay the bills as the work piled up'.[64]

The interests of the FBI and SAIC were not so well aligned, and the government struggled to control SAIC's behaviour. The failure of the VCF project led to a significant waste of taxpayers' money and limited the FBI's ability to carry out its national security mission. Multiple accountability holders criticised the FBI publicly for this failure, but ultimately neither the bureau and its leadership nor the prime contractor faced significant punishment. Considering the accountability model used in this book, the government's inability to efficiently plan and manage the contracting process, and the absence of punishment for the failures of this modernisation effort, suggest that accountability was lacking.

Inefficiency at the NSA: The Trailblazer Programme

The NSA also faced a series of problems when it sought to upgrade its IT systems to better process and analyse the increasingly diverse SIGINT sources it started to collect in the 1990s. These problems caught the attention of congressional overseers and the news media as early as November 2001.[65] Public attention notably focused on the failure of the Trailblazer project, which came to embody acquisition flaws at the NSA. Following 9/11, the Director of the NSA gathered the political impetus to push this project forward and contracted it out to a host of big defence companies in fall 2002.[66] From the onset, the NSA was confused as to what Trailblazer would actually provide and defined its requirements poorly.[67] Just like in the example of the FBI's VCF, early errors were exacerbated by political pressure to accelerate completion of the project and bring the NSA into the twenty-first century. Inadequate management and oversight led to overpayments, cost overruns and significant delays.

A group of NSA officials became increasingly concerned about Trailblazer and alerted Diane Roark, a Republican staffer on the House intelligence committee. Roark contacted senior executive branch officials, but did not manage to trigger any significant investigation. In 2002, the same group of NSA colleagues filed a complaint with the DoD IG alleging that 'NSA actions in the development of THINTHREAD and TRAILBLAZER resulted in fraud, waste, and abuse.'[68] The IG accepted the complaint and a subsequent audit revealed inadequate management and oversight as well as overpayment of contractors. In its final report, the inspector found that the NSA 'is inefficiently using resources to develop a digital network exploitation system that is not capable of fully exploiting the digital network intelligence available to analysts from the Global Information Network. . . . The NSA transformation effort may be developing a less capable long-term digital network exploitation solution that will take longer and cost significantly more to develop.' These findings were strongly contested by the management of the NSA.[69]

The NSA's continuing trouble with its major acquisitions pushed the Senate Armed Services Committee to set a deadline for the SIGINT agency to 'put its books in order', and Congress subsequently decided to take NSA's authority to sign major acquisition contracts, and give it to the Under Secretary of Defense for Acquisitions, Technology and Logistics to 'stimulate better executive branch oversight of NSA systems acquisition'.[70] This decision shows how, at the political level, congressional accountability holders can punish government agencies for their failures. Despite increasingly obvious flaws and concern, Trailblazer continued. By 2005, NSA Director Michael Hayden recognised publicly that the programme had cost hundreds of millions of dollars in extra costs and was months behind schedule with no completion date in sight. Reflecting on this situation, Hayden would later say that 'it was just far more difficult than anyone anticipated'.[71] Eventually, the *Baltimore Sun* published a series of articles about NSA mismanagement, fraud and waste, which raised the issue at a new level. Trailblazer was terminated in 2007 without fulfilling its objectives, and after more than a billion dollars of taxpayer money had been disbursed.[72] Overall, the spotlight that intelligence officials, Congress and the media had kept on this costly intelligence acquisition programme did not prevent the persistence of seemingly intractable problems.

The NSA, Congress and the contractors all bear some responsibility in the failure of Trailblazer. According to historian Matthew Aid, the agency is 'guilty of buying a bill of goods from contractors without checking to see if it is feasible. The contractors are guilty of promising the moon and not delivering, and Congress is guilty for failing to oversee it from beginning to end.'[73] Aid overlooks the fact that the NSA was publicly reprimanded by Congress and lost some of its contracting authorities. However, he is not entirely wrong. No publicly available evidence suggests that the contractors involved in the programme suffered consequences for their failure. One of the main contractors, SAIC, was merely blamed because it 'did not provide enough people with the technical or management skills to produce' the sophisticated system that was requested by the NSA.[74] Despite its shortfalls, SAIC remained one of the few prime contractors able to develop and implement such a major modernisation project, and was subsequently awarded the contract for a revised version of Trailblazer.[75] This absence of punishment raises interesting questions about the government's willingness and ability to maintain strong accountability for procurement failures. Government accountability holders are unlikely to impose harsh punishments on contractors when public officials share some responsibility, and when the intelligence community needs a strong industrial base to thrive.

Poorly developed acquisition programmes have plagued the US national security apparatus for decades, generating hundreds of government reports, congressional hearings and public debates. Elements of the intelligence community have struggled to define requirements for major acquisitions and carefully manage the development of cutting-edge technologies, leading to significant cost overruns and delays.[76] These inefficiencies reinforce the notion that outsourcing is a necessity more than a deliberate policy developed to make the government more efficient. Reflecting on the failure of the Trailblazer programme, former Director Hayden said: 'We learned within Trailblazer that when we asked industry for something they had or something close to what they already had, they were remarkable in providing us a response, an outcome. When we asked them for something that no one had yet invented, they weren't any better at inventing it than we were in doing it ourselves.'[77] Rather than avoiding private involvement altogether – a decision that would deprive the intelligence community of a valuable pool of expertise – Hayden suggests breaking down major projects into smaller incremental steps to make them more achievable and easier to control. On the whole the VCF and Trailblazer stories emphasise the need to rethink how intelligence agencies collaborate with the private sector to acquire major products and services. To start with, government agencies should provide clear, stable and reasonable demands to their contractors. However, this solution requires officials to have enough expertise to formulate viable plans, which is not always the case.

Contractors in the Interrogation Room

The accountability problems plaguing intelligence contracting have not been limited to the acquisition of new IT capabilities. In Iraq, Afghanistan and in Guantanamo Bay, the US government relied on contractor support to conduct interrogation operations. Senior intelligence officers with knowledge of these operations have explained that contractors' involvement in these sensitive operations was born out of necessity. Simply put, there were not enough experienced government personnel to conduct these missions.[78] Contractors' involvement in these sensitive intelligence collection programmes was marked by a series of controversies.

On 28 April 2004, the CBS network programme *60 Minutes* exposed a torture scandal at the Abu Ghraib detention centre in Iraq. Although the news media and public interest groups such as Amnesty International and Human Rights Watch had already highlighted US mistreatment of detainees, the *60 Minutes* story and its shocking photographs raised the affair to an international level, triggering a worldwide outcry.[79] The human rights abuses committed at Abu Ghraib became one of the most widely publicised incidents involving US intelligence contractors.[80]

The US government started investigating allegations of abuses prior to the public scandal. In January 2004, Major General Antonio Taguba (US Army) was directed to investigate the 800th Military Police Brigade's detention and internment operations with a specific focus on allegations of maltreatment at the Abu Ghraib prison, and according to his report at least two civilian interrogators working for CACI and contracted by the 205th Military Intelligence Brigade were involved in the abuses.[81] Government investigations found several breaking points in the process of procuring interrogations – a type of HUMINT collection – for the DoD. Competition requirements were not followed, and the use of interagency contracting processes was not properly justified. To outsource interrogation, the Army used a contract awarded by the General Services Administration and assigned for administration to the Department of Interior. This complex arrangement allowed the Army to bypass a directive that banned the private provision of interrogators.

Existing standards and procedures were also misused when contracts for activities such as human intelligence support, interrogation and screening followed a procedure designed for contracting engineering and information technology services. For the GAO, this improper use of existing procedures raised questions about 'the integrity of the federal procurement process'.[82] Another government report pointed out the 'lack of an effective system of policies, procedures, and process controls', the 'lack of monitoring and oversight' and the 'eagerness' of procurement personnel who 'found shortcuts to federal procurement procedures'.[83] Outsiders have been more suspicious, and one commentator even considered that the US government used 'some creative accounting to keep the contract relatively obscure'.[84] Danielle Brian, the executive director of the Project on Government Oversight, a public interest group based in Washington, DC, questions 'how can a person at Interior know what qualities you're looking for in a contractor doing something as sensitive as interrogating prisoners of war?'[85] In this particular case, although legal standards and procedures existed, they were not implemented adequately.

Beyond these concerns with the procurement process, the government's monitoring of contractors was lacking. Although the military chain of command is supposed to ensure the ascendancy of public authority over private means, investigations pointed out the absence of doctrine guiding 'intelligence leaders in the contract management or command and control of contractors in a wartime environment'.[86] Military supervisors were apparently confused over their legal responsibilities for contractor personnel, and this confusion was reinforced by the absence of contracting officer technical representatives on site. Subsequent investigations revealed that contractor personnel lacked 'qualifications, experience, and training', and their performance was not overseen appropriately.[87] Torin Nelson, a former CACI interrogator who worked at the Abu Ghraib prison, confirmed that he and other civilian interrogators were 'often free to conduct operations as they best saw fit'.[88]

The CACI contract was terminated when the outsourcing of interrogation made media headlines.[89] While soldiers were eventually convicted of the detainee abuses at Abu Ghraib, so far none of the contractors who were involved have been criminally prosecuted, and the reasons for this situation remain unclear. Regulatory gaps might have been a key obstacle. Criminal prosecution under the Military Extraterritorial Jurisdiction Act was not possible at the time because the DoD did not directly employ these contractors. For scholar Laura Dickinson, the Bush administration lacked political willingness and was 'reluctant to initiate prosecutions of contractors implicated in the abuse'.[90] This situation may still change for the better following a decision by a US Court of Appeals to revive the possibility that CACI employees will be prosecuted under the Alien Tort Statute for their involvement in the abuses.[91] In a separate settlement, the firm L-3 Services Inc. – whose contractors provided translation services to support abusive interrogations – paid

$5.28 million to seventy-one former inmates who were abused at Abu Ghraib and other detention facilities.[92] This decision suggests that under the right conditions – when rules have clearly been broken and public pressure is sufficient – contractors can be forced to acknowledge their wrongdoing and pay for it. Regardless of the outcome of these cases, court decisions or settlements were long overdue. Intelligence accountability sometimes demands an urgency that is anathema to due legal process.

Since the beginning of the global war on terrorism, only one intelligence contractor has been convicted for a case of human rights abuse. In June 2004, David A. Passaro, a former CIA independent contractor, was indicted for 'knowingly and intentionally' assaulting an Afghan prisoner, which 'resulted in serious bodily injury'.[93] The Afghan prisoner ultimately died from these injuries, and Passaro was convicted of assault in a US Federal Court under the Special Maritime and Territorial Jurisdiction.[94] To this day, Passaro remains the only person connected to the CIA to have been convicted for a human rights abuse during the global war on terrorism. The conviction of this contractor proves that accountability for contractors working overseas is possible. Interestingly, Passaro's sentence contrasts with other cases involving CIA employees.

After an Iraqi detainee, suspected terrorist Manadel al-Jamadi, died during an interrogation at Abu Ghraib, the Department of Justice decided to open a torture and war crimes grand jury investigation into the role of the CIA employee leading the interrogation, Mark Swanner. A military autopsy concluded that al-Jamadi's death was caused by homicide, but the administration declined to prosecute Swanner because it judged that the admissible evidence was insufficient 'to obtain and sustain a conviction beyond reasonable doubt'.[95] The contract translator who assisted Swanner during the interrogation was granted immunity against criminal prosecution in exchange for his cooperation during the investigation. In other cases, CIA officers involved in prisoner abuses have only been reprimanded.[96] The involvement of government officials in all these abuses suggests that the participation of private contractors was not a necessary condition for them to occur. While contractors were held to different accountability standards than their government counterparts, these standards were not systematically lower.

The involvement of contractors in these scandals was a turning point in the public debate on outsourcing. Media coverage of the Abu Ghraib abuses significantly intensified the executive, judicial, legislative and societal scrutiny of intelligence contractors. Accountability holders started to discuss some of the core issues raised by outsourcing, including the definition of inherently governmental responsibilities, and the government's ability to control contractors' behaviour.[97] In a series of hearings held by the Senate Armed Services Committee, members of Congress publicly questioned senior administration officials on the role of contractors in interrogations. Senator Warner (R-VA) asked: 'How is it in our nation's interest to have civilian contractors, rather than military personnel, performing vital national security functions, such as prisoner interrogations, in a war zone? When soldiers break the law, or fail to follow orders, commanders can hold them accountable for their misconduct. Military commanders don't have the same authority over civilian contractors.' Senator Akaka (D-HI) wondered 'what are the roles of the private contractors at this and other detention facilities in Iraq and Afghanistan? And who monitors and supervises these contracted employees?' In his answer, Secretary of Defense Rumsfeld pointed out that civilian contractors are 'responsible to military intelligence who hire them, and have the responsibility for supervising them'.[98] In the *Washington Post*, Representative Janice Schakowsky (D-IL) wondered whether contractors were 'taking orders from their CEOs and shareholders and then telling our soldiers what to do'.[99] To this day, the boundaries between inherently governmental and commercial activities are not always clear.

Crossing the Line

The mobility of personnel and close ties between the intelligence community and the private sector have caused public concern about potential conflicts of interest. Since the 1990s an increasing number of government employees have quit intelligence agencies to work for private companies. According to *Washington Post* research, 'at least 91 of the [Central Intelligence] agency's upper-level managers have left for the private sector' from 2001 to 2011.[100] In many cases, these former officials work for private companies on government contracts because the government is the biggest buyer of intelligence services and goods on the market. The career of Mike McConnell, a former Vice Admiral in the US Navy, epitomises the revolving door between the public and private sectors. McConnell was successively head of intelligence for the Joint Chiefs of Staff during the first Gulf War of 1991, Director of the NSA from 1992 to 1996, Senior Vice President at Booz Allen Hamilton, Chairman of the Intelligence and National Security Alliance (INSA) from 2005 to 2007, Director of National Intelligence from 2007 to 2009, and Executive Vice President and leader of the Intelligence Business at Booz Allen Hamilton.[101]

Similar public-private experiences can be found when researching the profiles of congressional intelligence staffers. A Senate intelligence committee staffer was a SAIC intelligence contractor working for the Pacific Command from 2003 to 2007, before she joined the committee as professional staff member. Another staffer worked at Raytheon, a major defence contractor, just after leaving his post as deputy staff director of the committee. A deputy staff director of the Senate intelligence committee between 2000 and 2009 left to work for Lockheed Martin. Other staffers found jobs in the lobbying industry in Washington, DC after their time serving the committee.[102]

These career paths do not constitute conflicts of interest *per se* and officials have the right to pursue their career once they have left government. Public-private mobility and interactions are desirable to the extent that government and industry need to understand how to work together. Thus the boardrooms of most major intelligence contractors are filled with former senior intelligence officials.[103] Nevertheless, the existence of a revolving door at this level poses important questions about the ability of key accountability holders to maintain a clear distinction between public and private interests, and impartially oversee the companies they worked for or plan to work for. Former DNI McConnell raised this issue himself when he recognised, in an op-ed for the *New York Times*, that during his time at Booz Allen, in many respects he 'never left' the government.[104] Companies should not be blamed for doing what they are permitted to do and buying access. The government is wholly responsible for establishing a lax system that allows retired senior executives – both civilian and military – to work almost immediately after leaving government for firms they have previously dealt with.

The money that some companies devote to lobbying members of Congress causes similar concerns. SAIC spent $1,460,000 in 2007 to lobby in the area of intelligence, and Verizon Communications Inc. spent $5,300,000. The same year, the SAIC voluntary political action committee provided contributions to four senators and eight representatives sitting in the intelligence committees.[105] Representatives are particularly important targets for private companies, since they hold the governmental purse and can decide on special funding requests or earmarks. According to a study of the totality of the earmarks that went to companies in 2005, 'on average, companies generated $28 in earmark revenue for every dollar they spent lobbying'.[106] Although lobbying is a legal activity, critics have long been concerned that this system creates political dependencies on commercial companies' money, and skews national security politics towards private interests.

On the margin, the rapprochement between public and private interests and organisations creates an environment that fosters conflicts of interest.[107] However, the mere existence of public-private interactions does not prove the private sector is systematically exerting undue influence on government accountability holders and the standards they defend. The key issue behind the dilution of the public-private boundary is to ensure that private incentives and behaviours remain aligned to the public interest. This is particularly important when contractors carry out sensitive functions like intelligence collection and analysis, but also when they interact with other contractors on behalf of the government. At the Abu Ghraib detention centre, contractors wrote statements of work for which they were the beneficiaries, and they routinely directed and authorised each other's work.[108] Although it is normal to involve contractors in the procurement process so that they can refine their offer, the increasingly important role they have played in this context inevitably raises concerns about potential conflicts of interest. Defining clear and enforceable boundaries between core public and private activities is essential to avoid controversy, but it is not enough. Boundaries need to be respected. On both counts, the US government (not the private sector) has created and maintained a very lax system.

In two notable cases, public officials crossed the line and accepted bribes from contractors in exchange for favours. Journalist Marcus Stern revealed in 2005 that national security firm MZM Inc. had purchased a $700,000 house for then Rep. Randy Cunningham (D-CA). An FBI investigation found that Cunningham had received over $2 million in bribes in exchange for using his position as a member of the House appropriations and intelligence committees to earmark contracts to MZM Inc. for a new counterintelligence project at the DoD.[109] This case was first brought to the attention of the DoD in 2004 when the IG received a hotline complaint. Once public, the story sparked near immediate reactions by the Democratic Party and public interest groups that called for a full-scale investigation.[110] The evidence uncovered by the investigation was so overwhelming that it eventually forced Cunningham and Mitchell Wade, the founder of MZM Inc., to plead guilty. Cunningham was sentenced to eight years and four months in prison in March 2006, and Wade to two and a half years in prison as well as a $250,000 fine.[111]

This scandal demonstrated how an elected official, supposed to hold the intelligence community and its contractors to account, could shirk his responsibility to further private interests. The Cunningham affair led investigators to a second case involving defence contractor Brent Wilkes, then owner of data mining company ADCS Inc., and former CIA Executive Director Kyle Foggo. Foggo had been under investigation from the CIA IG for his potential involvement in the Cunningham case. Although the Cunningham connection did not reveal any wrongdoing, on 13 February 2007 Foggo and Wilkes were indicted for another case of bribery. Wilkes was later sentenced to twelve years' imprisonment and Foggo pleaded guilty to a single count of fraud concerning bribery and misconduct over a contract, while prosecutors agreed to dismiss twenty-seven other charges.

These cases of bribery show that mechanisms controlling the regularity of the procurement process within the DoD and the CIA were imperfect but not inexistent. Both examples demonstrate the crucial accountability role played by inspectors general, at the crossroads of the executive and judiciary branches of government. Considering Congress, the case of the former CIA senior official was barely mentioned during a congressional hearing of the Committee on the Judiciary concerning the resignation of a US attorney. It was only when a legislator was directly concerned – in the Cunningham affair – that Representatives notably reacted.[112] Overall, both of these cases drew sustained public attention to the conflicts of interest that can arise when the distinction between public authority and private interest collapses. In such cases, outsourcing can offer opportunities for unscrupulous individuals to disregard ethical, legal and professional standards, and use their position to seek favours instead of serving the public interest. Remarkably, accountability problems emerged when public officials made the wrong decision, and were not a direct result of outsourcing. While relevant authorities – mostly inspector generals and the courts – could not prevent the occurrence of incidents, they were ultimately able to investigate Cunningham, Wade, Foggo and Wilkes's conduct and take action to punish their wrongdoing. These examples, just like the labour mischarging emphasised earlier in the chapter, confirm that concerns about the blurring of the boundary between public and private interests are genuine. They also demonstrate the important role played by inspectors general and the courts in checking the behaviour of government officials and contractors.

Conclusion

This chapter has demonstrated the existence of an accountability regime for intelligence contractors in the global war on terrorism. This regime was primarily visible at the administrative level, where federal acquisition processes and the US system of intelligence accountability allowed government officials to maintain some degree of control over the acquisition of goods and services. Considering the core conditions for accountability to occur, government access to information on intelligence activities was complicated but not prevented by outsourcing. In each of the examples presented in this chapter, government officials were able to access key information on contractors' behaviour, generally after they engaged in wrongdoing. Regulatory standards did exist, and were used to punish the mistakes and excesses of some government officials and contractors. However, punishing contractors was not always evident or possible, especially in the cases of the failed modernisation programmes at the FBI and the NSA, where contractors did not clearly break the law and government authorities failed to provide clear direction.

Government authorities hold most of the responsibility for the failures and excesses of intelligence outsourcing. The government sets the rules and sturctures, awards and supervises contracts, and manages individual contracts and contractors. Officials' lack of understanding regarding what their agency needed, and how they could effectively acquire new IT capabilities, played a significant role in the failures of the FBI's VCF and the NSA's Trailblazer projects. In these two cases and at Abu Ghraib, government officials failed to apply existing regulations and procedures to effectively monitor contractors. Cunningham and Foggo, two public officials, accepted bribes from intelligence contractors and failed to uphold the public interest. In turn, the shortcomings of these public authorities were tolerated, not to say exploited, by contractors. This leads to the conclusion that government accountability shortfalls negatively affected the outsourcing of intelligence in the global war on terrorism.

The accountability regime for contractors in the global war on terrorism was imperfect, and government officials were forced to react to problems that were not fundamentally new but were precipitated by rapid outsourcing and unscrupulous individuals. The reactive posture adopted by most accountability holders highlights the need to strengthen upstream control and improve the government's ability to monitor the intelligence outsourcing process to prevent the emergence of problems, or react to them as early as possible. The problems presented in this chapter crystallised accountability holders' attention around key issues such as the inefficiency of major intelligence acquisition projects and the blurring of public and private boundaries. Threats to public officials' integrity, fundamental rights and efficient government can be found throughout the history of US intelligence. Yet, following significant personnel cuts and the advent of the global war on terrorism, the US government's struggles to mitigate these risks became more apparent.[113] Accountability failures brought intelligence outsourcing to the fore, and pushed government authorities to improve the accountability regime for intelligence contractors.

Notes

1. Tim Shorrock, 'The Corporate Takeover of US Intelligence'; Tim Shorrock, *Spies for Hire*, pp. 21–2; Dana Priest, 'America's Security Overload', *The Daily Beast*, 21 September 2011; Michaels, 'All the President's Spies', pp. 929–30.
2. Sanders, *Results of the Fiscal Year 2007 US Intelligence Community*, p. 4.
3. Guttman, 'Government by Contract', pp. 12–13.
4. Hayden, interview with *Frontline*.
5. National security expert A, interview with author, 10 June 2011, Washington, DC; National security expert B, interview with author, 17 June 2011, Washington, DC.
6. Guttman, 'Public Purpose and Private Service', p. 894.
7. National security expert B, interview with author.
8. National security lawyer B, interview with author, 26 July 2011, Washington, DC; Congressional Budget Office, Contractors' Support of US Operations in Iraq, p. 8.
9. US Congress, Public Law 105–270, *Federal Activities Inventory Reform Act*, 105th Congress, 2nd session, 19 October 1998, section 5. The other main definition of inherently governmental functions is provided by the Office of Management and Budget Circular A-76 Revised, 29 May 2003, A-2. The OMB definition is not fundamentally different than the one provided by the FAIR Act.
10. White House, Office of Federal Procurement Policy, Policy Letter 93-1, Management Oversight of Service Contracting, May 18, 1994, app. C-17.
11. Federal Acquisition Regulation 46.104 (a) and (b).

12. Federal Acquisition Institute, COTR Training Blueprint, Section 1, App C-18; Office of the Director of National Intelligence, Office of the Inspector General, *Evaluation of the Administration and Management of ODNI Core Contracts Supporting Critical Missions*, 2011, pp. 4–5.
13. Kate M. Manuel and Rodney M. Perry, *Selected Legal Mechanisms Whereby the Government Can Hold Contractors Accountable for Failure to Perform or Other Misconduct*, CRS Report, 23 September 2015, p. 2.
14. 'Avoiding Federal Debarment: Some Firms Keep Getting Contracts Despite History of Fraud', *Washington Post*, 21 August 2000, A19; Kate M. Manuel, *Debarment and Suspension of Government Contractors: An Overview of the Law Including Recently Enacted and Proposed Amendments*, Congressional Research Service Report for Congress, 19 November 2008; Department of Defense, Office of the Under Secretary of Defense for Acquisition, Technology and Logistics, *Report to Congress on Contracting Fraud*, January 2011, pp. 4–5.
15. For example of agency-specific regulations, see the Defense Federal Acquisition Regulation Supplement and the Department of State Acquisition Regulation.
16. Wright, 'Procurement Authorities of the CIA', pp. 1198, 1211.
17. Radsan, '*Sed Quis Custodiet Ipsos Custodes*', p. 230; Mark Lowenthal in US Senate, Senate Committee on Homeland Security and Governmental Affairs, Subcommittee on Oversight of Government Management, the Federal Workforce, and the District of Columbia, Background: *Intelligence Community Contractors: Are We Striking the Right Balance?*, 112th Congress, 1st session, 20 September 2011, p. 17.
18. Eric Rosenbach and Aki J. Peritz, 'Confrontation or Collaboration? Congress and the Intelligence Community: The Role of Private Corporations in the Intelligence Community', Intelligence and Policy Project of Harvard Kennedy School's Belfer Center for Science and International Affairs, July 2009, p. 3.
19. Dickinson, *Outsourcing War and Peace*, p. 50.
20. US Congress, Public Law 106–523, *Military Extraterritorial Jurisdiction Act*, 106th Congress, 2nd session, 22 November 2000, section 3267 (1)(A); US Congress, Public Law 108–375, *Ronald W. Reagan National Defense Authorization Act for Fiscal Year 2005*, 108th Congress, 2nd session, 28 October 2004, section 1088; Dickinson,

Outsourcing War and Peace, p. 50; Corn, 'Contractors and the Law', p. 171.

21. US Congress, Public Law 109–364, *John Warner National Defense Authorization Act for Fiscal Year 2007*, 109th Congress, 2nd session, 17 October 2006, section 2083; Dickinson, *Outsourcing War and Peace*, p. 51; Corn, 'Contractors and the Law', pp. 171–3; Price, 'Private Contractors, Public Consequences', pp. 210–15.
22. Jennifer K. Elsea, 'Private Security Contractors in Iraq and Afghanistan: Legal Issues', Congressional Research Service Report for Congress, 7 January 2010, p. 18.
23. Frederick Kaiser, US Senate, Committee on Homeland Security and Governmental Affairs, Oversight of Government Management, the Federal Workforce, and the District of Columbia Subcommittee, *Government-wide Intelligence Community Management Reforms*, hearing, 110th Congress, 2nd session, 29 February 2008, p. 21.
24. Rostker, *A Call to Revitalize the Engines of Government*, p. 7; Dickinson, *Outsourcing War and Peace*, p. 54; Corn, 'Contractors and the Law', p. 171.
25. Avant, *The Market for Force*, p. 66; Percy, 'Regulating The Private Security Industry', p. 37.
26. McCubbins and Schwartz, 'Congressional Oversight Overlooked', pp. 165–79; Zegart, 'The Domestic Politics of Irrational Intelligence Oversight', pp. 1–25; Johnson, 'Intelligence Shocks, Media Coverage, and Congressional Accountability, 1947–2012', pp. 1–21.
27. George W. Bush, 'The President's State of the Union Address', 29 January 2002, available at <http://georgewbush-whitehouse.archives.gov/news/releases/2002/01/20020129-11.html> (accessed 29 May 2018).
28. Michael V. Hayden, interview with *Frontline*, 19 August 2010, available at <http://www.pbs.org/wgbh/pages/frontline/are-we-safer/interviews/michael-hayden.html> (accessed 29 May 2018).
29. Terri Everett, Office of the Director of National Intelligence, 'Procuring the Future: 21st Century Acquisition', pp. 9–12, presentation given at conference organised by the DIA, Boulder, Colorado, 14 May 2007, available at <http://www.fas.org/irp/dni/everett.ppt> (accessed 28 May 2018); Office of the Director of National Intelligence, Office of the Inspector General, *Critical Intelligence Community Management Challenges*, 12 November 2008, p. 11; Intelligence and National Security Alliance, *Critical Issues for Intelligence Acquisition Reform*, 2008, p. 2; Nemfakos et al., *Workforce Planning in the Intelligence Community*, p. 26.

30. National security expert B, interview with author; Director of National Intelligence, FY 2013 Congressional Budget Justification, Volume I, National Intelligence Program Summary, February 2012.
31. US Congress, Public Law 81–110, *Central Intelligence Agency Act of 1949*, 81st Congress, 1st session, 20 June 1949, section 17; Snider, *The Agency and the Hill*, pp. 68–9, 147–9, 373.
32. US Senate, Select Committee on Intelligence, *Nomination of John L. Helgerson to be Inspector General, Central Intelligence Agency*, 107th Congress, 2nd session, 15 and 25 April 2002, p. 7.
33. Central Intelligence Agency, *Semiannual reports to the Director of Central Intelligence, January–June 2004, January–June 2007*, p. 36.
34. Central Intelligence Agency, *Semiannual report, January–June 2001*, p. 66; Central Intelligence Agency, *Semiannual report, January–June 2008*, p. 31; Central Intelligence Agency, *Semiannual report to the Director, July–December 2008*, p. 43.
35. Roberts, *Report Accompanying the Intelligence Authorization Act for Fiscal Year 2007*, p. 29.
36. Central Intelligence Agency, *Semiannual report to the Director of Central Intelligence, July–December 2002*, p. 3; Central Intelligence Agency, *Semiannual report, January–June 2005*, p. 60; Central Intelligence Agency, *Semiannual report, July–December 2005*, p. 2.
37. For multiple cases of labour mischarging by NSA contractors see Department of Defense, Inspector General, Defense Criminal Investigative Service, *Pervasive Labor Mischarging by Contract Employees of the National Security Agency*, 31 October 2012; US Court of Appeals, Fourth Circuit, United States of America, v. James E. Jackson, Case No.09-4753, 24 June 2010.
38. US District Court of Virginia, Western District, Charlottesville Division, United States of America, v. Kenneth Harvey and Michael Kronstein, Criminal Nos. 3:06-cr-00023-1, 3:06-cr-00023-2, 9 October 2009.
39. Schooner, 'Fear of Oversight', p. 682.
40. Michaels, 'The (Willingly) Fettered Executive', p. 856.
41. US GAO, B293026.4; B293026.5, SOS Interpreting, Ltd., 25 August 2004.
42. Armed Services Board of Contract Appeals, Appeal of Cubic Defense Applications, Inc. Under Contract No. N00039-03-C-0024, ABSCA No. 56097, 2 October 2007.
43. US House of Representatives, Permanent Select Committee on Intelligence, *Intelligence Authorization for Fiscal Year 2004*, Report 108–381, 108th Congress, 1st session, 19 November 2003, p. 46;

US Senate, Select Committee on Intelligence, *Nomination of Honorable Porter J. Goss to be Director of Central Intelligence*, 108th Congress, 2nd session, 14 and 20 September 2004, p. 11; US Senate, Select Committee on Intelligence, *Nomination of Ambassador John D. Negroponte to be Director of National Intelligence*, 109th Congress, 1st session, 12 April 2005, p. 140; US Senate, Select Committee on Intelligence, *Nomination of Lieutenant General Michael V. Hayden, USAF, to be Principal Deputy Director of National Intelligence*, 109th Congress, 1st session, 14 April 2005, p. 69.

44. See US Department of Justice, Office of the Inspector General, Audit Division, *The Federal Bureau of Investigation's Management of the Trilogy Information Technology Modernization Project*, Audit Report 05–07, February 2005, Appendix 2 – Prior Reports on the FBI's Information Technology, pp. 42–8; US Senate, Committee on Appropriations, Subcommittee on Commerce, Justice, and State, the Judiciary, and Related Agencies, *Federal Bureau of Investigation's Information Technology Modernization Program, Trilogy*, S. Hrg. 109–76, 3 February 2005.
45. Glenn A. Fine, Inspector General, US Department of Justice, testimony before the US Senate Committee on Appropriations, Subcommittee on Commerce, Justice, State and the Judiciary, 3 February 2005, p. 10.
46. Government Accounting Office, *Information Technology: FBI Needs an Enterprise Architecture to Guide Its Modernization Activities*, GAO-03-959, September 2003; Robert S. Mueller, Director of the Federal Bureau of Investigation, testimony before the US Senate, Committee on Appropriations, Subcommittee on Commerce, Justice, State and the Judiciary, 3 February 2005, available at <https://www.fbi.gov/news/testimony/fbis-virtual-case-file-system> (accessed 29 May 2018).
47. McGroddy and Lin, *A Review of the FBI's Trilogy Information Technology Modernization Program*, pp. 1, 43.
48. US Department of Justice, Office of the Inspector General, *An Investigation of the Belated Production of Documents in the Oklahoma City Bombing Case*, 19 March 2002; US Department of Justice, *A Review of FBI Security Programs*. Commission for Review of FBI Security Programs, March 2002; Zelikow et al., *The 9/11 Commission Report*, p. 77.
49. US Senate, Committee on Appropriations, Subcommittee on Commerce, Justice, State and the Judiciary, *Special Hearing: Federal Bureau of Investigation's Information Technology Modernization*

Program, Trilogy, 3 February 2005, Washington, DC, p. 3; Glenn A. Fine, Inspector General, US Department of Justice, testimony before the US Senate Committee on Appropriations, Subcommittee on Commerce, Justice, State and the Judiciary, 3 February 2005, p. 10; Kim and Brown, 'The Importance of Contract Design', p. 687.

50. Glenn A. Fine, Inspector General, US Department of Justice, testimony before the US Senate Committee on Appropriations, Subcommittee on Commerce, Justice, State and the Judiciary, 3 February 2005, p. 10.
51. US Department of Justice, *The Federal Bureau of Investigation's Management of the Trilogy Information Technology Modernization Project*, p. 25.
52. Ibid. pp. iii–iv, 23, 29.
53. McGroddy and Lin, *A Review of the FBI's Trilogy Information Technology Modernization Program*, p. 5.
54. Ibid. p. 43.
55. Ibid. pp. 1–2.
56. US Department of Justice, *The Federal Bureau of Investigation's Management of the Trilogy Information Technology Modernization Project*, p. 27.
57. Government Accountability Office, *Federal Bureau of Investigation: Weak Controls over Trilogy Project Led to Payment of Questionable Contractor Costs and Missing Assets*, GAO-06-306, February 2006, p. 32.
58. McGroddy and Lin, *A Review of the FBI's Trilogy Information Technology Modernization Program*, p. 5; Government Accountability Office, *Federal Bureau of Investigation: Weak Controls*, p. 5.
59. US Department of Justice, The Federal Bureau of Investigation's Management of the Trilogy Information Technology Modernization Project, pp. 28–9; Government Accountability Office, *Federal Bureau of Investigation: Weak Controls*, p. 13.
60. Robert S. Mueller, Director of the Federal Bureau of Investigation, testimony before the US Senate, Committee on Appropriations, Subcommittee on Commerce, Justice, State and the Judiciary, 3 February 2005, available at <https://www.fbi.gov/news/testimony/fbis-virtual-case-file-system> (accessed 29 May 2018).
61. US Department of Justice, *The Federal Bureau of Investigation's Management of the Trilogy Information Technology Modernization Project*, p. v.
62. Government Accountability Office, *Federal Bureau of Investigation: Weak Controls*, p. 8. For more on the FBI problems, see Tromblay,

'Information Technology (IT) Woes and Intelligence Agency Failures', pp. 817–32.

63. Glenn A. Fine, Inspector General, US Department of Justice, testimony before the US Senate Committee on Appropriations, Subcommittee on Commerce, Justice, State and the Judiciary, 3 February 2005, p. 10; Kim and Brown, 'The Importance of Contract Design', p. 688.
64. Dan Eggen and Griff Witte, 'The FBI's Upgrade That Wasn't: $170 Million Bought an Unusable Computer System', *Washington Post*, 18 August 2006, A1.
65. Walter Pincus, 'Intelligence Shakeup Would Boost CIA; Panel Urges Transfer of NSA, Satellites, Imagery From Pentagon', *Washington Post*, 8 November 2001, A1; US Congress, House Permanent Select Committee on Intelligence and Senate Select Committee on Intelligence, *Report of the Joint inquiry into Intelligence Community Activities Before and After the Terrorist Attacks of September 11, 2001*, December 2002, p. 77; US Senate, Select Committee on Intelligence, Committee Activities, *Special Report*, 3 January 2001 to 22 November 2002, 108th Congress, 1st session, 21 May 2003, p. 14.
66. Bamford, *The Shadow Factory*, pp. 325–30; Department of Defense, Office of the Inspector General, *Requirements for the Trailblazer and Thinthread Systems*, Report 05-INTEL-03, 15 December 2004, pp. 1, 38; Siobhan Gorman, 'Little-Known Contractor Has Close Ties with Staff of NSA', *Baltimore Sun*, 29 January 2006, available at <http://articles.baltimoresun.com/2006-01-29/news/0601290158_1_saic-information-technology-intelligence-experts> (accessed 29 May 2018); Mayer, 'The Secret Sharer', pp. 46–56.
67. US Senate, *Joint Inquiry Into Intelligence Community Activities Before and After Terrorist Attacks of September 11, 2001*, Report No.351, 107th Congress, 2nd session, 23 January–22 November 2002, p. 55.
68. Department of Defense, *Requirements for the Trailblazer and Thinthread Systems*, pp. i, 95, 107–10.
69. US District Court for the Northern District of Maryland, United States of America v. Thomas Andrews Drake, Case 1:10-cr-00181-RDB, Document 75, filed 15 March 2011, p. 3, available at <http://static1.firedoglake.com/28/files/2011/05/110315-Defense-Support-Whistleblow.pdf> (accessed 29 May 2018); Ellen Nakashima, 'Former NSA Executive Thomas A. Drake May Pay High Price For Media Leak', *Washington Post*, 14 July 2010, C1.

70. US Congress, Public Law 108–136, *National Defense Authorization Act for Fiscal Year 2004*, 108th Congress, 1st session, 4 June 2003, section 804; Ariel Sabar, 'Congress Curbs NSA's Power to Contract with Suppliers', 20 July 2003, *Baltimore Sun*, available at <http://articles.baltimoresun.com/2003-07-20/news/0307200276_1_nsa-eavesdropping-agency> (accessed 29 May 2018); Aid, 'Prometheus Embattled', p. 44.
71. US Senate, Select Committee on Intelligence, *Nomination of Lieutenant General Michael V. Hayden*, pp. 21–2, 69–71.
72. Siobhan Gorman, 'System Error', *Baltimore Sun*, 29 January 2006, A1; Gorman, 'Computer Ills Hinder NSA'; Gorman, 'NSA Rejected System That Sifted Phone Data Legally', *Baltimore Sun*, 18 May 2006; Hosenball and Thomas, 'Hold the Phone; Big Brother Knows Whom You Call', pp. 22–3; Marvin C. Ott, statement before the Subcommittee on Oversight of Government Management, the Federal Workforce, and the District of Columbia, US Senate Committee on Homeland Security and Governmental Affairs, 110th Congress, 2nd session, 29 February 2008.
73. Alice Lipowicz, 'Trailblazer Loses Its Way', *Washington Technology*, 10 September 2005, available at <https://washingtontechnology.com/articles/2005/09/10/trailblazer-loses-its-way.aspx> (accessed 29 May 2018).
74. Gorman, 'System Error'.
75. Donald L. Barlett and James B. Steele, 'Washington $8 Billion Shadow', *Vanity Fair*, 28 February 2007; Former NSA Senior Executives/Veteran Intelligence Professionals for Sanity (VIPS), 'Memorandum for the President, Input for Your Decisions on NSA', 7 January 2014, available at <https://consortiumnews.com/2014/01/07/nsa-insiders-reveal-what-went-wrong/> (accessed 29 May 2018).
76. See for example the failure of the NRO's Future Imagery Architecture: Philip Taubman, 'Death of a Spy Satellite Program', *New York Times*, 11 November 2007, p. 1.
77. Michael Hayden, *Nomination of Lieutenant General Michael V. Hayden, USAF, to be Principal Deputy Director of National Intelligence*, p. 21.
78. Naval Inspector General, Vice Admiral Albert T. Church, III, Executive Summary, February 2005, <https://cryptome.org/church-report.htm> (accessed 29 May 2018); Harris, 'Intelligence Incorporated', p. 46.
79. Video: CBS Network, *60 Minutes II. Abuse at Abu Ghraib*, 28 April 2004, New York; Seymour Hersh, 'Torture at Abu Ghraib', *New*

Yorker, 10 May 2004, p. 42. On media reactions to the Abu Ghraib abuses, see Ricchiardi, 'Missed Signals'; Andén-Papadopoulos, 'The Abu Ghraib Torture Photograph'.

80. Ariana Eunjung Cha and Renae Merle, 'Line Increasingly Blurred Between Soldiers and Civilian Contractors', *Washington Post*, 13 May 2004, A1; Joshua Chaffin, 'Contract Interrogators Hired to Avoid Supervision', *Financial Times*, 21 May 2004, A9; Hersh, 'Torture at Abu Ghraib;' Julian Borger, 'US Military in Torture Scandal: Use of Private Contractors in Iraqi Jail Interrogations Highlighted by Inquiry into Abuse of Prisoners', *Guardian*, 30 April 2004, A1; Danielle Brian cited in Ellen McCarthy, 'CACI Contract: From Supplies to Interrogation', *Washington Post*, 17 May 2004, E1.
81. Antonio M. Taguba, *Article 15-6 Investigation of the 800th Military Police Brigade*, 12 March 2004, pp. 6, 48.
82. Government Accountability Office, *Interagency Contracting: Problems with DOD's and Interior's Orders to Support Military Operations*, GAO-05-201, April 2005, pp. 2, 7–8; Department of the Interior, Office of the Inspector General, 'Memorandum from Earl E. Devaney to Assistant Secretary for Policy, Management and Budget, in Review of 12 Procurements Placed Under General Services Administration Federal Supply Schedules 70 and 871 by the National Business Center' (Assignment No. W-EV-OSS-0075-2004), 16 July 2004; Guttman, 'Government By Contract', p. 12.
83. Department of the Interior, Office of the Inspector General, 'Memorandum from Earl E. Devaney', p. 3.
84. Hughes, *War on Terror Inc.*, p. 193.
85. Robert O'Harrow, Jr. and Ellen McCarthy, 'Private Sector Has Firm Role at the Pentagon', *Washington Post*, 9 June 2004, E1.
86. Maj. Gen. Geoffrey Miller, Deputy Commander for Detainee Operations, Multinational Force-Iraq, in US Senate, Armed Services Committee, hearing, 108th Congress, 2nd session, 19 May 2004; Department of Defense, Office of the Inspector General, *AR 15-6 Investigation of the Abu Ghraib Detention Facility and 205th Military Intelligence Brigade* (U) (also called the Jones-Fay report), 25 August 2004, p. 19.
87. Department of Defense, *AR 15-6 Investigation of the Abu Ghraib Detention Facility*, pp. 18, 33, 49–50, 52; Department of Defense, Independent Panel to review DoD Detention Operations, *Final Report*, 24 August 2004, p. 69; Government Accountability Office, *Interagency Contracting*, pp. 1–2, 8; Department of the Interior, 'Memorandum from Earl E. Devaney', pp. 1–2; Department of the Army, Office of the Inspector General, *Detainee Operations Inspection*, 21 July 2004,

pp. 87–9; Government Accountability Office, *Interagency Contracting*, pp. 1–2.

88. Ariana Eunjung Cha and Renae Merle, 'Line Increasingly Blurred Between Soldiers and Civilian Contractors', *Washington Post*, 13 May 2004, A1.
89. Harris, 'Intelligence Incorporated', p. 46.
90. Dickinson, *Outsourcing War and Peace*, pp. 66–7; Department of Defense, *AR 15-6 Investigation of the Abu Ghraib Detention Facility*, p. 50.
91. Editor, 'Will Anyone Pay for Abu Ghraib?', *New York Times*, 5 February 2015; Josh White, 'Reservist Sentenced to 3 Years for Abu Ghraib Abuse', *Washington Post*, 28 September 2005, A12; US Court of Appeal for the Fourth District, Al Shimari et al. v. CACI Premier Technology, Inc.; CACI International, Inc., Case No. 13-1937, 30 June 2014; Center for Constitutional Rights, 'Al Shimari v. CACI et al.', available at <http://ccrjustice.org/ourcases/current-cases/al-shimari-v-caci-et-al> (accessed 29 May 2018); US District Court for the Central District of California, Emad Khudhayir Shahuth Al-Janabi v. Steven A. Stefanowicz et al., Civil Action No.08CV-02913, 5 May 2008.
92. Pete Yost, 'Abu Ghraib Settlement: Defense Contractor Engility Holdings Pays $5M to Iraqi Torture Detainees', *Huffington Post*, 8 January 2013.
93. US District Court for the Eastern District of North Carolina (Western Division), United States of America v. David A. Passaro, Case No. 5:04-CR-211-1, Indictment, 17 June 2004.
94. US District Court for the Eastern District of North Carolina (Western Division), United States of America v. David A. Passaro, Memorandum in Support of Motion to Dismiss for Lack of Jurisdiction, 1 November 2004, 5; *PBS Newshour*, 'Convicted Former CIA Contractor Speaks Out About Prisoner Interrogation', 20 April 2015, available at <http://www.pbs.org/newshour/bb/convicted-former-cia-contractor-speaks-prisoner-interrogation/> (accessed 29 May 2018).
95. Department of Justice, Office of Public Affairs, *Statement of Attorney General Eric Holder on Closure of Investigation into the Interrogation of Certain Detainees*, 30 August 2012; BBC, 'CIA Interrogation Probe Ends Without Any Charges', available at <http://www.bbc.co.uk/news/world-us-canada-19432553> (accessed 29 May 2018); Jane Mayer, 'Deadly Interrogation', *New Yorker*, 14 November 2005, pp. 44–5; Mark Thompson, 'Haunted by Homicide: Federal Grand Jury Investigates War Crimes and Torture in Death of "the Iceman" at Abu Ghraib, Plus Other Alleged CIA Abuses', *Time*, 13 June 2011.

96. Marian Wang, 'CIA Officials Involved in Abuse and Wrongful Detention Rarely Reprimanded, Sometimes Promoted', 9 February 2011, available at <http://www.propublica.org/blog/item/cia-officials-involved-in-abuse-and-wrongful-detention-rarely-reprimanded-s> (accessed 29 May 2018).
97. Rep. Henry A. Waxman (D-CA), letter to the Honorable Tom Davis, Chairman, Committee on Government Reform, US House of Representatives, 12 May 2004; Charles Babington and Helen Dewar, 'Lawmakers Demand Answers On Abuses in Military-Run Jails', *Washington Post*, 6 May 2004, A12.
98. US Senate, Armed Service Committee, S. Hrg. 108-868 – Review of Department of Defense Detention and Interrogation Operations, 7, 11, 19 May, 22 July, 9 September 2004, pp. 4, 44.
99. Cha and Merle, 'Line Increasingly Blurred'.
100. Julie Tate, 'A Post-9/11 Brain Drain at the CIA', *Washington Post*, 13 April 2011, A1; Rostker, *A Call to Revitalize the Engines of Government*, p. 12.
101. Glenn Greenwald, 'Mike McConnell, the WashPost and the Dangers of Sleazy Corporatism', 29 March 2010, available at <http://www.salon.com/news/opinion/glenn_greenwald/2010/03/29/mcconnell> (accessed 29 May 2018); Priest and Arkin, *Top Secret America*, pp. 188–91; Shorrock, *Spies for Hire*, pp. 38–40, 48–60.
102. LinkedIn, 'Amy Hopkins', available at <http://www.linkedin.com/pub/amy-hopkins/40/b/497> (accessed 29 May 2018); Center for Responsive Politics, 'Filippone, Bob', available at <http://www.opensecrets.org/revolving/rev_summary.php?id=70959> (accessed 29 May 2018); Center for Responsive Politics, 'Dubee, Melvin', available at <http://www.opensecrets.org/revolving/rev_summary.php?id=75505> (accessed 29 May 2018); Center for Responsive Politics, 'Revolving Door: Search Results; Congressional Committee search: Select Intelligence Committee', available at <http://www.opensecrets.org/revolving/search_result.php?cmte=Select+Intelligence&id=SITL> (accessed 29 May 2018).
103. See Ellen McCarthy, 'Intelligence Work Comes to CACI via Acquisitions', *Washington Post*, 8 July 2004, E1.
104. Mark Mazzetti and David E. Sanger, 'Bush Announces Pick for Intelligence Post', *New York Times*, 5 January 2007.
105. US Senate, Lobbying Disclosure Act Database, Filing Year: 2007, Issue Code: INTELLIGENCE, available at <http://soprweb.senate.gov/index.cfm?event=submitSearchRequest> (accessed 29 May 2018); US Senate, Lobbying Contribution report for SAIC Voluntary

Political Action Committee, LD-203 YEAR-END REPORT, available at <http://soprweb.senate.gov/index.cfm?event=getFilingDetails&filingID=ca6c4c36-5735-468b-a235-a33738adb67e> (accessed 29 May 2018).

106. Eamon Javers, 'Inside the Hidden World of Earmarks', *BusinessWeek*, 17 September 2007, p. 56.
107. For a similar argument see Scheuer, *Imperial Hubris*, p. 249.
108. Department of Defense, Office of the Inspector General, Deputy Inspector General for Intelligence, *Allegations of Mismanagement and Waste within the Counterintelligence Field Activity*, Report No.06-INTEL-15, 29 September 2006, p. 14; Department of Defense, *AR 15-6 Investigation of the Abu Ghraib Detention Facility*, p. 49.
109. Marcus Stern, 'Lawmaker's Home Sale Questioned: Cunningham Defends Deal with Defense Firm's Owner', *Copley News Service*, 2 June 2005, available at <http://www.lexisnexis.com/uk/nexis/search/newssubmitForm.do> (accessed 29 May 2018); Marcus Stern and Joe Cantlupe, 'FBI Looking at Sale of US Rep. Cunningham's Home', *Copley News Service*, 17 June 2005, available at <http://www.lexisnexis.com/uk/nexis/search/newssubmitForm.do> (accessed 29 May 2018); Randal C. Archibold, 'Ex-Congressman Gets 8-Year Term in Bribery Case', *New York Times*, 4 March 2006, A1; *Report of the Special Counsel for the Cunningham Enquiry, Executive Summary, Cunningham's Plea*, pp. 1–3, available at <http://www.fas.org/irp/congress/2006_rpt/harman101706.pdf> (accessed 29 May 2018); Department of Justice, *Defense contractor Mitchell Wade pleads guilty to bribing former Congressman 'Duke' Cunningham, corrupting Department of Defense officials, and election fraud*, 24 February 2006, p. 3; Maurice J. Hattier, State of New York, Suffolk County, Affidavit, 05-1215M, p. 11, available at <http://legacy.utsandiego.com/news/politics/cunningham/images/070717hattieraffidavit.pdf> (accessed 29 May 2018).
110. Hattier, Affidavit, p. 52; Jeffrey H. Birnbaum and Renae Merle, 'Lawmaker-Contractor Deals Questioned; Congressman's Relationship with Defense Firm Chief Sparks Call for Ethics Probe', *Washington Post*, 17 June 2005, A29; Patrick O'Connor, 'Delay Defends Cunningham's Home Sale', *The Hill*, 15 June 2005, p. 3; *Report of the Special Counsel for the Cunningham Enquiry, Executive Summary, Cunningham's Plea*, pp. 1–2.
111. Onell R. Soto, 'Bribery Probe Continues Despite Lawmaker's Guilty Plea', *Union-Tribune San Diego*, 30 November 2005; Tony

Perry, 'Cunningham Receives Eight-Year Sentence', *Los Angeles Times*, 3 March 2006; Del Quentin Wilber, 'Ex-Contractor Gets 2½ Years in Prison in Cunningham Case', *Washington Post*, 16 December 2008, A3.

112. Dean Calbreath and Jerry Kammer, 'Poway Contractor Provided a Loaner', *Copley News Service*, 10 September 2005; Dean Calbreath, 'No. 3 CIA Official Investigated on Ties to Wilkes', *San Diego Union-Tribune*, 4 March 2006; Mark Mazzetti and David Johnston, 'CIA Aide's House and Office Searched', *New York Times*, 13 May 2006, p. 10, A1; US District Court, Southern District of California, United States of America v. Kyle Dustin Foggo, Criminal Case No. 07 CR 0329 LAB, 13 February 2007, available at <http://media.washingtonpost.com/wp-srv/business/documents/indictment_foggo_wilkes.pdf> (accessed 29 May 2018); Matthew Barakat, 'Kyle "Dusty" Foggo, Former CIA#3 Gets More Than 3 Years in Prison', *Huffington Post*, 26 February 2009.
113. Savas, *Privatization and Public-Private Partnerships*, p. 209.

5 Improving Government Oversight of Intelligence Contractors

Following the conceptual model used in this book, a thorough examination of the accountability regime for contractors should not stop at the emergence of problems but should also consider accountability holders' responses to these problems. Elements of the intelligence community and Congress have long been aware of some of the accountability problems with intelligence outsourcing, but policy-makers did not pay much attention to these problems until a series of high-profile incidents broke out in the early 2000s. These scandals drew public attention to the extensive ties between the intelligence community and the private sector, and comforted critics who argued that contractors were out of control.

Behind the media headlines, a host of factors fostered government responses to the accountability problems involving intelligence contractors. The intelligence reform undertaken by the administration of George W. Bush and culminating in the establishment of the ODNI in 2005 provided new opportunities to manage and regulate issues – like human capital policies and acquisition management – affecting the relationship between the intelligence community and its contractors. At the political level, the sense of emergency that had characterised the aftermath of the 9/11 attacks started to fade. In these conditions, the executive and legislative branches of government sought to respond to some of the problems of intelligence outsourcing. These efforts have largely been overlooked by critics, yet they constitute an essential part of the story of intelligence outsourcing.

From 2006 onward, government authorities increased their efforts to oversee intelligence contractors and redefine the contour of public-private boundaries in the national intelligence effort. Within the executive branch, leading agencies like the ODNI and the CIA collected data to help intelligence and congressional leaders understand the role played by contractors in the national intelligence effort. Government accountability holders used this information to develop new guidance and better control the role of contractors in the intelligence community. They focused their attention on three sets of issues: reinforcing contract management to minimise the risks of wrongdoing; defining core government activities; and balancing the roles of government employees and contractors in the intelligence workforce. Government measures in these three areas prove, once again, that contractors are not 'out of control'. Yet these decisions could not solve all the issues confronting intelligence outsourcing and the US system of intelligence accountability.

Gathering Evidence on Intelligence Contractors

Executive and legislative interest in intelligence outsourcing predates the global war on terrorism, but available evidence suggests that contractors started drawing more attention from senior intelligence officials and congressional committees from 2006 onwards.[1] When the ODNI was established in 2005 it was granted authority to coordinate the intelligence community and ensure the integration of its workforce, and to manage the National Intelligence Program (NIP), including the major systems acquisitions funded as a part of this programme.[2] Given these responsibilities, intelligence outsourcing naturally became an important issue for the ODNI. In the early days of the ODNI, when the agency was literally a dozen persons strong, the position of Chief Human Capital Officer was created to develop and execute intelligence community-wide human resource strategies, plans and policies. The ODNI leadership hoped to use human capital policies to instil a sense of community among the sixteen US intelligence agencies. Ronald Sanders, the first official to take this position, remembers that 'more effectively managing the intelligence community's contract workforce was one of the very first things' ODNI leaders set out to do when the agency was established.[3]

Beyond the negative media coverage on intelligence contractors, one of the factors that drew senior officials' attention to the need for strategic workforce planning was a Senate intelligence committee audit of personnel growth in the intelligence community that revealed a significant gap in knowledge about the roles and cost of contractors.[4] The role this audit played in triggering accountability holders' attention adds nuance to the conventional argument that scandals drive intelligence oversight, and shows that anticipatory forms of oversight activities – or police-patrols, to refer to the seminal model developed by McCubbins and Schwartz – can contribute to flag issues that require attention. In this case, the intelligence committee's audit combined with a series of scandals and a favourable political environment to foster more active oversight efforts.

Before the establishment of the ODNI, the Director of Central Intelligence's community management staff, who used to be in charge of developing policies for the entire intelligence community, had not really considered the aggregate effects of sourcing decisions on the overall intelligence workforce. As incredible as it sounds, senior decision-makers had never looked at the civilian, military and contractor components of the intelligence workforce as a whole, and despite the existence of federal requirements to inventory commercial activities, little data had been collected to help understand the roles contractors were playing in the national intelligence effort.[5] Prior to 2006, the sixteen US intelligence agencies had 'no single standard to count or distinguish contractors', and the aggregate numbers of contractors working for the community remained unknown.[6]

With hindsight, officials have emphasised that the government procurement model makes counting contractors more complicated than counting government employees. For example, contractors sometimes work part-time on multiple contracts, and this reality complicates comparisons between full-time government employees and their contractor equivalents. Yet, the difficulty of the task does not explain the absence of an overall effort to collect and harmonise data on the aggregate number of intelligence contractors before the establishment of the ODNI. Focusing on organisational cultures provides a more convincing explanation. In a community known for its problems of information sharing, various agencies and officials – including human capital and procurement officers – followed different procedures and were not expected to coordinate their use of contractors.[7] In this context, developing a unified vision for the use of intelligence contractors was beyond their reach.[8]

This strategic deficiency in the executive control of contractors had the disturbing consequence of limiting congressional oversight of intelligence. When intelligence agencies do not have the necessary information and capabilities to control their workforce, congressional overseers can hardly be expected to keep an eye on the evolution of this workforce. The information gaps uncovered by the SSCI audit on the intelligence workforce and the intelligence scandals that caught the headlines in the mid-2000s combined to draw congressional attention to the problems of intelligence outsourcing. However, congressional oversight of intelligence was also limited by political tensions, which prevented representatives from passing intelligence authorisation bills from 2005 to 2008. In the absence of authorisation, senior intelligence managers had, from a legal standpoint, 'unlimited flexibility' to spend the funds appropriated to the intelligence community as they saw fit.[9] A former senior ODNI official notes that his organisation did not abuse the 'vacuum' created by the absence of authorisation, and kept providing information and justifying its policies to Congress.[10] Although they did not pass, these intelligence authorisation bills are worthy of interest because they indicate some of the intelligence committees' concerns.

Congressional committees started paying more attention to intelligence contractors in spring 2006, before the mid-term elections. Following the publication of a news article on intelligence contracting, Representative David Price (D-NC), a member of the House appropriations committee, expressed concern about the place of contractors in the intelligence community budget and noted that this issue required immediate attention.[11] Congressional committees soon started requesting more information on intelligence contractors. A House report accompanying the 2007 intelligence authorisation bill required:

> (1) the DNI to report to Congress on regulations issued by agencies within the Intelligence Community regarding minimum standards for hiring and training of contractors, functions appropriate for private sector contractors, and procedures for preventing waste, fraud, and abuse; (2) contractors awarded Intelligence Community contracts to provide a transparent accounting of their work to their contracting officers within Intelligence Community agencies; (3) the DNI to submit an annual report to Congress on the contracts awarded by Intelligence Community agencies; and (4) the DNI to make recommendations to Congress on enhancing the Intelligence Community's ability to hire, promote, and retain highly qualified and experienced professional staff.[12]

Discussing the 2007 intelligence budget, the SSCI complained that it had 'seen no metrics that would link the additional proposed personnel to improvements in the Intelligence Community's ability to detect, predict, analyse, and counter current and future threats to the United States'.[13] Put simply, the intelligence community expanded its workforce without knowing whether it would improve its capabilities at the margins. This approach can be related to the exponential growth of intelligence requirements in the early days of the global war on terrorism.

Less than a month later, the publication of the ODNI five-year strategic human capital plan, released as an annex to the 2006 national intelligence strategy, provided a clear signal that the intelligence community leadership had identified a series of issues it was determined to fix. The document pointed out:

> increasingly, the IC finds itself in competition with its contractors for our own employees. Confronted by arbitrary staffing ceilings and uncertain funding, components are left with no choice but to use contractors for work that may be borderline 'inherently governmental' – only to find that to do that work, those same contractors recruit our own employees, already cleared and trained at the government expense, and then 'lease' them back to us at considerably greater expense.[14]

Instead of setting limits on the numbers and types of contractors within each agency, the plan highlighted the community's desire to determine 'the optimum mix of military, civilian, contractor, and other human resources'.[15] To make this possible, the ODNI emphasised the need to eliminate the staff ceilings restricting the number of government employees within each agency, one of the most discussable factors behind the expansion of labour contractors in the intelligence community.[16] However, implementing this plan required data on the intelligence community's human capital, something the intelligence community continued to lack. A few months after the publication of this plan, the House intelligence committee complained that US officials did not 'have an adequate understanding of the size and composition of the contractor workforce, a consistent and well-articulated method for assessing contractor performance, or strategies for managing a combined staff-contractor workforce'.[17] Under such conditions, it is legitimate to speculate whether or not functions vital to national security were being contracted beyond the government's capability for control.

To fill the knowledge gap about contractors, intelligence leaders established a series of working groups. At the CIA, Director Hayden created a study group 'to review CIA's use of contractors and develop a management strategy' in November 2006. In retrospect, it is clear that this study group was established because CIA management lacked information about its contractors.[18] According to General Hayden, this knowledge gap can be explained by the fact that the Agency's contractor workforce grew as a result of a series of relatively independent decisions to contract within each directorate.[19] The CIA study group on contractors concluded that responsibility for earlier shortfalls regarding the management of contractors lay with the agency's leadership, something Hayden recognised publicly.[20]

The ODNI initiated a broader effort 'to capture information on the number and costs of contractors throughout the Intelligence Community'.[21] However, data collection was confounded by the lack of common definitions, and this led the Office of Management and Budget to establish an official definition of core contractors as those providing 'direct support to core IC mission areas'.[22] The establishment of a contractor inventory working group at the ODNI helped in overcoming problems of information sharing. The impetus to gather and analyse data on the role of contractors in the intelligence community eventually bore fruit, leading to the production of the first ever *Inventory of Core Contract Personnel in the Intelligence Community*. The Senate intelligence committee described this inventory as 'a good first step' and welcomed the 'preliminary snapshot of the total number of full time equivalent (FTE) contractors by expenditure center' provided by this inventory.[23]

Thanks to this effort, the ODNI was able to reveal that 27 per cent of the intelligence community's workforce, approximately 37,000 contractors, was engaged in 'core' intelligence tasks like intelligence collection, operations and analysis in 2007.[24] The *Inventory of Core Contract Personnel* showed that intelligence collection and operations, intelligence analysis and production, and research and technology accounted for most of the expenses devoted to core contractors in the NIP (see Figure 5.1 below). Given the absence of an overall human capital plan prior to 2006, there was no clear government rationale for this repartition. The ODNI used this inventory to shed light on the justifications for intelligence outsourcing and confirmed the unique character of some of the services provided by the private sector, with 56 per cent of core contract personnel reported to provide 'unique expertise' to the intelligence community in 2007. The figure, though it did not include the employees working under the Military Intelligence

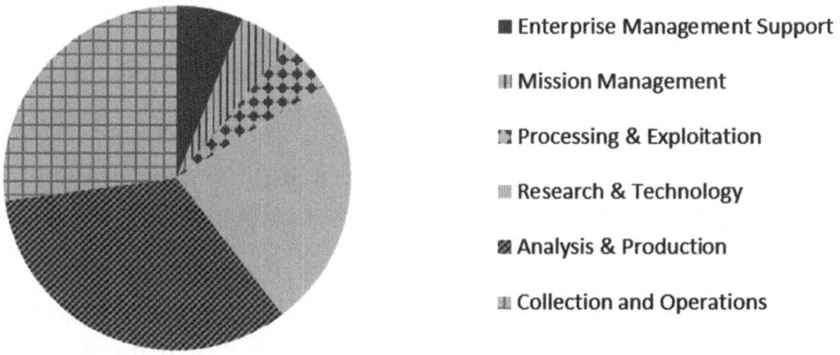

Figure 5.1 National Intelligence Program contract personnel full-time equivalents: by function (FY 2007). Source: Office of the Director of National Intelligence, FY 2007 Results, US Intelligence Community, Inventory of Core Contractor Personnel, p. 4.

Program (MIP),[25] corroborates one of the main points made in this book: contractors are an essential component of the national intelligence effort that deserves attention from key accountability holders. In its inventory, the ODNI further confirmed that some of the decisions to outsource were based on rationales such as cost-effectiveness, the uncertain nature of intelligence activities, and surge requirements – all of which are explained in Chapter 3.[26]

In subsequent years, the congressional intelligence committees continued to require information on intelligence contractors and mandated the ODNI to provide annual personnel assessments including more refined inventories on core contractors.[27] The 2010 intelligence authorisation act, the first to be passed by Congress after a four-year hiatus, directed each component of the intelligence community to provide estimates of the number and costs of core contract personnel for the upcoming year, and required the ODNI to put together an extensive report on intelligence contractors covering key issues like the workforce balance between government and contractor employees.[28] US intelligence agencies were required to collect and process data on their use of contractors and report their findings to the ODNI, which could then use the data to explain the role of intelligence contractors to the OMB and Congress. This process incited intelligence agencies to systematically gather information, explain and optimise their reliance on contractors.[29]

Despite its effort to oversee the intelligence workforce, the ODNI has struggled to put together reliable inventories of contract personnel. Shortcomings and variations in the methodologies and definitions used to collect data on contractors have limited the comparability of the information that is collected, and complicated the management of contractors at the strategic level. Key information, such as the type of functions carried out by contractors, was still missing from the inventories in 2014. These problems are not unique, but they are more pressing in the intelligence community given the way in which intelligence activities can affect national security. As long as data are missing or incompatible, it will be very difficult to develop detailed plans to balance the intelligence workforce and control the role of contractors in the national intelligence effort. Much progress has been achieved since the beginning of the global war on terrorism, but further efforts are needed to keep improving yearly inventories and fine-tune the role and number of contractors in the intelligence community.[30]

As intelligence leaders and congressional committees started receiving more information on the contractor workforce, they were able to refine their understanding of intelligence outsourcing and turn their attention to a number of key issues. The rest of this chapter provides an overview of the progress these accountability holders have made in three areas: contract management, the definition of core governmental functions, and balancing the public and private components of the intelligence workforce.

Managing Contracts and Contractors

Contract management is one of the key issues on which intelligence accountability holders have focused their oversight efforts. At the CIA, the study group on contractors recommended taking an 'efficient approach to contracting' and centralising the management of contracts. The group also underlined the need for 'better workforce management through procedural and administrative changes'.[31] To improve contract management the CIA decided to make the contracting process more rigorous, emphasise performance-based models and revamp training for contracting officer technical representatives. These decisions aimed to improve the standards guiding the use of contractors and their implementation. The CIA management also sought to limit the revolving door phenomenon. In a public statement, the Director announced that 'all Requests for Proposals and contracts issued after 1 June [2007] will bar contracting firms from bidding back within 18 months former CIA employees who resigned before retirement eligibility'. Director Hayden argued that he did not want the CIA to become 'a farm team for contractors'.[32] This effort was supposed to help mitigate conflicts of interest, yet it was criticised because it applied only to contractors and not to the individuals sitting on companies' boards. The ban was also limited in time, while personal relationships often are not.[33]

To reinforce the importance of acquisition management within the intelligence community, the ODNI created the position of Deputy Director of National Intelligence for Acquisition in 2007.[34] This new post provided leadership, but problems persisted. A 2008 report by the ODNI IG pointed out that acquisition management remained a core challenge for the intelligence community and found that 'some IC elements lack strong program and procurement offices; clearly defined program requirements, performance measures, and acceptance terms; and program management systems to support the acquisition decision-making process'. The report noted that acquisition continued to suffer from 'instances of noncompliance, cost and schedule overruns and poor process discipline', and oversight efforts had been 'impeded by a perceived lack of trust, communication, and accountability in the IC acquisition community'.[35] These issues are very similar to those that had confronted the Trailblazer and VCF projects a few years earlier.

Congressional committees also expressed concerns, and called for new policies to improve acquisition management and contractors' performance. An intelligence committee report encouraged 'the DNI to issue a formal policy establishing a procedure by which the Intelligence Community would be empowered to withhold incentives from companies with poor contract performance'. The document urged 'the Deputy DNI for Acquisition to consider whether established firewalls are sufficient to prevent any potential conflict of interest'.[36] A HPSCI report focused more directly on wrongdoing and decried the supposed 'absence of procedures for overseeing contractors, ensuring the recognition of criminal violations and preventing and redressing of financial waste, fraud and abuse'.[37] As we have seen in the previous chapter, procedures did exist at the time to report and punish contractors' wrongdoing, even though they were not perfect. Thanks to these procedures the SSCI was, for example, able to request a 'list of all contractors that have been the subject of an investigation by the inspector general of any element of the Intelligence Community during the previous fiscal year or that are or have been the subject of an investigation during the current fiscal year'.[38]

These efforts on the part of Congress to inform itself and request executive action are notable, but they were insufficient on their own to prevent further problems. Contract management is primarily an issue of policy implementation, and while committees can request changes, their implementation depends on the willingness and ability of the executive branch to tackle long-standing and complex problems. Likewise, while the ODNI can develop new guidance and policies at the strategic level, their existence and success depends on decisions made at the agency level. Some agencies, like the CIA, took clear measures to minimise the risks posed by conflicts of interest. However, broader management issues relating to contract performance, especially for major projects, are a more complex matter that has long puzzled practitioners and scholars alike, and is likely to remain in the foreseeable future.

Defining Core Government Functions

The vast number of contractors working in the intelligence community, and their involvement in sensitive intelligence activities, raised concerns about the need to find a balance between government and contractor personnel in order to maintain core capabilities in government. An essential part of this effort entailed identifying long- and short-term mission requirements and related workforce needs in order to ensure that the intelligence community would retain appropriate core capabilities over the long term.[39] From this perspective, too much outsourcing could cause a permanent loss of expertise and endanger the functioning of government.

In 2007, the United States continued to lack a clear definition of the tasks for which government employees should always be responsible.[40] The congressional intelligence committees were concerned that the intelligence community did not have 'a clear definition of what functions are "inherently governmental" and, as a result, whether there [were] contractors performing inherently governmental functions'.[41] The focus on red lines was reinforced after General Hayden, then Director of the CIA, testified to the Senate that his agency might have been relying on contractors to carry out interrogations.[42] This possibility, as Senator Feinstein (D-CA) highlighted, raised important questions about the definition of governmental activities and the 'legality of using contractors to perform interrogations involving so-called enhanced interrogation techniques'.[43] Following a proposition made by Senators Feinstein and Feingold (D-WI), the Senate intelligence committee required:

> a one-time report to the congressional intelligence committees by the DNI describing the activities within the Intelligence Community that the DNI believes should only be conducted by governmental employees but that are being conducted by one or more contractors, an estimate of the number of contractors performing each such activity, and the DNI's plans, if any, to have such activities performed solely by governmental employees.[44]

The final versions of the 2009 intelligence authorisation bill explicitly prohibited interrogation by CIA contractors.[45] Rep. Janice Schakowsky (D-IL) hoped that the bill would 'take detention-related activities out of the hands of private contractors and put the responsibility back where it belongs, in the hands of authorized government personnel'.[46] However, the bill never passed 'because of partisan differences over language on interrogation techniques'.[47] The 2009 National Defense Authorization Act was more successful, and barred the DoD from employing contract interrogators.[48] However, the ban has only held in appearance since this law allowed the Secretary of Defense to waive the restriction. According to a government expert, this loophole suggests that Congress did not consider interrogation to be inherently governmental.[49] Regardless of its application, this measure can be criticised because banning the outsourcing of specific functions shirks the problem of contractors' supervision instead of addressing it. The 2009 defence authorisation further directed the OMB to develop a single consistent definition of an 'inherently governmental function', establish criteria for agencies to identify critical functions, and 'provide guidance to improve internal agency staffing decisions to ensure that federal employees are filling critical management roles'.[50] A few months later, President Obama – who as a senator had sponsored bills to improve accountability for security contractors – weighed in and directed the OMB to 'clarify when governmental outsourcing for services is and is not appropriate'.[51] It would take one more year for the OMB to produce a new policy on inherently governmental functions.

Adding to the existing congressional concern about the involvement of contractors in interrogations, CIA director Leon Panetta revealed to the House and Senate Intelligence Committees that contractors had been involved in the development of a controversial covert action programme. The programme, which started in 2004 and was shut two years later, reportedly relied on Blackwater to set up teams that would kill high-value terrorist targets.[52] Following his appointment as Director of the CIA in February 2009, Leon Panetta became alarmed about this programme and, given the level of congressional interest in the outsourcing of intelligence at the time, decided to brief the committees on this decision. Contractors' involvement in some of the most sensitive CIA operations became public knowledge when mainstream newspapers like the *New York Times* and *Washington Post* reported that 'CIA Hired Blackwater for Assassin Program'.[53] Public pressure on intelligence leaders to define clear red lines on who should conduct core intelligence activities had reached its apex.

A few months later, the ODNI released a seminal intelligence community directive (ICD) entitled 'Intelligence Community Core Contract Personnel'.[54] This directive established an intelligence community-wide policy for managing the use of core contract personnel, thereby recognising that contractors had become an integral part of the intelligence workforce. Under government policies, intelligence managers have to pay particular attention to the activities performed by core contractors. ICD 612, which was updated in 2011, helped achieve this requirement and introduced a common definition of core contract personnel as:

> Personnel that provide only direct support to core IC mission areas that include: (1) collection activities and operations (technical and human intelligence), (2) intelligence analysis and production, (3) basic and applied technology research and development, (4) acquisition and program management, (5) enterprise information technology, and (6) management or administrative support to these functions.[55]

Establishing this common understanding was important to standardise and ease the gathering of data on core contractors across the intelligence community. The document also put an emphasis on strategic workforce planning, and required intelligence elements to 'determine, review, and evaluate the actual and projected number and uses of core contract personnel in support of their intelligence mission'.[56] Keeping a close eye on contractors is an essential step in maintaining the delicate balance between military, civilian and contractor personnel.

ICD 612 further clarified the circumstances in which core contract personnel can be used, including when there is an immediate surge, a need for unique expertise, insufficient staffing resources, a need to transfer institutional knowledge or a need to ensure a more efficient or effective provision of services. However, rather than encouraging further outsourcing, the directive invited intelligence agencies to 'reemploy Federal civilian annuitants as [US government] employees under the National Intelligence Reserve Corps and other applicable authorities rather than as independent contractors'.[57] This language prefigured a broader push towards insourcing – the practice of using an organisation's own personnel instead of contractors – to balance the overall intelligence workforce. To guarantee the implementation of the ODNI policy, the Chief Human Capital Officer subsequently set up a board including representatives from all of the US intelligence agencies, tasked with the development of supplemental guidance.[58] Further initiatives sought to better align the intelligence community workforce – government and contractor employees – against the national intelligence priorities, and maintain and develop core skills within the intelligence community's acquisition workforce.[59] On the whole, ICD 612 was a significant step in the history of intelligence outsourcing. The directive rationalised the use of contractors and helped establish more solid foundations to manage the intelligence community's human capital.

The regulatory effort to refine the definition of core government functions reached a new milestone when the OMB's Office of Federal Procurement Policy (OFPP) released a policy letter on the *Performance of Inherently Governmental and Critical Functions* in 2010.[60] This document expanded upon existing authorities and clarified some of the limits of outsourcing in the United States. The letter established two new tests for identifying inherently governmental functions based on the nature of the function and the exercise of discretion. According to these tests, functions that entail the exercise of sovereign power and those that commit the government to new courses of action, requiring the exercise of discretion in applying federal authority or the making of value judgements, are inherently governmental.[61] The OMB guidance mentions multiple examples of inherently governmental functions that are of interest, such as the direction and control of intelligence and counterintelligence operations, the direct conduct of criminal investigations, the conduct of foreign relations and the determination of foreign policy, the direction and control of federal employees, the determination of agency policy, the determination of federal programme priorities for budget requests, awarding, administering and terminating prime contracts, the selection of individuals for federal government employment and the drafting of congressional testimony and correspondence.[62] This list provides some clarification, but allows room for interpretation. First, the letter does not precisely define key terms like 'direct control' and 'intelligence operations'. Second, the list is not intended to be exhaustive.

The OFPP letter also mentions another category of tasks that are 'closely associated to inherently governmental functions' and provides examples such as services that involve budget preparation, planning activities, analysis, evaluation of another contractor's performance and assistance in contract management. For instance, the management tasks contracted out to Miretek, which supervised FBI contracts for the Trilogy project, could qualify as a closely associated function. The third and final type of function identified in this policy is 'critical functions', or functions that are necessary for an agency to effectively perform and maintain control over functions that are core to its missions and operations. The letter encourages agencies to identify such functions and ensure government personnel perform them or have the capacity to manage them. What exactly constitutes critical functions is not set in stone. The OMB considers that 'a function's criticality is dependent on an agency's mission and operations', and therefore refused to provide a list of functions that could be considered as critical.[63] Overall, the rule of thumb followed by the letter is that the more important the mission – ranging from critical to closely associated to inherently governmental functions – the more significant government control should be. This framework encourages government agencies to define a spectrum of tasks that can and cannot be conducted with the help of contractors.

Considering the application of this new policy, the OMB guidance is quite precise and this should encourage the refinement of existing procedures across the intelligence community. The office directed agencies to 'take specific actions, before and after contract award, to prevent contractor performance of inherently governmental functions and overreliance on contractors in "closely associated" and critical functions'.[64] In these areas, the OMB considered that 'special consideration' should be given to using federal employees, and if contractors were relied upon, then 'special management attention' should be devoted to them to 'guard against their expansion into inherently governmental functions'.[65] Special consideration can, for instance, entail assigning enough qualified government employees to oversee contractor activities, making contractors' contributions easily identifiable and 'taking appropriate steps to avoid or mitigate conflicts of interest'.[66]

Depending on its interpretation and application within each government agency, the policy letter could constitute a landmark in the history of intelligence outsourcing. However, the letter is a policy document and as such it lacks the force and effect of law. Initial guidance to implement the OFPP letter was issued in the fall of 2013 by the Chief Human Capital Officer of the intelligence community. To this day, further guidance may be needed from the ODNI to harmonise various agencies' understanding of what functions are critical to their mission, and how the risks related to contractors performing these functions can be managed.[67] The broad spectrum of activities carried out by intelligence agencies can sometimes be difficult to categorise, and actions that are closely associated to inherently governmental functions, like conducting due diligence and analysing contractors' proposals for services, could very well slip into the realm of inherently governmental functions during the course of a contract. Some agencies may be tempted to distance themselves altogether from the OFPP policy letter. The CIA, for example, has traditionally considered such letters as 'expressions of executive branch policy rather than requirements'.[68] Some elements of the intelligence community have the authority to hire personal services contractors, who are not explicitly prohibited from performing inherently governmental functions.[69] In sum, new regulations can only do so much, and exceptions can never be ruled out. It is difficult to believe that, in a situation of crisis and under great political pressure to perform, an agency would not consider relying on contractors to carry out inherently governmental functions if a mission was considered to be an absolute necessity. The government's efforts to define red lines should not prevent further discussion on the most effective ways of monitoring contractors' behaviour in various settings, including cases in which contractors might conduct inherently governmental functions.

Balancing the Intelligence Workforce

The need to reach an appropriate balance between government employees and contractors is another issue accountability holders have sought to tackle. The government needs civil servants to maintain control over the contractor workforce, especially when the latter engage in core intelligence activities. After 2006, select intelligence agencies launched an effort toward insourcing to increase the number of government employees in their workforce. This shift started at the CIA, where Director Hayden launched an initiative called the 'go-blue program' in reference to the colour of the security badges worn by government employees. The aim was to reduce the Agency's reliance on contractors by 10 per cent before the end of 2008.[70] When reflecting upon this decision, Hayden acknowledged this percentage was 'arbitrary' and explained that he followed his instinct as Director of the CIA. Though workforce planning should not be reduced to such decisions, there is little question that the Agency's workforce needed to be rebalanced at the time.

When enough data was gathered, the CIA leadership discovered in the mid-2000s that agency contractors were more involved in core tasks like collection and analysis than in support tasks. The go-blue programme was used to rebalance the workforce according to the principle that contractors should ideally contribute more to support tasks than core functions.[71] Once the CIA had replenished some of its core workforce, it began shifting 'contract support out of intelligence analysis and collection and either into back-room support functions or out altogether'.[72] The challenge was to downsize the contractor workforce without going too far. Too much insourcing could very well degrade important capabilities and lead to another wave of outsourcing in the future.[73] According to Charles E. Allen, a former Assistant Director of Intelligence for Collection who went on to work at the Chertoff Group with Michael Hayden, Hayden's decision to insource did not affect the efficiency of the CIA.[74] From his and Hayden's point of view, the go-blue programme was a success.

To facilitate the shift towards insourcing, congressional authorisations offered more flexibility for intelligence leaders to manage their workforce. In 2007, the SSCI raised personnel caps, allowing a 20 per cent growth of full-time government positions in the community, and no longer required the ODNI 'to count re-employed retirees against [its] employment ceilings'.[75] This measure was well received by the ODNI, which was able to 'civilian-ise' contract positions and 'optimize the balance between military and civilian personnel on one hand and contract personnel on the other'.[76] Nevertheless, the intelligence committee's decision was also criticised for being 'insufficient to meet the demand set by policy-makers'.[77] The intelligence community needed more flexibility to fill capabilities gaps with government personnel. In subsequent years, Congress continued to show support for insourcing. Following the estimation that the average annual cost of a core contractor was largely higher than that of a US government civilian employee (respectively $250,000 and $126,500), the SSCI recommended reducing the intelligence community's 'dependence' on contractors in the long term.[78] Contrary to what the proponents of economic privatisation and new public management had predicted, outsourcing increasingly appeared to be a costly policy. To provide more flexibility, Congress subsequently waived the pension offset that made the re-employment of former intelligence officers difficult, and provided greater authority to intelligence leaders so that they could convert activities performed by contract personnel into government positions.[79]

With the support of congressional committees, intelligence leaders and even the President, the in-sourcing movement propagated throughout the intelligence community.[80] At the DIA, measures were taken to ease former employees' return to government service, and the need for workforce flexibility and adaptation was highlighted by Deputy Director David Shedd when he said that 'demographics tell us in our society the average young person will have four or five careers. The intelligence community has to be able to adapt and adjust to that and bring that talent back in at various stages.'[81] The effort to cut the contractor workforce also continued at the CIA. In 2011, during his nomination hearing to become Director of the CIA, General David Petraeus confirmed that the effort to reduce the agency's reliance on contractors was ongoing 'for a variety of different reasons', including budget constraints.[82] The NSA developed plans to convert several hundred contractor positions into government employees over the 2011–15 timeframe.[83] The ODNI and the Department of Homeland Security's Office of Intelligence and Analysis (I&A) initially relied heavily on contractors to help them find their feet after their establishment in the mid-2000s. As the two organisations grew, they eventually decided to cut down on contractors. In 2012, the ODNI planned to reduce its reliance on core contractors by almost 17 per cent.[84] While contract personnel made up to 63 per cent of the personnel at DHS I&A, the presence of contractors subsequently declined to 27 per cent of the workforce in 2014.[85]

On the whole, according to then DNI Clapper, the intelligence community reduced contractor full-time equivalents by 40 per cent between 2007 and 2014, and expected to continue decreasing its reliance on contractors thereafter.[86] In 2013, contractors accounted for an estimated 18 per cent of the intelligence workforce.[87] The reduction of intelligence contractors has met with some criticism. One commentator criticized the administration of Barack Obama for its 'ideological opposition to contracting'. Efforts to trim staff and lower costs can lead to the firing of experienced and capable contractors, and their subsequent replacement with less experienced government employees or contractors.[88] In the absence of publicly available evidence, the overall magnitude and consequences of such actions remain unclear.

Conclusion: The Nature of Intelligence Oversight

This chapter has shown how the executive and legislative branches gathered information on intelligence outsourcing to tackle some of the core issues surrounding the use of contractors since the end of the Cold War. Following the involvement of the private sector in a series of core intelligence activities and scandals, a new period of regulation in the history of intelligence outsourcing started in the mid-2000s. Under pressure from Congress, the intelligence community initially collected data to better articulate the rationales and the scope of intelligence outsourcing. With the support of key agencies, the ODNI was able to address a number of human capital and acquisition issues, facilitate congressional oversight and public understanding of intelligence contracting, and eventually regulate the use of contractors at the strategic level. This capacity to support executive control from the top of the community is a welcome addition to the US system of intelligence accountability, and contrasts with the view that intelligence oversight is primarily an operational matter.[89] However, the role of the ODNI should not be overestimated and remains contingent on the support of key intelligence agencies within the community.

Using the information they collected, the executive and legislative branches concentrated their oversight efforts on three core issues: improving contract management, defining core governmental functions and balancing the intelligence workforce. The government achieved progress across these three areas, but the extent to which the accountability gaps presented in the previous chapter were filled is debatable. While the involvement of contractors in abusive interrogations seems unlikely to reoccur following government investigations, congressional attention and new regulations, further accountability problems – including contractors' involvement in cases of fraud, waste and abuse, and government acquisition inefficiencies – cannot be ruled out. The government's efforts to systematise data collection on the intelligence community's workforce, to refine the definitions of core intelligence functions and to downsize the contractor workforce stand out as three important milestones in the recent history of intelligence outsourcing. Yet these measures can, at best, be expected to reduce – not to eliminate – the occurrence of accountability problems.

When examining the government's efforts to improve the accountability regime for intelligence contractors, this chapter has shed light on the nature of intelligence accountability as a dual process that blends administrative and political efforts. The political nature of oversight can impact both positively and negatively on intelligence accountability. From this perspective, the public debate on contractors – despite a number of inaccuracies and exaggerations – acted positively, to the extent that it encouraged executive efforts to understand and explain the state of the intelligence workforce. While outsourcing is primarily a technical issue of policy implementation, political figures like agency directors and members of Congress felt that accountability problems with intelligence contractors were important enough to warrant their attention, thus fostering change. Growing public concern about contractors also made it worth reporting on, which inflated some of the communication channels between the executive and legislative branches of government. The correlation between media reporting, congressional interest and executive control is apparent across the main accountability issues examined in Chapters 4 and 5, and confirms the utility of the model of accountability as a process presented at the start of this book. A more traditional approach, based on the distinction between the three branches of government, would have made it more difficult to emphasise how accountability holders interact around specific issues that arise on their agenda.

While the role of contractors in the national intelligence effort did attract some political interest, it never became a major concern for the government. Interagency working groups, inspectors general and federal courts investigated the practices surrounding intelligence contracting, but no blue-ribbon commission was set up. At most, the accountability issues raised by the use of intelligence contractors constituted a mid-level policy problem, warranting detailed attention from congressional committees, intelligence leaders and the bureaucracy.

Politics also impacted negatively on accountability when Congress failed, for the first time in its history, to pass intelligence authorisations. A Congressional Research Service report noted that authorisations were not passed because members chose not 'to compromise disagreements either amongst themselves or with the White House on issues they considered important'.[90] Referring to the unprecedented refusal of the majority leader to bring the 2006 and 2007 intelligence authorisation bills to the floor, Senator Rockefeller (D-WV) pointed it out as an 'inexplicable and unpardonable failure' that will 'result in less effective oversight'.[91] Without the authority granted by congressional authorisations, senior intelligence officials were free to disregard the preferences expressed in the intelligence committees' bills and lacked the clout necessary to implement key policies promptly. Despite this hurdle, they sought to inform Congress and filled some of the accountability gaps plaguing the management of intelligence contractors.

Overall, the intelligence community reacted to some of the challenges posed by the outsourcing boom by refining its human capital policies and processes to improve the management of contractors. Given the long history of public-private intelligence collaboration, it is surprising to observe that basic policies and procedures to keep track of the contractor workforce and manage its growth were not in place before 2006. It is only when a series of scandals emerged and reports flagged problems that accountability moved to a political level, forcing key decision-makers to take remedial action. One of the reasons behind the apparent absence of strategic workforce planning in the early 2000s is that, following the 9/11 attacks, priorities were directed towards action, mostly collection and operations, rather than workforce and acquisition management. It was only later, when the sense of urgency reduced and the shortfalls of intelligence outsourcing became apparent, that key decision-makers were able to pause and devote more attention to the roles and missions performed by contractors in the national intelligence effort.

However, this context does not explain why previous administrations did not put adequate procedures and regulations in place earlier. In the specific case of the ODNI, the youth of the organisation explains why personnel management was lacking, until at least 2006. The organisation needed time to understand intelligence contracting, 'to manage it, to optimize it', but the situation was more contentious in the cases of more well-established agencies like the CIA.[92] Given the history of public-private intelligence collaboration, most agencies had decades to set up a system to evaluate and control the place of contractors in the intelligence workforce. In an ideal world, such a system would have been better able to cope with the post-9/11 surge in intelligence requirements and the boom in intelligence outsourcing. Instead, officials failed to anticipate this boom, and the government made significant efforts to identify accountability problems and improve a host of policies and processes surrounding intelligence outsourcing. These efforts contradict the claim that intelligence contractors have been unaccountable. In fact, the main issue with intelligence outsourcing was not only the lack of government control, but also what stood behind it: the imperfect and reactive nature of intelligence accountability, both at the political and administrative levels. The next chapter considers what can be done to keep improving intelligence outsourcing, and by extension the US system of intelligence accountability.

Notes

1. Walter Pincus, 'Increase in Contracting Intelligence Jobs Raises Concerns', *Washington Post*, 20 March 2006, A3.
2. Office of the Director of National Intelligence, *Questions and Answers on the Intelligence Community Post 9/11*, p. 4, available at <http://www.dni.gov/content/Question_and_Answer_IC.pdf> (accessed 29 May 2018); US Congress, Public Law 108–458, *Intelligence Reform and Terrorism Prevention Act*, 108th Congress, 2nd session, 17

December 2004, section 1011; Office of the Director of National Intelligence, *Intelligence Community Directive Number 105, Acquisition*, 15 August 2006; US Code (2015), Title 41, Chapter 7, Section 403 (9).

3. Sanders, interview with author.
4. Nemfakos et al., *Workforce Planning in the Intelligence Community*, p. 6.
5. US Congress, Public Law 105–270, *Federal Activities Inventory Reform*, 105th Congress, 2nd session, 19 October 1998.
6. Sanders, *Results of the Fiscal Year 2007 US Intelligence Community Inventory of Core Contractor Personnel*, pp. 3, 13; Scott Shane, 'Government Keeps a Secret After Studying Spy Agencies', *New York Times*, 26 April 2007, p. 21, A1.
7. Jones, 'Intelligence Reform: The Logic of Information Sharing', pp. 384–401.
8. Former senior official, interview with author, 7 April 2015. Michael Hayden, in Video: C-SPAN, *Privatization of US Intelligence*; Office of the Director of National Intelligence, *Key Facts About Contractors*, p. 2, available at <https://www.fas.org/irp/news/2010/07/ic-contract.pdf> (accessed 29 May 2018); US Senate, Select Committee on Intelligence, *Nomination of Lieutenant General James Clapper, Jr., USAF, Ret., to be Director of National Intelligence*, 111th Congress, 2nd session, 20 July 2010, p. 16; Paula J. Roberts, statement before the US Senate Committee on Homeland Security and Governmental Affairs, Subcommittee on Oversight of Government Management, the Federal Workforce, and the District of Columbia, 112th Congress, 1st session, 20 September 2011, p. 31.
9. In the absence of intelligence authorization, the intelligence appropriation bills passed as a part of the Defense budget became a point of reference.
10. Sanders, media conference call, p. 12; National security expert A, interview with author, 10 June 2011, Washington, DC.
11. Tim Shorrock, 'The Spy Who Billed Me', *Mother Jones*, January/February 2005, available at <http://motherjones.com/politics/2005/01/spy-who-billed-me> (accessed 29 May 2018); Rep. David Price (D-NC), 'House Passes Price Amendment to Examine Private Intelligence Contractors – Congressman Hopes to Shed Light on a "Major Shift" in Intel Community', 26 April 2006, available at <http://price.house.gov/index.php?option=com_content&task=view&id=2882&Itemid=100260> (accessed 29 May 2018); Shorrock, *Spies for Hire*, p. 370.

12. US House of Representatives, Committee on Rules, *Report to accompany H. Res. 774, Providing for consideration of H.R. 5020, Intelligence Authorization Act for fiscal Year 2007*, Report 109–438, 109th Congress, 2nd session, 25 April 2006, section 308.
13. US Senate, Select Committee on Intelligence, *Report Accompanying the Intelligence Authorization Act for Fiscal Year 2007*, Report 109–259, 109th Congress, 2nd session, 25 May 2006, p. 40.
14. Office of the Director of National Intelligence, *The US Intelligence Community's Five Year Strategic Human Capital Plan, An Annex to the US National Intelligence Strategy*, 22 June 2006, p. 6.
15. Ibid. p. 1.
16. Ibid. pp. 14, 17.
17. US House of Representatives, Permanent Select Committee on Intelligence, *Report on Intelligence Authorization Act for Fiscal Year 2008*, Report 110–131, 7 May 2007, p. 42.
18. Video: C-SPAN, *Privatization of US Intelligence.*
19. Michael V. Hayden, interview with author, 8 August 2011, Washington, DC. A similar argument is made concerning the whole intelligence community in Nemfakos et al., *Workforce Planning in the Intelligence Community*, p. 45.
20. Stephen Barr, 'This CIA Mission – Better Contract-Workforce Management – Isn't Classified', 11 June 2007, *Washington Post*, D1; Central Intelligence Agency, *Director's Statement on Contractor Study*, 30 May 2007, available at <https://www.cia.gov/news-information/press-releases-statements/press-release-archive-2007/statement-on-contractor-study.html> (accessed 29 May 2018).
21. US House of Representatives, Permanent Select Committee on Intelligence, *Intelligence Authorization Act for Fiscal Year 2009*, Report 110–665, 110th Congress, 2nd session, 21 May 2008, p. 49.
22. Patrick F. Kennedy, deputy director of national intelligence for management, 'Memorandum M-06-6019: IC Contractor Inventory', 1, quoted in Nemfakos et al., *Workforce Planning in the Intelligence Community*, pp. 26–7.
23. US Senate, Select Committee on Intelligence, *Intelligence Authorization for Fiscal Year 2008*, Report 110–75, p. 11. The US intelligence budget is subdivided into a series of categories ranging from programmes, to disciplines, to capabilities, to expenditure centres and projects. See Elkins, *Managing Intelligence Resources*, pp. 5–9.
24. This number is based on information provided by the ODNI: Sanders, *Results of the Fiscal Year 2007 US Intelligence Community Inventory of Core Contractor Personnel*, pp. 12–14; Office of the

Director of National Intelligence, *Questions and Answers on the Intelligence Community Post-9/11*, p. 4; Sanders, media conference call, p. 6.

25. This figure is based on the National Intelligence Program and does not include the Military Intelligence Program.
26. Office of the Director of National Intelligence, *FY 2007 Results*, US Intelligence Community, *Inventory of Core Contractor Personnel*, p. 5 (on file with author); Sanders, *Results of the Fiscal Year 2007 US Intelligence Community Inventory of Core Contractor Personnel*, p. 3; Government Accountability Office, *Civilian Intelligence Community. Additional Actions Needed to Improve Reporting on and Planning for the Use of Contract Personnel*, GAO-14-204, 29 January 2014, p. 22.
27. US House of Representatives, *Conference report on Intelligence Authorization Act for Fiscal Year 2008*, Report 110–478, 110th Congress, 1st session, 6 December 2007; US Senate, Select Committee on Intelligence, *Intelligence Authorization Act for Fiscal Year 2007*, Report 109–259, 109th Congress, 2nd session, 25 May 2006, p. 40; Tim Roemer, testimony before the House Permanent Select Committee on Intelligence, Subcommittee on Intelligence Community Management, Director of National Intelligence 500 Day Plan, 6 December 2007, p. 5; US Senate, Select Committee on Intelligence, *Intelligence Authorization for Fiscal Year 2008*, Report 110–75, 110th Congress, 1st session, 31 May 2007, p. 11; US Senate, Select Committee on Intelligence, *Nomination Hearing of Mike McConnell to be Director of National Intelligence*, 110th Congress, 1st session, 1 February 2007, pp. 14, 31; US Senate, Committee on Homeland Security and Governmental Affairs, Subcommittee on Oversight of Government Management, the Federal Workforce, and the District of Columbia, *Intelligence Community Contractors: Are We Striking the Right Balance?*, hearing, 112th Congress, 1st session, 20 September 2011; US Congress, *Intelligence Authorization Act for Fiscal Year 2010*, Section 305(a); US Congress, Public Law 113–293, *Intelligence Authorization Act for Fiscal Year 2015*, 113th Congress, 2nd session, 19 December 2014, section 327.
28. US Congress, Public Law 111–259, *Intelligence Authorization Act for FY 2010*, 111th congress, 2nd session, 7 October 2010, sections 305(a) and 339.
29. Sanders, *Results of the Fiscal Year 2007 US Intelligence Community Inventory of Core Contractor Personnel*, pp. 1, 7, 13.

30. Director of National Intelligence, *The National Intelligence Strategy of the United States of America*, August 2009, pp. 8, 16–17; Director of National Intelligence, *The 2014 National Intelligence Strategy of the United States of America*, pp. 12–14; Government Accountability Office, *Civilian Intelligence Community*, p. 28.
31. Barr, 'This CIA Mission – Better Contract-Workforce Management – Isn't Classified'.
32. Central Intelligence Agency, *Director's Statement on Contractor Study*; Walter Pincus and Stephen Barr, 'CIA Plans Cutbacks, Limits on Contractor Staffing', *Washington Post*, 11 June 2007, A2; US Senate, Committee on Homeland Security and Governmental Affairs, Subcommittee on Oversight of Government Management, the Federal Workforce, and the District of Columbia, *Intelligence Community Contractors: Are We Striking the Right Balance?*, Post-Hearing Questions for the Record Submitted to Paula Roberts From Senator Daniel Akaka, 112th Congress, 1st session, 20 September 2011, p. 73.
33. Shorrock, *Spies for Hire*, p. 32.
34. Office of the Director of National Intelligence, Public Affairs Office, 'DNI Names New Deputy for Acquisition', ODNI News Release no. 13-07, 8 May 2007, available at <http://www.dni.gov/press_releases/20070508_release.pdf> (accessed 29 May 2018); Office of the Director of National Intelligence, Public Affairs Office, 'DNI Announces 100 Day Plan for Integration and Collaboration', ODNI News Release no.12-07, 11 April 2007, available at <http://www.dni.gov/press_releases/20070411_release.pdf.
35. Office of the Director of National Intelligence, *Critical Intelligence Community Management Challenges*, pp. 10–11.
36. US House of Representatives, Permanent Select Committee on Intelligence, *Intelligence Authorization Act for Fiscal Year 2009*, Report 110–665, pp. 38–9. See also: US Senate, Select Committee on Intelligence, *Intelligence Authorization for Fiscal Year 2008*, Report 110–75, pp. 41–2; US Senate, Select Committee on Intelligence, *Intelligence Authorization Act for Fiscal Year 2009*, Report 110–333, section 315.
37. US House of Representatives, Permanent Select Committee on Intelligence, *Intelligence Authorization Act for Fiscal Year 2009*, Report 110–665, p. 50.
38. US Senate, Select Committee on Intelligence, *Intelligence Authorization for Fiscal Year 2009*, Report 110–333, pp. 5–6.

39. Sanders, *Results of the Fiscal Year 2007 US Intelligence Community Inventory of Core Contractor Personnel*, pp. 11–15; John F. Hackett, Information Management Office, Office of the Director of National Intelligence, letter to the author, 19 March 2012.
40. Barr, 'This CIA Mission – Better Contract-Workforce Management – Isn't Classified'.
41. US House of Representatives, *Intelligence Authorization Act for Fiscal Year 2008*, Report 110–131, 110th Congress, 1st session, May 7 2007, p. 42; US Senate, Select Committee on Intelligence, *Nomination Hearing of Mike McConnell to be Director of National Intelligence*, p. 14.
42. US House of the Representatives, Permanent Select Committee on Intelligence, *Annual Worldwide Threat Assessment*, 110th Congress, 2nd session, 5 February 2008, p. 26. This was later confirmed in the so-called 'CIA torture report'; see US Senate, Select Committee on Intelligence, *Committee Study of the Central Intelligence Agency's Detention and Interrogation Program*, 13 December 2012, p. 65.
43. Senator Feinstein (D-CA), letter to the Honorable Michael B. Mukasey, Attorney General of the United States, 6 February 2008, available at <http://www.feinstein.senate.gov/public/index.cfm/press-releases?ID=f4862661-a162-9308-9347-cd080733551d> (accessed 29 May 2018); US House of the Representatives, Permanent Select Committee on Intelligence, *Annual Worldwide Threat Assessment*, 110th Congress, 2nd session, 5 February 2008, p. 26.
44. US Senate, Select Committee on Intelligence, *Intelligence Authorization Act for Fiscal Year 2009*, Report 110–333, 110th Congress, 2nd session, 8 May 2008, pp. 16, 68.
45. Ibid. section 322; US House of Representatives, Select Committee on Intelligence, *Intelligence Authorization Act for Fiscal Year 2009*, Report 110–665, section 425.
46. Rep. Schakowsky (D-IL), 'Price-Schakowsky Bill Would Prohibit Intel Contractors From Detainee Operations', 6 May 2008, available at <http://price.house.gov/index.php?option=com_content&task=view&id=2735&Itemid=100260> (accessed 29 May 2018).
47. Joe Mazzafro, 'Too Many Contractors; Too Much Cost?', 8 September 2008, available at <http://www.afcea.org/content/?q=node/1701> (accessed 29 May 2018).
48. US Congress, Public Law 111–84, National Defense Authorization Act for FY 2010, 111th Congress, 1st session, 28 October 2009, section 1038.

49. Daniel I. Gordon, testimony before the US Senate Committee on Homeland Security and Governmental Affairs, p. 6.
50. US Congress, *Duncan Hunter National Defense Authorization Act for Fiscal Year 2009*, section 321.
51. Barack Obama, 'Memorandum on Government Contracting to Heads of Executive Departments and Agencies', 4 March 2009, available at <http://www.whitehouse.gov/the_press_office/Memorandum-for-the-Heads-of-Executive-Departments-and-Agencies-Subject-Government> (accessed 29 May 2018).
52. Boot, 'Afterword: The CIA and Erik Prince', pp. 348–9; Risen and Mazzetti, 'Blackwater Guards Tied to Secret Raids by the CIA'.
53. Warrick and Smith, 'Sources Say CIA Hired Blackwater for Assassin Program'.
54. Office of the Director of National Intelligence, media conference call with Dr Ronald Sanders, Intelligence Community Chief Human Capital Officer, 14 January 2010, p. 12.
55. Government Accountability Office, *Civilian Intelligence Community. Additional Actions Needed to Improve Reporting on and Planning for the Use of Contract Personnel*, GAO-12-204, January 2014, p. 49.
56. Office of the Director of National Intelligence, *Intelligence Community Directive Number 612, Intelligence Community Core Contract Personnel*, 30 October 2009, p. 3.
57. Ibid. p. 2. See also Voelz, *Managing the Private Spies*, pp. 58–60.
58. Office of the Director of National Intelligence, *Evaluation of the Administration and Management of ODNI Core Contracts Supporting Critical Missions*, 2011, p. 13.
59. Office of the Director of National Intelligence, *IC Base Force Study for FY2011-2015*, cited in Office of the Director of National Intelligence, *Human Capital Vision 2020*, 2014, p. 9; US Senate, *Intelligence Community Contractors: Are We Striking the Right Balance?*, 37, 77.
60. Office of Management and Budget, Office of Federal Procurement Policy, *Work Reserved for Performance by Federal Government Employees – Notice of Proposed Policy Letter*, 75 Federal regulation 16188–9, 31 March 2010; Office of Management and Budget, Office of Federal Procurement Policy, *Performance of Inherently Governmental and Critical Functions*, Policy Letter 11–01, *Federal Register* 76/176, 12 September 2011, pp. 56227–42.
61. This definition is based on the FAIR Act: US Congress, Public Law 105–270, *Federal Activities Inventory Reform Act of 1998*, 105th Congress, 2nd session, 19 October 1998, section 5.

62. Office of Management and Budget, *Performance of Inherently Governmental and Critical Functions*, p. 56240. These examples have now been included in the federal acquisition regulation; see Code of Federal Regulations, 48 CFR 7.503 – Policy.
63. Office of Management and Budget, *Performance of Inherently Governmental and Critical Functions*, p. 56233.
64. Ibid. p. 56228.
65. Office of Management and Budget, *Performance of Inherently Governmental and Critical Functions*, p. 56227; Office of Management and Budget, Office of Federal Procurement Policy, Letter 92-1, App C-16; Code of Federal Regulations, 48 CFR 37.114 – Special acquisition requirements.
66. Daniel I. Gordon, statement before the Subcommittee on Oversight of Government Management, the Federal Workforce, and the District of Columbia, Committee on Homeland Security and Governmental Affairs, US Senate, *Intelligence Community Contractors: Are We Striking the Right Balance?*, hearing, 112th Congress, 1st session, 20 September 2011, p. 3; Office of Management and Budget, *Performance of Inherently Governmental and Critical Functions*, 56228; Code of Federal Regulations, 48 CFR 37.114 – Special acquisition requirements.
67. Manuel, *Definitions of 'Inherently Governmental Function' in Federal Procurement Law and Guidance*, p. 21; Stephanie O'Sullivan, Principal Deputy Director of National Intelligence, statement for the record, Senate Homeland Security and Governmental Affairs Committee, 'The Intelligence Community: Keeping Watch Over its Contractor Workforce', hearing, 13 February 2014, p. 6; L. Elaine Halchin, *The Intelligence Community and Its Use of Contractors: Congressional Oversight Issues*, Congressional Research Service Report, 18 August 2015, p. 17.
68. Wright, 'Procurement Authorities of the CIA', p. 1225.
69. Government Accountability Office, *Civilian Intelligence Community. Additional Actions Needed to Improve Reporting on and Planning for the Use of Contract Personnel*, GAO-12-204, January 2014, p. 8.
70. Sanders, *Results of the Fiscal Year 2007 US Intelligence Community Inventory of Core Contractor Personnel*, p. 10. Blue is the colour of the security badges worn by government officials. Contractors typically wear green and sometimes pink badges, depending on their security clearance. In Washington parlance, contractors in the field of national security are often called 'green-badgers'.

71. Hayden, interview with author.
72. Sanders, *Results of the Fiscal Year 2007 US Intelligence Community Inventory of Core Contractor Personnel*, p. 8.
73. Lisa Singh, 'Jacques Gansler: "Global war" on contractors must stop', 15 January 2010, available at <http://blog.executivebiz.com/2010/01/jacques-gansler-global-war-on-contractors-must-stop/> (accessed 29 May 2018); Walter Pincus, 'Defense Agency Proposes Outsourcing More Spying', *Washington Post*, 19 August 2007, A3.
74. Charles E. Allen, US Senate, Committee on Homeland Security and Governmental Affairs, Subcommittee on Oversight of Government Management, the Federal Workforce, and the District of Columbia, *Intelligence Community Contractors: Are We Striking the Right Balance?*, hearing, 112th Congress, 1st session, 20 September 2011, p. 26
75. Sanders, *Results of the Fiscal Year 2007 US Intelligence Community Inventory of Core Contractor Personnel*, p. 6.
76. Ibid. pp. 3, 8; US Senate, Select Committee on Intelligence, *Intelligence Authorization for Fiscal Year 2008*, Report 110–75, pp. 2–3, 38.
77. J. Michael Waller, 'Private Intelligence Contracting Is Here to Stay', *Serviam Magazine* (July–August 2008), available at <https://www.iwp.edu/news_publications/detail/private-intelligence-contracting-is-here-to-stay> (accessed 29 May 2018).
78. US Senate Select Committee on Intelligence, *Intelligence Authorization Act for Fiscal Year 2009*, Mr Rockefeller Report to accompany S. 2996, Report 110–333, 110th Congress, 2nd session, 8 May 2008. On the methodological issues behind such comparisons see Berteau et al., 'DoD Workforce Cost Realism Assessment', pp. 12–19; Khattab, 'Revised Circular A-76: Embracing Flawed Methodologies', pp. 469–520; Acquisition Advisory Panel, *Report of the Acquisition Advisory Panel to the Office of Federal Procurement Policy and the United States Congress*, January 2007, pp. 7–8, 19.
79. US Congress, Public Law 111–84, *National Defense Authorization Act for Fiscal Year 2010*, 111th Congress, 1st session, 28 October 2009, section 1121; US Congress, Public Law 112–87, *Intelligence Authorization Act for Fiscal Year 2012*, 112th Congress, 1st session, 3 January 2012, section 103 (b).
80. President Obama publicly expressed his support for insourcing intelligence during an interview with Jay Leno on the *Tonight Show*. See White House, Office of the Press Secretary, 'Interview of the President by Jay Leno, The Tonight Show', 7 August 2013.

81. Jason Miller, 'DIA to Reform "Revolving" Door for Employees', *Federal News Radio*, 18 August 2011, available at <http://www.federalnewsradio.com/239/2501052/DIA-to-reform-revolving-door-for-employees> (accessed 29 May 2018).
82. US Senate, Select Committee on Intelligence, *Nomination of General David H. Petraeus to be Director, Central Intelligence Agency*, S. Hrg.112–307, 112th Congress, 1st session, 23 June 2011, 29.
83. Nemfakos et al., *Workforce Planning in the Intelligence Community*, p. 28.
84. Office of the Director of National Intelligence, *Strategic Human Capital Plan 2012-2017, 2012, Appendix A – Workforce Data*, pp. 2, 7. In 2011, the ODNI workforce was composed of 43.6% contractors.
85. US Senate, Select Committee on Intelligence, *Additional Prehearing Questions for Mr Francis X. Taylor upon his nomination to be the Under Secretary for Intelligence and Analysis of the Department of Homeland Security*, 25 February 2014, p. 7. See also: Robert O'Harrow, 'Costs Skyrocket As DHS Runs Up No-Bid Contracts; $2 Million Security Project Balloons to $124 Million', *Washington Post*, 28 June 2007, A1.
86. Johnson, 'A Conversation with James R. Clapper, Jr.', p. 22; Executive Office of the President, *Fiscal Year 2012 Budget of the US Government*, p. 66, available at <https://www.gpo.gov/fdsys/pkg/BUDGET-2012-BUD/pdf/BUDGET-2012-BUD-8.pdf> (accessed 29 May 2018); Executive Office of the President, *Fiscal Year 2014 Budget of the US Government*, p. 77, available at <https://www.whitehouse.gov/sites/default/files/omb/budget/fy2014/assets/budget.pdf> (accessed 29 May 2018).
87. Nemfakos et al., *Workforce Planning in the Intelligence Community*, p. 17.
88. Anonymous, correspondence with author, March 2018.
89. See Lester, *When Should State Secrets Stay Secret?*, pp. 146–7.
90. Richard F. Grimmett, 'Intelligence Authorization Legislation: Status and Challenges', Congressional Research Service Report for Congress, 13 February 2012, p. 1.
91. Senator Rockefeller (D-WV), 'Department of Defense Appropriations Act, 2007 – Continued', *Congressional Record* 152/108, 6 September 2006, S9067; Executive Office of the President, Office of Management and Budget, Statement of Administration Policy, H.R. 2082 – *Intelligence Authorization Act for Fiscal Year 2008*, 11 December 2007; Executive Office of the President, Office of

Management and Budget, Statement of Administration Policy, H.R. 5959 – *Intelligence Authorization Act for FY 2009*, 16 July 2008; Library of Congress, Bill Summary and Status, 110th Congress (2007–2008), H.R. 2082, available at <http://thomas.loc.gov/cgi-bin/bdquery/z?d110:H.R.2082:> (accessed 29 May 2018); Mazzafro, 'Too Many Contractors; Too Much Cost?'.

92. Sanders, *Results of the Fiscal Year 2007 US Intelligence Community Inventory of Core Contractor Personnel*, p. 7.

6 The Future of Intelligence Outsourcing

Despite the government's efforts to improve the relationship between the intelligence community and its contractors, many questions remain. Drawing on the problems highlighted throughout the book, this chapter examines three core questions that shape intelligence outsourcing. The first issue concerns what (not) to outsource. The executive branch has now clarified what exactly it considers to be within its remit by defining inherently governmental and related functions. While this effort is laudable, current regulations leave room for interpretation and varying degrees of privatisation are likely to subsist throughout the intelligence community. Legal considerations aside, it is worth pondering the adequacy of outsourcing various types of core intelligence activities such as collection, covert action and analysis. The problems that have challenged intelligence outsourcing have pushed some commentators to argue that civil servants should always conduct particularly sensitive and complicated activities. Instead of drawing a red line, I argue that any intelligence activity can be outsourced as long as the government maintains effective control over its contractors. When the government delegates tasks and manages to keep a close eye on contractors, it does not shirk its responsibility to serve the public interest in national security.

Another equally important question is: when to outsource? Criteria such as the nature of modern government, the consequences of outsourcing, the government's ability to manage contractors and the perceived acceptability of outsourcing can be used to decide when to call upon commercial providers. For a long time, decision-makers lacked the tools necessary to reach coherent decisions about the sourcing of intelligence activities in the short, medium and long terms. One of the most important and difficult tasks the government confronts in this context is to find the right balance between insourcing and outsourcing. Excessive outsourcing could strip the government of its ability to steer the national intelligence effort. Conversely, too much insourcing could prevent the government from using valuable, and sometimes unique, private sector resources. Although significant improvements have been realised in this field thanks to the development of new policies, human capital planning has been implemented unequally across the intelligence community and plagued by issues of data reliability. The latest shift toward insourcing and recent budget cuts have increased concern that the politics of national security could further disrupt the market for intelligence and affect the capabilities of the intelligence community.

Once a decision to outsource has been reached, the government sponsor needs to consider how to do so effectively. This is the most challenging and important question raised by this book. In the last decade or so, inadequate standards of accountability and a lack of in-house expertise in contract management have plagued intelligence outsourcing. Persistent accountability problems with contractors can be tied to the fact that government managers have lacked the incentives, expertise and resources to carry out their duties in a more rigorous manner. Calls for a more networked system of accountability emphasise the role that non-governmental actors can play in triggering and implementing accountability. In light of this, better coordination between public and private accountability holders is the solution to the problems plaguing cross-sector collaboration. Yet if such coordination is to play a greater role within the US system of intelligence accountability, the key to implementing changes remains in the hands of the federal government, the primary guarantor of the public interest.

The intelligence community is now moving out of the surge cycle that characterised the first decade of the global war on terrorism. In a context of budget cuts, decision-makers are scaling back the national intelligence effort and the time is ripe to reconsider the role played by the private sector alongside the US intelligence community.[1] History suggests that the intelligence community will continue to contract out various tasks to the private sector, for a variety of reasons and in a variety of ways that will continue to evolve. A convincing case can be made that as long as intelligence outsourcing is carefully planned and controlled by the government, it will bring more benefits than drawbacks. The US intelligence community thus needs to continuously adapt and nurture cross-sector collaboration to build a national intelligence enterprise that is suited to the rigours of the security environment. Whether intelligence leaders and the bureaucracy will effectively manage to do so remains to be seen. In the meantime, examining what, when and how to outsource intelligence is a good first step.

What (Not) to Outsource?

Concerns about contractors' involvement in interrogations and other sensitive intelligence activities prompted the administration of Barack Obama to refine its policies on inherently governmental and related functions. Despite this regulatory effort, public-private boundaries remain susceptible to a variety of interpretations.[2] The flexibility offered by current regulations requires a frank discussion on the evolving boundaries of government in the realm of intelligence and national security. Some commentators concur on the point that certain tasks should only ever be done by government officials, and never contracted. Simon Chesterman, a legal scholar, convincingly argues that because of its democratic legitimacy, the government should define its own realm or prerogatives.[3] A more pragmatic stance holds that the government should always be able to set its own strategic priorities and plan for its requirements accordingly. For privatisation scholar E. S. Savas, the proper role of the government is to steer, not to row.[4] Steering requires a good understanding of the host of factors that can affect a boat's performance. While there is little question that the government has steered the national intelligence effort, at least since the US entry into the Second World War, it did not always seem to understand the direction taken by specific intelligence projects. The ill-conceived efforts to modernise the FBI and NSA information systems in the early 2000s both suggest that, in the IT domain, government authorities have sometimes lacked the knowledge and ability to set adequate priorities and requirements, and monitor the implementation of their policies. The main lesson learned from these examples is that outsourcing cannot act as a substitute for strategic leadership and management.

Most analyses implicitly or explicitly refer to the potential consequences of outsourcing intelligence functions to consider its use, and emphasise that the government is better positioned than the private sector to conduct some activities. Some authors assume that government officials have more integrity, either because they have taken an oath or because they have an incentive to protect their career in the public service. In contrast, contractors would be primarily driven by their profit interest. The Comptroller General of the United States thus noted that contractors' involvement in core government functions 'may result in decisions that are not in the best interest of the government and American taxpayer, while also increasing overall vulnerability to waste, fraud, or abuse'.[5] Glenn Hastedt, an intelligence expert, similarly remarks that 'one should not expect to see contractors evidence the same depth of loyalty as career employees'.[6] This is why government regulations require closer supervision when contractors are conducting core intelligence functions. Following this logic, some particularly sensitive functions should only be entrusted to government officials.

Morten Hansen, a researcher who has worked as a security contractor, argues that at the individual level, public and private employees are intrinsically driven by their national security mission. Many contractors have had a career in the government and were recruited on a similar basis to their government counterparts. Hansen adds that security clearance requirements make it difficult 'to conceal interests and loyalties that run counter to the national security objective'.[7] However, it would be wrong to assume that government employees and contractors are always selfless public servants. A synthesis of both approaches is possible by considering that contractors and government employees are motivated by monetary, personal and organisational interests as well as the possibility of contributing to national security. While personal interests might be similar across the public-private divide, the organisational cultures of government agencies and companies do differ. Accordingly, accountability holders should pay attention to the behaviour displayed by both types of employees and develop an understanding of how the different contexts in which they work affect their conduct.

Another argument considers that public authorities are better able or better suited to 'withstand the political costs of misadventure'.[8] The definition of public-private boundaries would therefore depend, at least partly, on what the public deems acceptable. The challenge is that determining the boundaries of the public's tolerance is 'neither feasible nor realistic'.[9] While the public might agree on the need for efficient and effective national security, it cannot systematically decide on the conduct of secret intelligence activities; this would impede the effectiveness of the national intelligence effort.

Based on the above perspectives, it is useful to consider intelligence by functions to take into account specific circumstances and reflect on the boundaries of the public realm. Given the secrecy, the extraordinary authority and relative legal immunity, the high level of discretion and the potential consequences accompanying sensitive intelligence operations, many observers have wondered whether contractors should carry out such activities.[10] A convincing case can be made that certain HUMINT efforts, even those that occur in controlled environments like interrogations, should not be outsourced because they can require the 'exercise of substantial discretion' and can 'directly affect the life, liberty, and property of both US persons and foreign nationals'.[11] Intelligence scholar William Lahneman argues that HUMINT is inherently governmental because it 'affects relationships between nations'.[12] Since disclosures, resulting from government decisions or leaks, are not uncommon in national security affairs, officials should also take potential public reticence to the outsourcing of sensitive intelligence operations into account before they decide to rely on the private sector. The CIA decision to contract out the design and implementation of some of its interrogations is a case in point. The release of the Senate intelligence committee report on the CIA detention and interrogation programme (the so-called torture report) in late 2014 confirmed the significant role contractors played in the Rendition, Detention, and Interrogation Group, and led to a public relations debacle for the agency.[13] This report pointed out a series of accountability shortfalls including government officials and contractors' involvement in various instances of wrongdoing, contractors' involvement in inherently governmental functions and possible conflicts of interest.

The risks posed by outsourcing interrogations – in terms of loss of government discretion, impact on human lives and public outrage – suggest that intelligence agencies might simply need to refrain from contracting out such functions whenever they can. However, in the absence of an alternative, related tasks like the translation of rare languages in the interrogation room might need to be outsourced. One cannot reasonably expect the intelligence community to keep in-house expertise in the more than 6,500 languages spoken around the world. Since the logic of necessity is likely to dictate the government's reliance on contractors, adequate accountability mechanisms need to be in place to control the involvement of contractors in all types of intelligence activity, including interrogation and other sensitive or controversial collection activities, which some observers consider inherently governmental. In these situations, keeping government officials in the field, where they can more directly control the work of contractors, is necessary.

One common argument holds that the use of force should not be outsourced, since contractors do not enjoy the same legitimacy as the state.[14] This argument has taken on a particular significance in the context of the 'drone war' and the involvement of the private sector in the administration of lethal force through targeted killings. There is little dissent from the view that key decisions regarding paramilitary actions, including targeted killings, should always remain in the hands of elected officials or their political appointees in order to ensure that the accountability relationship between the decision-maker and the US people is as straightforward as possible in matters of life and death. When and if such operations are outsourced, government officials must maintain the ability to control contractors' behaviour either in person or remotely. Ensuring that a government supervisor accompanies contractors is one way to do so. However, who is really in control when the private sector develops, constructs, ships, arms, flies the drones remotely, and a government official just presses the button?

To steer the boat, the government needs not only to be on board, but also to maintain enough expertise to assess contractors' decisions. Keeping control over contractors requires some overlap between public and private capabilities. A dose of pragmatism is also necessary because technical knowledge, rare skills, privileged access to certain human and digital networks and other forms of comparative advantage occasionally compel the government to rely on the private sector to conduct intelligence operations. When this kind of situation occurs, the existence of well-defined and effective operating procedures, developed and overseen by experienced and impartial government officials, is essential to guarantee public control over private means.

The outsourcing of intelligence analysis raises interesting questions on the analytic integrity of intelligence products, though ultimately there is no evidence that contracting out generates an economic type of politicisation, or economisation of intelligence. From a legal perspective it is possible to argue that outsourcing analysis risks 'delegating to contractors duties and functions reserved for governmental performance' because these can be 'intimately linked to the direction and control of intelligence and counterintelligence operations'.[15] Yet, based on similar statutes, analysis can be construed as 'developing options' and should therefore not be considered as inherently governmental.[16]

A more nuanced approach considers different types and levels of intelligence analysis. Outsourcing open source analysis is, from this perspective, relatively uncontroversial. Using publicly available information can, for instance, be an effective way for outsiders in academia and the private sector to forecast international events.[17] The commission that investigated the US intelligence failure in the run-up to the 2003 Iraq war recognised that 'the community may simply not be the natural home for real expertise on certain topics. Private sector companies investing millions in emerging markets are likely to have a better handle on current market conditions. Relying on these experts might free up community resources to work more intensely on finding answers no one else has.'[18] However, contracting out analyses on particularly sensitive topics such as the Iranian nuclear programme is more contentious and may give the impression that the government is not in charge any more, even though there is no fundamental reason to trust contractors any less than government employees, as long as analysts are cleared and competent.

Perhaps one of the most convincing arguments against the outsourcing of analysis holds that, at the highest level, intelligence products that are directly policy-relevant to questions of war and peace, such as the President's Daily Brief (PDB) or national intelligence estimates (NIE), should not be written by contractors. One former government official considered that if senior analysts in charge of similar products were to be private contractors, this would give 'an unfair advantage' to their company in the form of direct access to the President.[19] However, well-established companies do already have access to the President and other senior government officials; for instance, when their CEOs sit on the President's Intelligence Advisory Board.[20] Some commentators have expressed concern that outsourcing intelligence analysis may impact negatively on the integrity of an intelligence product and allow private interests to exert undue influence on government officials' decisions. Contractors could tailor the findings of their intelligence reports in order to please their governmental client and obtain the renewal or the continuation of their contract.[21] This is a notion that Richard Immerman, Assistant Deputy Director of National Intelligence for Analytical Integrity and Standards from 2007 to 2009, has rejected.[22] It is entirely conceivable that private sector analysts may feel under some sort of pressure when their next contract depends on their consumers' appreciation of what they delivered, but government analysts essentially face the same kind of pressure and have been known to alter their analysis to curry favour with their superior.[23]

Bias is not necessarily dependent on the involvement of the private sector in national security affairs. In fact, as an analyst suggests, outsourcing analysis could very well allow reports to be written outside of the constraining environment in which government analysts work, and thereby decrease organisational and political pressures.[24] All the agencies in the intelligence community have extensive review and coordination procedures for all analysts – government and contractor. These review processes are designed to ensure product quality and remove motivated biases from finished analyses. In the absence of clear evidence that outsourcing systematically skews analysis, there is no reason to stop doing so.

Investigative journalist Tim Shorrock has argued that 'the entire analysis operation' should be brought 'back into government so that Congress can have full oversight over what goes into intelligence reports'.[25] First, outsourcing intelligence analysis does not necessarily lead to decreased congressional oversight of intelligence reports. As noted earlier, congressional overseers can ask the intelligence community for any piece of evidence they deem relevant. Presumably, this includes reports prepared by intelligence contractors for their government consumers. Second, a legislature that would systematically oversee 'what goes into intelligence reports' might actually increase the risk of political bias tainting these reports. While Congress has an important oversight role to play with regard to intelligence policies, it should refrain from interfering in core intelligence practices like analysis. Third, requiring government agencies to conduct all the analysis that is required by intelligence consumers is simply unachievable.

Given the unpredictable nature of world affairs, intelligence capabilities cannot possibly cover the entire threat universe at any point in time. Intelligence agencies are bound to rely on the private sector for expertise and analysis on certain perishable and specific topics. As long as appropriate review procedures ensure the integrity of intelligence products, outsourcing analysis does not pose major problems. Important reports like the PDB or NIEs go through numerous rounds of review and are edited by senior government employees before they reach decision-makers. This process is designed to guard against human error and bias, and to filter out a potential economisation of intelligence. The fact that intelligence consumers typically rely on multiple sources of information before they make their decision further decreases the likelihood that a single 'tainted' report would distort the government's decisions.

Some types of activity are, by their very nature, difficult to outsource and public authorities may therefore wish to avoid outsourcing them. National security expert and former contract writer Joshua Foust has argued that when measuring performance is difficult, or even impossible, contracting out should be avoided.[26] The quality and impact of intelligence is notoriously difficult to assess, and as a result, Foust's standard might be unachievable in the realm of intelligence.[27] In addition, the intelligence community does not always outsource by choice but also through necessity. In the example of the FBI's Trilogy project, the government lacked the in-house expertise to upgrade its IT capabilities and struggled to develop and manage a complex contract. Given the FBI's lack of expertise, the political context and the nature of this project, there is little doubt that government officials would also have struggled to develop and manage the project if it had remained in-house. Regardless of the sourcing decision, developing cutting-edge capabilities is a highly complex and risky endeavour. From this perspective, delays and cost overruns will probably continue to affect the development and acquisition of new technological capabilities in the intelligence community. Despite these issues, the intelligence community has little choice but to invest in such projects because they are essential to keep an edge over its adversaries. While government officials should do all they can to manage the national intelligence effort effectively, they cannot be expected to overcome the uncertain nature of research and development programmes and intelligence.

By contrast, some intelligence functions have been outsourced without much controversy. This is the case in the involvement of the private sector in areas such as information technology support and catering, where measuring performance is doable and outsourcing does not risk encroaching on core government functions.[28] Nevertheless, outsourcing in these areas still requires agencies to maintain a stable pool of well-qualified government supervisors able to understand and control private sector activities. The leak of sensitive information orchestrated by NSA contractor Edward Snowden demonstrates the risk IT specialists, or for that matter any cleared government employee, can pose to information security.[29] Overall, the ability of public accountability holders to remain in charge of key decisions – those involving matters of life and death, constitutional freedoms and the commitment of resources – is the most important criteria determining the acceptability of outsourcing. Maintaining control over such decisions does not require a prohibition of outsourcing, but adequate standards of control and a workforce that is able to implement these standards.

When to Outsource?

Sourcing decisions are inevitably context-dependent, and as a result they can be approached from a variety of angles.[30] Recent history, from the downsizing of the intelligence community in the 1990s to the post-9/11 surge, suggests that strategic planning in this area has been insufficient. In an ideal world, the intelligence community would always contract out by choice, and not by default. Human capital and strategic planning can help identify core missions and capabilities, which government agencies should be prepared to provide in all circumstances. The ODNI achieved remarkable progress in this domain, but further efforts are needed to optimise the use of contractors.

Human capital planning necessarily starts with the creation of an inventory that helps agencies understand the state of their workforce and identify potential shortcomings. Despite the obligation to compile service contract inventories on an annual basis and the efforts to streamline human capital planning, the intelligence community continues to struggle gathering and making sense of this information. The lack of standardisation across the intelligence community and within each agency has complicated the drafting of inventories. Changes to the definition of contract personnel and issues of data reliability – caused by changes in the methodologies used to count full-time equivalents – have skewed some of the reporting on contractors. These limitations have made yearly comparisons difficult or even unachievable, and workforce trends have remained poorly understood as a result. The latest evidence suggests that the overall number of core contract personnel performing key functions in the civilian intelligence community, the reasons for their use and their cost are not reliably determined.[31] These shortcomings are particularly concerning since this information is necessary to effectively manage the mixed workforce of civilian, military and contractor personnel that composes the intelligence community.

On a more positive note, the intelligence community leadership is now well aware of these limitations and has already launched an initiative to better understand and tackle methodological discrepancies.[32] The appropriate workforce mix within the intelligence community is not static and varies from week to week and agency to agency, according to a host of needs, priorities and outside factors which need to be constantly evaluated and anticipated.[33] In the future, developing an ability to determine the intelligence community's use of contractors on a monthly or even weekly basis will help senior officials refine their reliance on private sector capabilities.

At the political level, the impetus towards insourcing has raised fears that the pendulum may swing back too far. Political considerations have historically affected sourcing decisions. Executive branch policies promoting privatisation and congressional decisions to maintain personnel ceilings on the intelligence workforce can disrupt human capital plans. In the last few years, the intelligence budget has decreased from $80.1 billion in 2010 to $73 billion in 2017. These cuts have forced a rationalisation of the US intelligence enterprise and even encouraged some companies to reconsider the pricing of the goods and services they provide to the intelligence community.[34] However, budget cuts can also have negative effects. The sequestration and pay freezes of 2013 have affected the government's ability to hire and retain government personnel, and delayed the intelligence community's efforts to balance its workforce.[35] In this context, lessons learned from the past should not be overlooked. The US government drastically cut the intelligence budget in the 1990s, only to expand it tremendously and call upon contractors to fill capability gaps in the global war on terrorism. Recent efforts to rein in the national intelligence effort may be worthwhile but they should not affect the base force of the intelligence community, including government expertise in acquisition. The government's ability to maintain civil servants in key positions is essential to keep core capabilities in government, but greater professional freedom and higher salaries in the private sector will continue to challenge the government's ability to do so.[36]

To this day, striking the optimal balance between government and contractor employees remains difficult, not least because it depends on the ever-changing national security environment and politics. This question is important because, at the margins, excessive outsourcing could strip the government of its ability to understand and control the activities it contracts out; conversely, too much insourcing could prevent the government from tapping into key private sector capabilities.[37] The government needs strong strategic planning to maintain a baseline of expertise in key competencies and foster a rich industrial base. In the short term, sourcing decisions are often made on a case-by-case basis by mid-level managers for whom time constraints and mission requirements can make outsourcing preferable or even necessary. This operational logic can sometimes conflict with senior officials' strategic considerations regarding the appropriate mix of government and contractor employees over the medium and long term. Mid-level intelligence managers play a central role in this process because they cope with, and ideally reconcile, requirements from above and below. They are uniquely positioned to consider the suitability of the private option and justify it based on pre-defined rationales like unique private sector expertise or surge requirements, or more controversially, efficiency.[38] Yet their position is poorly understood because intelligence scholarship has mostly focused on the views and experiences of senior officials, and has largely overlooked issues of human capital management.

In order to outsource to save money, the government needs appropriate information and decision-making instruments. In the past, government agencies have lacked sufficient information 'to assess the soundness of savings estimates'.[39] Measuring the relative cost-effectiveness of public and private options poses methodological problems, in particular when determining what factors to include in the calculation of the cost of employees.[40] Finding a reliable methodology for comparing public and private options is essential because as long as uncertainty about the cost of government and contractor employees remains, shifting from one to the other 'could prove to be a false savings'.[41] Supporters of outsourcing note that although contractors cost more than full-time civilians, 'the total expenditure to pay for civilian benefits and retirements far exceeds the short-term cost'.[42] This argument loses some of its relevance when contractors become a long-term feature of the intelligence community. Broader limits on objective knowledge can also impede outsourcing decisions. This is particularly the case for certain types of activities, such as intelligence analysis, that are notably hard to put metrics on. In the words of Mark

Lowenthal, a former Assistant Director of Central Intelligence for Analysis and Production, 'although improvements undoubtedly can be made in intelligence, determining how efficient an inherently inefficient and intellectual process can be remains elusive'.[43] Other intelligence activities, particularly operations and research and development, are more unpredictable, which can also complicate rational decision-making. On the whole, the means to make cost-effectiveness a sound rationale for outsourcing have been lacking, and this problem is unlikely to disappear given the uncertain nature of intelligence.

How to Outsource?

Outsourcing should only occur when adequate accountability standards are firmly established. These standards are important because they can help mitigate the risks of outsourcing. As the examples explored in Chapter 4 illustrate, the accountability regime for contractors has often seemed inadequate. In recent years, the risks posed by contractors have become particularly visible through a series of compromises to national security. The information security risks posed by contractors illustrate one of the core themes of this book: the tension between control and flexibility and its impact on public-private intelligence collaboration. Since the Snowden leaks, a host of information security breaches originating with contractors has pushed some commentators to conclude that outsourcing creates security risks.[44] In his controversial book on Edward Snowden, investigative journalist and former political science professor Edward Epstein suggests that Snowden was able to navigate through the cracks of NSA security because he worked as a contractor and was poorly vetted by the company in charge of his security clearance reinvestigation.[45] As far as security vetting is concerned, the same investigative and adjudicative standards apply to federal employees and contractors who receive a security clearance from the federal government. From this perspective, there is no reason why contractors would constitute more of a security risk than government employees. The historical record presented in Chapter 2 suggests that, on the whole, contractors have been involved in fewer cases of compromises to national security than government employees. Yet the growth of the overall intelligence workforce and problems of public-private coordination seem to have strained security.

Much like other concerns about the outsourcing of intelligence, the security risk posed by contractors can often be traced to shortfalls in government control. Government authorities have relied on 'faulty procedures' to vet intelligence workers, including contractors, in the rush to fill workforce gaps during the global war on terrorism.[46] A significant part of the US government vetting is done by contractors, and the vetting of contractors by other contractors gained increasing attention following the Washington Navy Yard shooting, a few months after the Snowden affair came to the fore in 2013.[47] In both cases, the company in charge of the background investigation of the perpetrator (respectively defence contractor Aaron Alexis, and intelligence contractor Edward Snowden), US Investigation Services (USIS), did not vet government contractors thoroughly. One of the issues confronted by USIS in the case of Edward Snowden is that the CIA would not share Snowden's file with a private concern. USIS was subsequently indicted in another affair for failing to conduct quality review on 665,000 background investigations it carried out from 2008 to 2012 for the US government. According to court documents, the company circumvented contractually required quality reviews of personnel working for DoD entities like the Defense Intelligence Agency to increase its profit margins.[48] In other words, government authorities failed to control whether USIS was fulfilling its contractual requirements.

Since then, a vulnerability introduced by a contractor who was the victim of a spear phishing attack allowed foreign hackers to access sensitive databases from the Office of Personnel Management, including personal information on over 21.5 million serving and former government employees who had received a security clearance. In 2016, an NSA contractor was arrested for stealing terabytes of sensitive government information over a twenty-year period.[49] The following year, another NSA contractor was arrested for leaking a report on alleged Russian meddling in the 2016 presidential election.[50] These examples all emphasise the urgent need for government authorities to develop better means to liaise with and control contractors' behaviour in the interest of national security, but they do not prove that contractors are out of control. Hundreds of thousands of contractors access sensitive government systems and contribute to national security every day; few compromise them.

The main challenge the government confronts when it outsources its activities is to find a balance between control and flexibility. Government acquisition regulations have long been criticised for their complexity, which is said to impede upon the free-market ideal. A common concern is that following the post-Cold War shift from outsourcing goods to outsourcing services, acquisition procedures may have become obsolete. Accordingly, certain commentators propose to change or simplify federal regulations to liberalise the market and make it more efficient.[51] The lengthiness of the government procurement process has been a major issue in this context, especially in the acquisition of technological solutions, which is often focused on large-scale 'system integrator contracts that do not easily allow for the agile adoption of new security products that keep up with the ever-changing threat'.[52] Yet the flexibility embodied by the notion of the free market is not achievable in a domain characterised by secrecy and specific government requirements.

While the legal framework for outsourcing can always be improved, existing regulations need to be applied effectively, and this requires appropriate control procedures and capabilities. In recent years, critics have focused on key stakeholders' lack of control over contractors. A report considering the state of intelligence contracting in the civilian intelligence community finds that more efforts are needed to enhance and refine internal controls and strategic plans that are agency- and mission-specific. The civilian elements of the intelligence community have reportedly 'made limited progress in developing policies and strategies on contractor use to mitigate risks'.[53] The latest evidence suggests that numerous intelligence agencies are still in the process of developing internal policies to address relatively new policies like the OFPP policy letter defining inherently governmental and critical functions. Public-private intelligence collaboration is in a state of transition, and it will take time before the regulatory movement that started in the mid-2000s becomes fully effective.

The application of standards and procedures to manage the mixed workforce within the intelligence community requires skilled public managers, able to make smart decisions about the provision of goods and services. Most observers agree that the intelligence community's contract management workforce needs better training and more personnel.[54] In its latest investigation on the subject, the GAO found that the intelligence community chief human capital officer 'does not have the staff resources for more extensive reviews' of contract personnel.[55] To tackle such staffing issues, Joseph Mazzafro, an intelligence officer turned contractor, recommends that the intelligence community protect its acquisition workforce 'with draconian non-compete rules that would make it economically impossible for the private sector to hire these acquisition professionals away from the government before retirement'.[56] This bold measure might be impossible to implement, and is unlikely to generate consensus.

The key to attracting and retaining talented individuals in crucial oversight positions, including those of contracting officer and COTR, is an incentive structure that facilitates the recognition of these positions and motivates these professionals to work more efficiently.[57] Buying is rarely perceived as a core mission of executive agencies, and the COTR field has been criticised for lacking performance incentives. The ODNI strategic human capital plan for 2012–17 reiterates a commitment to 'ensuring its acquisition workforce has the training, education, and experience necessary to ensure cost-effective acquisition outcomes and improved management of the contractor workforce'.[58] Initiatives in this area include the development of standard COTR performance objectives, specific training and certification and the establishment of a recognition and awards programme to increase acquisition awareness and interest.[59] These are important steps towards ensuring the government reinforces its ability to manage intelligence contracts and contractors in the following decades.

Changing the culture of the intelligence community to give contract management more importance will take time and attention. Better and more coherent career paths for acquisition personnel are needed to create a more 'stable and capable' acquisition workforce.[60] Further insourcing could reduce the need for a sizeable contract management workforce and refocus efforts on training current government experts.[61] However, this option is neither sufficient nor desirable, as it does not take into account the traditional ebb and flow of sourcing policies and the resulting need for contract managers over the long term. The government needs to be prepared to manage its combined workforce now – since contracting continues to be common across the intelligence community – as well as when the next surge in intelligence requirements occurs.

The prominence of contractors has created a need for the intelligence community and its managers to evolve and develop the skills necessary to coordinate activities and capabilities across the public-private divide. This need goes beyond managing the contractor workforce and encompasses broader, sometimes informal, relations with the private sector. Educating the intelligence workforce about some of the basic principles of business administration could reinforce the intelligence community's ability to understand and harness the capabilities of the private sector. Initiatives to engage with the private sector, like the Office of Partner Engagement at the ODNI, need to be pursued to continue information exchange and further institutionalise cross-sector collaboration.[62] Leadership, specifically through these initiatives, will be necessary to create greater synergy between the various entities that engage with the private sector across the intelligence community. Making the relationship between the intelligence community and its contractors more comprehensive, to the extent it is possible, has the potential to improve communication and cooperation across the public-private divide in the interest of national security.

Better Public–Private Coordination

The distance the government maintains from its contractors is one of the central questions that runs through the history of government contracting. Should the government keep contractors at arm's length and systematically offer contracts to the lowest bidder, or nurture relationships with specific companies to develop a responsive industrial base?[63] For some scholars, better coordination can be achieved thanks to a move away from hierarchical management towards a more networked and horizontal type of governance that includes the private sector and the interested public in intelligence and national security decisions.[64] From this perspective, the solution to the problems of intelligence outsourcing lies in better public-private coordination in the domain of accountability. The example of In-Q-Tel demonstrates the potential of 'new' modes of collaboration. One solution to the government's accountability shortfalls is to shape incentives to instil mutual trust and cooperation between the public and private sectors. At the organisational level, companies could play a greater role as the guarantors of the US accountability regime.[65]

Corporations are the first and closest point of control over their own personnel. They have the specialised knowledge and expertise to carry out control appropriately, and are also well placed to be aware of breaches by their competitors. From this perspective, peer pressure and competition can contribute to the professionalisation of the industry and generate higher standards of behaviour across the board.[66] This is the case when companies protest against contract awards decisions made by government agencies. Corporations, some commentators argue, are well disposed towards their regulation since they have a long-term interest in maintaining a good public image in order to gain comparative advantage against their public and private competitors.[67] From the government perspective, self-regulation is also unlikely to be onerous.[68]

In practice, however, self-regulation is insufficient to palliate the range of problems that have affected outsourcing. In the field of private security, researchers have found that codes of conduct are more likely to regulate those violations that are deemed to be minor breaches of law.[69] The most obvious problem is that codes of conduct are not legally binding, and as a result, sanctions are not credible and are rarely applied. As long as they are given a choice, companies are unlikely to take the initiative to share information they hold with any trade association or government entity supposed to enforce a code of conduct, especially if it contradicts their for-profit orientation.[70] This type of behaviour was clearly demonstrated by USIS when it preferred not to divulge an information security breach that compromised one of its computer networks to its DHS contracting officer.[71] From the perspective of the private sector, reporting one's shortcomings could deter would-be clients if mistakes were made public.[72] In the highly compartmentalised context of the national security enterprise, it is also unlikely that peers or consumers will be able to systematically identify companies' breaches.

Solutions will need to be found to refine the place and role of contractors in national security affairs, and to allow both the government and business sectors to draw on their complementary strengths, communicate and plan together for the future of national security. The deficiencies of self-regulation point to the role of the government in setting and guaranteeing further means of control by, for example, using contracts to require specific training and accreditation from independent experts or industry association.[73] In her study of the impact of PSC on military effectiveness, Molly Dunigan proposes that such training should be paid for by PSC or deducted from their government contracts.[74] Various incentives, including fines, but also tax relief for complying companies and performance evaluations, can be used by government agencies to foster better public-private collaboration.[75] The key challenge is to use them effectively. While the government needs to demonstrate trust towards its private partners, it should continue to verify whether contractors deserve this trust.

The accountability model guiding public-private collaboration must remain partly hierarchical to maintain public authority over private means. In the field of national security, where the government faces high expectations from its citizens and has relatively little room for error, it remains difficult to conceive of accountability other than in this traditional way. As the accountability model used in this book posits, accountability is a relationship between a principal, typically the government, and an agent, in this case a contractor, in which the latter answers to the former. This relationship can take multiple forms, and government officials are also held to account by other stakeholders like the courts and companies. However, the core process and rules of democratic intelligence accountability remain and should remain defined by the government, and its workforce of public officials.

The Case for Adaptation

Reform is often touted as a panacea in the fields of national security intelligence and defence, but what is really needed to improve public-private collaboration is adaptation. Since the Second World War, and even more so since the end of the Cold War, the theme of reform has been the focus of any number of reports. A study by the RAND Corporation counted sixty-three distinct acquisition reform initiatives undertaken between the 1960s and 2002, and another one considered seventeen major intelligence reviews from 1945 to 2005.[76] Research has related changes in this domain to organisational structures, policies, culture and practices, and leadership.[77] Overall, very few major reform initiatives have wrought fundamental change. Indeed, bureaucratic and political incentives to reform are notoriously unsuccessful in the realm of intelligence and national security. Reform is politically risky, not rewarding enough, and not worthy of political capital in most circumstances.[78] In the twenty-first century, debates about intelligence reform and reorganisation reached a peak after the 9/11 attacks and ultimately led to the adoption of the Intelligence Reform and Terrorism Prevention Act of 2004.[79] The benefits of this reform remain debated.[80] Although the act did not directly address challenges in the areas of intelligence accountability and outsourcing, it established the ODNI, and the policies developed by this new office improved the accountability regime for contractors.

Experience suggests that although intelligence accountability and outsourcing have attracted some political attention in Washington, DC since the mid-2000s, a major reform effort is unlikely. Significant intelligence scandals in the last decade have not wrought fundamental changes in the system of intelligence accountability in the way the Church committee did back in 1975. The solution to the problems of intelligence accountability and outsourcing will not come through a radical overhaul of the system. In the field of intelligence and national security, incremental change is more suitable than a major, one-time reform initiative. Michael Warner and Kenneth McDonald note that 'intelligence is too large, too complicated, and too important either to fix at a stroke or to leave alone',[81] and the same is true of intelligence outsourcing. Continuous adaptation is a better option because it does not require anticipating the nature of future challenges – an 'extraordinarily difficult' task according to strategist James Wirtz.[82] Intelligence accountability holders often have to fine-tune a series of political and organisational trade-offs between liberal democratic values and national security imperatives, formality and informality, and autonomy and subordination. Similar choices need to be made, for example between insourcing and outsourcing, flexibility and regulation, to adapt the government's reliance on contractors so that intelligence leaders keep control over and effectively leverage their mixed workforce. Accountability holders need to consider on a regular basis how government policies, processes and capabilities cope with the broader security environment, and review and adjust intelligence outsourcing accordingly. Otherwise chaotic collaboration might, one more time, affect intelligence accountability and the intelligence community's ability to fulfil its national security mission.

Since the mid-2000s, policy-makers and senior intelligence officials have made significant efforts to better manage intelligence outsourcing. Their efforts have not led to major reform, but change has been incremental under the leadership of key decision-makers in the executive and legislative branches of government.[83] The sense of crisis that followed the 9/11 attacks has now vanished and a host of political events, ranging from scandals to elections, have provided key accountability holders with opportunities to reflect on intelligence practices and refine government policies. In this light, tackling the problems of intelligence outsourcing can be considered as an opportunity to reinforce democratic accountability and safeguard the ascendancy of the relationship between public authority and private means.[84] The intelligence community leadership is now well aware that workforce and acquisition issues need to be reassessed regularly in function of evolving mission needs. This is a positive evolution, but the recurrence of accountability problems beleaguering intelligence contracting suggests that accountability holders need to remain on their guard.

The case for domestic adaptation is persuasive but the politics of intelligence will need to evolve if adaptation is to be successful. At the political level, the willingness of political intelligence accountability holders to uphold high standards of accountability has been one of the central challenges facing intelligence accountability in the United States. The scholarly consensus underlines the lack of incentives for policy-makers to carry out their intelligence oversight duty. Mark Lowenthal, a former intelligence practitioner, explains the conservatism of the executive branch as a consequence of the fact that 'many policy makers understand some of the fragility of the intelligence community and fear the responsibility of making things worse'.[85] Recent research finds that representatives lack interest in intelligence oversight, and the roots of the problem, it is argued, lie with poor incentives.[86]

One way to approach the problem of accountability holders' incentives focuses on the role of money in the US political system and correlates electoral success, political funding from private companies and 'suspect appropriation choices and corruption'. The logical recommendation is to start 'changing the incentive structure that currently exists for any member of Congress'.[87] For example, this could entail the abrogation of congressional earmarks and changing the funding system of political campaigns. Such a move is unlikely to be generated by issues of security contracting and intelligence accountability alone. Representatives have benefited from pork-barrel politics for decades, and they are unlikely to deprive themselves of a system that can help them win votes. Moreover, the role of money in politics and national security is not the only problem with regards to intelligence accountability and contracting. Another central issue highlighted throughout this book is the evolution of intelligence management practices. Developing a stable and well-trained acquisition workforce is arguably the main challenge for intelligence outsourcing. This is mostly an administrative issue, but focusing on elected government officials is nevertheless essential since, in a democratic society, they constitute a significant force for change.

Societal actors, including media and outside experts, have a key role to play in this context. They can research contracting practices and point out problems. Disclosures of information and balanced media reporting can raise public pressure in favour of better intelligence accountability and, by extension, push government authorities to keep an eye on contractors. Scholars also have a role to play, particularly in the field of Intelligence Studies, which has long overlooked the role played by contractors in intelligence affairs and relevant debates about privatisation in the cognate fields of public administration and international relations. This book has sought to bring the private sector into the study of intelligence and refine our understanding of outsourcing as a core intelligence practice. The examples discussed throughout the book illustrate a number of accountability problems, and this chapter has identified a number of recommendations to improve human capital planning, acquisition management and intelligence accountability. The key to implementing these changes and improving the accountability regime for contractors remains in the hands of the federal government.

Notes

1. Steven Aftergood, 'Security-Cleared Population Declined by 12% Last Year', *Secrecy News*, 27 April 2015, available at <http://fas.org/blogs/secrecy/2015/04/clearances-2014/> (accessed 29 May 2018); Joe Davidson, 'Intelligence Chief Says Cuts Now May Bring Unexpected Dangers Later', *Washington Post*, 9 April 2013, B4.
2. Kate M. Manuel, *Definitions of 'Inherently Governmental Function' in Federal Procurement Law and Guidance*, Congressional Research Service Report R42325, 23 December 2014, p. 21; National Security Lawyer conversation with author, 10 August 2011; Office of the Director of National Intelligence, *Key Facts about Contractors*, p. 1, available at <https://www.fas.org/irp/news/2010/07/ic-contract.pdf> (accessed 29 May 2018).
3. Chesterman, 'We Can't Spy if We Can't Buy', p. 1073.
4. Savas, *Privatization and Public-Private Partnerships*, p. 7; Lahneman, 'Outsourcing the IC's Stovepipes'.
5. Government Accountability Office, *Defense Acquisitions: DOD's Increased Reliance on Service Contractors Exacerbates Long-standing Challenges*, statement of David M. Walker, Comptroller General of the United States, testimony before the Subcommittee on Defense, Committee on Appropriations, US House of Representatives, 23 January 2008, GAO-08-621T, p. 3.
6. Hastedt, 'An *INS* Special Forum', p. 799.
7. Hansen, 'Intelligence Contracting', p. 74.

8. Kinsey and Patterson, 'Conclusion', in *Contractors and War*, p. 300.
9. Schooner, 'Fear of Oversight', p. 719.
10. Chesterman, *One Nation Under Surveillance*, pp. 113, 118, 206; Harris, 'Intelligence Incorporated', 46; Kimberly Dozier, 'Official Resigns Over Alleged Spy Ring', 27 September 2011, available at <http://www.businessweek.com/ap/financialnews/D9Q0NE680.htm> (accessed 29 May 2018); Shorrock, *Spies for Hire*, p. 380.
11. Gale, 'Intelligence Outsourcing in the US Department of Defense', pp. 74–5.
12. Cited in Nguyen, 'Current Trends in Intelligence Outsourcing Affect Work Force Stability', p. 77.
13. US Senate, Select Committee on Intelligence, *Committee Study of the Central Intelligence Agency's Detention and Interrogation Program*, 13 December 2012, p. 2. For media reactions, see Karen De Young, 'CIA Report Details Intimate Role of Doctors in Interrogations', *Washington Post*, 14 December 2014, A1; Greg Miller and Adam Goldman, 'Report Charts CIA Prisons' Rise, Fall', *Washington Post*, 12 December 2014, A1; Editorial Board, 'The Senate Report on the CIA's Torture and Lies', *New York Times*, 9 December 2014.
14. On government legitimacy, see Verkuil, *Outsourcing Sovereignty*.
15. Chesterman, *One Nation Under Surveillance*, p. 98.
16. Chesterman, 'We Can't Spy if We Can't Buy', pp. 1072–3.
17. Office of the Director of National Intelligence, Intelligence Advance Research Projects Activity (IARPA), *Aggregative Contingent Information (ACE)*, available at <http://www.iarpa.gov/index.php/research-programs/ace> (accessed 29 May 2018).
18. The Commission on the Intelligence Capabilities of the United States Regarding Weapons of Mass Destruction, *Report to the President of the United States*, 31 March 2005, p. 400.
19. Former government official, interview with author.
20. For example, a vice-president for AT&T served on President George W. Bush's Foreign Intelligence Advisory Board. White House, Office of the Press Secretary, 'Nominations and Appointments', 5 October 2001, available at <http://georgewbush-whitehouse.archives.gov/news/releases/2001/10/20011005-8.html> (accessed 29 May 2018).
21. Shorrock, *Spies for Hire*, p. 37; Leander, 'The Power to Construct International Security', pp. 812–14; Chesterman, *One Nation Under Surveillance*, pp. 120–1.
22. Richard H. Immerman, email correspondence with author, 29 March 2013.

23. Rovner, *Fixing the Facts*, pp. 18–34.
24. Intelligence analyst, conversation with author, 2014.
25. Tim Shorrock, interview with author, 30 June 2011, Washington, DC.
26. Joshua Foust, US Senate, Committee on Homeland Security and Governmental Affairs, Subcommittee on Oversight of Government Management, the Federal Workforce, and the District of Columbia, *Intelligence Community Contractors: Are We Striking the Right Balance?*, hearing, 112th Congress, 1st session, 20 September 2011, p. 20.
27. Ratcliffe, *Intelligence-led Policing*, p. 212; Zelik et al., 'Understanding Rigor in Information Analysis', Proceedings of the Eighth International NDM Conference, Pacific Grove, CA, June 2007.
28. Rothkopf, 'Business versus Terror', p. 62; Gale, 'Intelligence Outsourcing in the US Department of Defense', pp. 105–7.
29. Office of the Director of National Intelligence, National Counterintelligence Executive Frank Montoya Jr., letter to Michelle Schmitz, Office of the Inspector General, US Office of Personnel Management, *Technical and quality review of the April 2011 Single Scope Background Investigation – Periodic Reinvestigation on Mr Snowden*, 23 August 2013; Intelligence and National Security Alliance, 'Next Steps for Security Reform', pp. 3, 10–11; Hastedt, 'An *INS* Special Forum', p. 799.
30. Camm, 'How to Decide When a Contractor Source Is Better to Use Than a Government Source', pp. 237, 246; Bowman, 'Legal Issues of Outsourcing Military Functions in Wartime', p. 456; Gale, 'Intelligence Outsourcing in the US Department of Defense', pp. 63–4, 69, 70; Voelz, *Managing the Private Spies*, p. 36.
31. The civilian intelligence community includes the CIA, DHS Office of Intelligence and Analysis, Department of Energy's Office of Intelligence and Counterintelligence, Department of State's Bureau of Intelligence and Research, Department of Treasury's Office of Intelligence and Analysis, DEA Office of National Security Intelligence, FBI, and ODNI. Government Accountability Office, *Civilian Intelligence Community*, pp. 11, 16, 18, 20, 28.
32. O'Sullivan, 'The Intelligence Community: Keeping Watch Over its Contractor Workforce', pp. 9–10.
33. Nemfakos et al., *Workforce Planning in the Intelligence Community*, pp. 15, 33–44.
34. O'Sullivan, 'The Intelligence Community: Keeping Watch Over its Contractor Workforce', p. 8.
35. Ibid. p. 6.

36. Shane Harris, 'The Outsiders', *Government Executive* 42/11 (2010), 48; Harris, 'Intelligence Incorporated', p. 47.
37. Rostker, *A Call to Revitalize the Engines of Government*, p. 13. See also: Office of Management and Budget, *Analytical Perspectives, Budget of the US Government, Fiscal Year 2011*, 1 February 2010, p. 105.
38. Michael Rubin, 'Privatize the CIA', *Weekly Standard* 12/20, 5 February 2007, available at <http://staging.weeklystandard.com/Content/Public/Articles/000/000/013/220wwnna.asp> (accessed 29 May 2018).
39. General Accounting Office, statement of David R. Warren, Director, Defense Management Issues, National Security and International Affairs Division, *Defense Outsourcing, Challenges Facing DOD as It Attempts to Save Billions in Infrastructure Costs*, hearing before the Subcommittee on Readiness of the House Committee on National Security, 105th Congress, 1st session, 12 March 1997, p. 18.
40. David Berteau et al., *DoD Workforce Cost Realism Assessment, Report of the CSIS Defense-Industrial Initiative Group*, May 2011; Elaine Halchin, *Sourcing Policy: Selected Developments and Issues*, CRS Report for Congress, p. 39.
41. Mazzafro, 'Too Many Contractors; Too Much Cost?'; Gale, 'Intelligence Outsourcing in the US Department of Defense', pp. 110–13.
42. Nguyen, 'Current Trends in Intelligence Outsourcing', p. 75.
43. Lowenthal, *Intelligence: From Secrets to Policy*, p. 343.
44. Philip Ewing and Tony Romm, 'Edward Snowden Leak Exposes Cracks in Contractor System', *Politico*, 9 June 2013, available at <http://www.politico.com/story/2013/06/edward-snowden-leak-contractor-92472.html> (accessed 29 May 2018).
45. Epstein, *How America Lost its Secrets*, pp. 28–37.
46. Robert O'Harrow Jr., Dana Priest and Marjorie Censer, 'NSA Leaks Put Focus on Intelligence Apparatus's Reliance on Outside Contractors', *Washington Post*, 10 June 2013.
47. Office of Management and Budget, *Suitability and Security Processes Review*, Report to the President, February 2014, p. 1.
48. US House of Representatives, Committee on Oversight and Government Reform, Rep. Elijah E. Cummings, *Contracting Out Security Clearance Investigations: The Role of USIS and Allegations of Systemic Fraud*, 113th Congress, 11 February 2014, p. 12; Elijah E. Cummings, opening statement, US House of Representatives, Committee on Oversight and Government Reform, hearing on *DC*

Navy Yard Shooting: Fixing the Security Clearance Process, 113th Congress, 11 February 2014, p. 2; US District Court for the Middle District of Alabama, Northern Division, United States of America v. US Investigations Services, Inc., Civil Action no., 11-CV-527-WKW, 22 January 2014, pp. 11–22.

49. Julie Hirschfeld Davis, 'Hacking Exposed 21 Million in US, Government Says', *New York Times*, 10 July 2015, A1; Ellen Nakashima, 'Government Alleges Former NSA Contractor Stole "Astonishing Quantity" of Classified Data Over 20 Years', *Washington Post*, 20 October 2016, A1.
50. Charlie Savage and Alan Blinder, 'Guilty Plea for Leak of Top Secret Report on Russian Election Hacking', *New York Times*, 27 June 2018, A14.
51. National security lawyer C, interview with author, 4 August 2011, Arlington, VA; Bowman, 'Legal Issues of Outsourcing Military Functions in Wartime', p. 423; Stanger, *One Nation Under Contract*, p. 182; Mazzafro, 'Too Many Contractors; Too Much Cost?'
52. President's Review Group on Intelligence and Communications Technologies, *Liberty and Security in a Changing World*, 12 December 2013, p. 251.
53. Government Accountability Office, *Civilian Intelligence Community*, pp. 23–4, 31.
54. Stiens, 'Uncontracting: The Move Back to Performing In-House', pp. 178–80; Guttman, 'Government By Contract', p. 12; Mazzafro, 'Too Many Contractors; Too Much Cost?'; Dickinson, 'Outsourcing Covert Activities', p. 532; Matt Armstrong, 'In-sourcing the Tools of National Power for Success and Security', *Small Wars Journal*, 3 January 2008; Allen, *Intelligence Community Contractors: Are We Striking the Right Balance?*, p. 19; Edward L. Haugland, testimony before the US Senate Committee on Homeland Security and Governmental Affairs, Subcommittee on Oversight of Government Management, the Federal Workforce, and the District of Columbia, *Intelligence Community Contractors: Are We Striking the Right Balance?*, hearing, 112th Congress, 1st session, 20 September 2011, p. 36; O'Sullivan, 'The Intelligence Community: Keeping Watch Over its Contractor Workforce', p. 19.
55. Government Accountability Office, *Civilian Intelligence Community*, p. 17.
56. Mazzafro, 'Too Many Contractors; Too Much Cost?'.
57. Haugland, US Senate, Committee on Homeland Security and Governmental Affairs, p. 36; Verkuil, *Outsourcing Sovereignty*, p. 175.

58. Office of the Director of National Intelligence, *Strategic Human Capital Plan 2012–2017*, p. 9.
59. Office of the Director of National Intelligence, Appendix B, *Strategic Human Capital Plan Initiatives*, p. 15.
60. Bruneau, 'Contracting Out Security', p. 661; Fox, *Defense Acquisition Reform*, pp. 201–2.
61. Stiens, 'Uncontracting: The Move Back to Performing In-House', p. 178.
62. Ackerman, 'Intelligence Tries a New Public-Private Partnership', p. 55; Center for Strategic and International Studies, 'Director of National Intelligence Private Sector Engagement Initiative', available at <http://csis.org/programs/transnational-threats-project/transnational-threats-project-past-initiatives/director-natio> (accessed 29 May 2018); INSA, 'ODNI Industry Days', available at <http://www.insaonline.org/index.php?id=559> (accessed 29 May 2018); ODNI, 'Partner Engagement', available at <http://www.dni.gov/index.php/about/organization/partner-engagement-who-we-are> (accessed 29 May 2018).
63. Nagle, *A History of Government Contracting*, pp. 2–6.
64. Goldsmith and Eggers, *Governing by Network*; Aldrich, 'Beyond the Vigilant State: Globalisation and Intelligence', pp. 892, 894, 901–2; Peter Gill, 'Not Just Joining the Dots But Crossing the Borders and Bridging the Voids: Constructing Security Networks after 11 September 2001', pp. 41–5; Voelz, *Managing the Private Spies*, p. 63; Stanger, *One Nation Under Contract*, p. 181; Dickinson, 'Outsourcing Covert Activities', p. 532; De Nevers, '(Self) Regulating War? Voluntary Regulation and the Private Security Industry', pp. 491–2; Busch and Givens, 'Public-Private Partnerships in Homeland Security: Opportunities and Challenges', p. 10; Johnson, *National Security Intelligence*, pp. 184–5.
65. Michaels, 'All the President's Spies', p. 906.
66. Avant, *The Market for Force*, p. 223; Caparini, 'Applying a Security Governance Perspective to the Privatisation of Security', p. 275; Maogoto et al., *Legal Control of the Private Military Corporation*, p. 140.
67. Perrin, 'Promoting Compliance of Private Security and Military Companies with International Humanitarian Law', p. 627; Singer, *Corporate Warriors*, p. 217.
68. Percy, 'Regulating the Private Security Industry', p. 57.
69. Gillard, 'Business Goes o War: Private Military/Security Companies and International Humanitarian Law', p. 548.

70. Caparini, 'Applying a Security Governance Perspective to the Privatisation of Security', p. 275.
71. Robert Block, 'Unisys Denies Coverup of Security Breaches', *Wall Street Journal*, 25 September 2007, A15.
72. Singer, *Corporate Warriors*, p. 222.
73. Dickinson, 'Public Law Values in a Privatized World', pp. 383, 403–23; Dickinson, *Outsourcing War and Peace*, p. 73.
74. Dunigan, *Victory for Hire*, p. 161.
75. Willis et al., 'Information Sharing for Infrastructure Risk Management: Barriers and Solutions', pp. 362–3.
76. Hanks et al., *Reexamining Military Acquisition Reform: Are We There Yet?*, pp. 101–3; Warner and McDonald, *US Intelligence Community Reform Studies Since 1947*; Zegart, *Spying Blind*, pp. 32–42; Lowenthal, *Intelligence: From Secrets to Policy*, pp. 383–6.
77. Sims and Gerber, *Transforming US Intelligence*, p. xi; Taylor and Goldman, 'Intelligence, Reform: Will More Agencies, Money, and Personnel Help?', p. 423; Lowenthal, *Intelligence: From Secrets to Policy*, p. 329.
78. Durbin, *The CIA and the Politics of US Intelligence Reform*, p. 3; Betts, 'The New Politics of Intelligence', p. 8; Zegart, 'September 11 and the Adaptation Failure of US Intelligence Agencies', pp. 94–6; Wirtz, 'A Review of: "Bureaucracy Does Its Thing"', pp. 578–80.
79. Pillar, 'Adapting Intelligence to Changing Issues', p. 157; Sims and Gerber, *Transforming US Intelligence*, p. xi.
80. Turner, 'Intelligence Reform and the Politics of Entrenchment', pp. 386–8.
81. Warner and McDonald, *US Intelligence Community Reform Studies Since 1947*, p. 43.
82. Wirtz, 'A Review of: "Bureaucracy Does Its Thing"', p. 580.
83. Central Intelligence Agency, *Director's Statement on Contractor Study*, 30 May 2007, at <https://www.cia.gov/news-information/press-releases-statements/press-release-archive-2007/statement-on-contractor-study.html> (accessed 29 May 2018); Sanders, *Results of the Fiscal Year 2007 US Intelligence Community Inventory of Core Contractor Personnel*; Senator Feinstein (D-CA), letter to the Honorable Michael B. Mukasey, Attorney General of the United States, 6 February 2008, at <http://www.feinstein.senate.gov/public/index.cfm/press-releases?ID=f4862661-a162-9308-9347-cd080733551d> (accessed 29 May 2018); Representative Price (D-NC), *Congressional Record* 153/19, 4 October 2007, p. H26634.

84. Avant, *The Market for Force*, p. 255; Kinsey, *Corporate Soldiers and International Security*, p. 135; Dickinson, 'Outsourcing Covert Activities', p. 536.
85. Lowenthal, *Intelligence: From Secrets to Policy*, p. 343.
86. Zegart and Quinn, 'Congressional Intelligence Oversight: The Electoral Disconnection', pp. 744–66; Zegart, 'The Domestic Politics of Irrational Intelligence Oversight'; Johnson, 'Accountability and America's Secret Foreign Policy', pp. 107–9, 112–13. On the lack of political will to regulate private security companies, see for example Chesterman and Fisher, 'Conclusion: Private Security, Public Order', in *Private Security, Public Order*, p. 223.
87. Stanger, *One Nation Under Contract*, p. 180.

Conclusion

The US intelligence community's reliance on contractors challenges accountability both in theory and in practice. When intelligence is outsourced, accountability cannot be approached through the sole prism of executive control, congressional oversight and judicial review, as is so often the case in the academic literature. To explore the evolving accountability regime for intelligence contractors, this book has proposed a new model of intelligence accountability as a process that brings together a variety of stakeholders across the three branches of government and broader society. In practice, these stakeholders' willingness and ability to hold contractors to account differs and evolves.

The history of intelligence outsourcing shows that contractors have been involved in a number of excesses that undermined government efficiency and human rights, and challenged public accountability holders' ability to serve the public interest. While government officials have sometimes lacked the resources and the willingness to hold contractors to account, intelligence outsourcing did not fundamentally alter the conditions required for accountability to occur. From the perspective of those charged with administering the accountability process, outsourcing complicated, but did not prevent, access to information from intelligence contractors. Accountability standards have long regulated intelligence outsourcing, but their mere existence has never been sufficient to hold contractors consistently to account. Senior accountability holders within the executive and legislative branches *always* retained the authority to devise better means to access private sector information, improve accountability standards and implement them. Their authority to control contractors never disappeared, but they have used it inconsistently throughout the years.

The history of intelligence offers multiple examples of the government's ability to harness contractors' capabilities without causing major accountability issues. The U-2 spy plane project and the CIA incubator In-Q-Tel can both be regarded as outsourcing successes that gave strategic advantages to the US intelligence community and its political masters. These examples are important because they prove that outsourcing does not necessarily weaken intelligence accountability. But intelligence contractors were also involved in cases of fraud, waste and abuse that highlight the shortcomings of the US system of intelligence accountability. Contractors worked on the CIA project MKUltra, which resulted in a series of human rights abuses. Decades later, they were at the centre of a series of controversies ranging from failed IT modernisation programmes at the NSA and the FBI to prisoner abuses at Abu Ghraib and the corruption of senior government officials. Behind the headlines, some elements of the intelligence community – like the CIA Office of Inspector General – managed to use their authority to keep a watchful eye on contractors and anticipate or respond to their excesses. In the main examples of accountability failure analysed in this book (in Chapters 2 and 4), government officials' inability or unwillingness to maintain existing standards of accountability explains contractors' excesses. These examples show that the ascendancy of public authority over private means does not guarantee the absence of wrongdoing.

The conceptual model developed in this book examines accountability beyond the emergence of problems. This approach reveals the efforts led by the executive and legislative branches to adapt and clarify the policies regulating contractors' behaviour. Findings in this area challenge the dominant view that contractors are unaccountable in two ways. First, the book demonstrates that the government has developed an accountability regime for contractors. Second, the recent history of intelligence shows that officials have adapted this regime when accountability failures became obvious in the mid-2000s. Despite the government's efforts in this area, the state of public-private collaboration remains imperfect. Given the intelligence community's history of reaching out to the private sector, some commentators might be surprised that officials did not do a better job at managing private intelligence providers in the last two decades. Critics should bear in mind the complexity of outsourcing sensitive and complex intelligence functions in a classified setting, and the immense political pressure to keep the nation safe by any means necessary.

The deficiencies and excesses of public-private intelligence collaboration, and by extension the shortcomings of intelligence accountability in the United States, can largely be related to government officials' decisions. The beginning of the global war on terrorism, just like the early Cold War, was characterised by a significant expansion of the US intelligence community, during which the market for intelligence thrived. In the context of crisis that followed the 9/11 attacks, senior decision-makers put an emphasis on effectiveness to achieve national security, and some accountability issues were initially relegated to the backbench. The expansion of intelligence outsourcing was carried out in a hurry instead of being carefully planned. When accountability problems became a pressing political issue in the mid-2000s, government officials in the executive and legislative branches began to devote significant attention to the management and oversight of intelligence contractors. As is often the case in government and in intelligence affairs, accountability was reactive more than proactive.

The government's responsibility for the problems of outsourcing should not absolve contractors from their mistakes. Responsibility in a partnership is shared, and both the government and its contractors have historically overlooked established accountability processes when they deemed it beneficial. Yet government responsibility is greater in the realm of intelligence because public officials, not CEOs, are the primary guarantors of national security. In the words of the US Constitution, a government of the people was established to 'provide for the common defense'.[1] Most commentators expect government officials to serve the public interest in national security and contractors to serve their private interests, but the reality of intelligence outsourcing is more complex. Government officials and contractors can hold each other to account and serve the public interest. In other cases, contractors and officials decide to pursue their own interest at the expense of effective national security. In sum, there is no necessary correlation between the public or private status and interest of a stakeholder.

Lessons Learnt

Alexis de Tocqueville in *Democracy in America* argued that 'The great privilege of the Americans does not simply consist in their being more enlightened than other nations, but in their being able to repair the faults they may commit.'[2] The history of public-private intelligence in the early twenty-first century proves America has retained its ability to address its faults. Government authorities responded to some of the most obvious problems plaguing intelligence outsourcing when they defined new red lines, rebalanced the number of contractor and government personnel in the intelligence workforce and reinforced select acquisition capabilities from the mid-2000s onwards. These government responses have engendered a series of legacies – including new regulations and practices such as yearly contractor inventories – but also highlighted persistent challenges. Officials have made significant efforts to tackle some of the main accountability problems involving contractors, but problems are unlikely to disappear. The government's ability to understand, regulate and effectively manage outsourcing remains a work in progress.

An important lesson learnt from the experience of the 1990s and early 2000s is that government institutions need to adapt their accountability capabilities and sourcing policies to the security environment and operational tempo. In times of crisis, when surge requirements force the government to increase its reliance on contractors, the growth of public-private collaboration must be matched by a growth in the capabilities of the acquisition workforce in order to maintain appropriate control over intelligence outsourcing. The government needs to be ready for such surges and retain at all times a sufficient number of skilled employees within its ranks to effectively control, oversee and sometimes limit the ebb and flow of public-private collaboration. Government control is particularly important in domains that are likely to remain mission-critical, such as intelligence collection and analysis. In addition to these capabilities, effective managerial processes are necessary to understand workforce needs and plan for them over the long term. The lack of contract management expertise within the government workforce remains one of the main issues affecting public-private intelligence collaboration.

Improving Intelligence Accountability

The evolution of intelligence outsourcing is inextricably linked to the US system of intelligence accountability, and the attention intelligence accountability holders – ranging from private intelligence providers to government officials and policy-makers – devote to contractors. These stakeholders' actions are framed by different incentives, and it is crucial to find ways to keep them invested in the oversight of contractors.

Government accountability holders in the executive branch have seen their role evolve significantly in the last decades. The growth of outsourcing warrants a more active role of manager by intelligence officers. Intelligence contractors need to embrace the true meaning of collaboration, in which successes but also failures are shared. So far, there is little evidence that the private sector is ready to do so, and finding more incentives to foster trust and cooperation, mostly through dialogue, between the public and private sectors remains an important task.

The government's efforts to adapt the accountability regime for contractors were, for the most part, a reaction to accountability problems. This situation emphasises one of the main issues with intelligence accountability: it tends to be reactive. Security practices often run ahead of the law and meaningful oversight, and this reality affects intelligence accountability, especially when dramatic shifts occur in national security priorities. Political involvement and significant government responses typically follow accountability scandals, and even then they tend to be insufficient, not least because they are based on compromises. In the aftermath of 9/11, intelligence accountability holders in the executive and legislative branches did react to a series of scandals that highlighted a number of issues with the oversight of intelligence contracts and contractors. Their accountability responses progressively improved the accountability regime for contractors, but they did not make it perfect. In an ideal world, effective accountability measures would prevent the (re)occurrence of problems, but this is not always possible. More accountability problems are bound to emerge, first at an administrative level, and occasionally at the political level.

The history of intelligence outsourcing raises questions about the factors influencing key accountability holders' willingness to uphold high standards of intelligence accountability, and their capacity to anticipate as best as they can and respond to the occurrence of problems. In times of crisis, government officials tend to focus on duties other than intelligence oversight. From this perspective, the core problem of accountability (and, by extension, of outsourcing) remains the lack of political commitment to systematically oversee the intelligence community and its contractors. There is no obvious solution to this problem in the short term, but in the long term, developing a better public understanding of the uses and limits of intelligence can help to improve democratic accountability.

The main driver of government activity in a democracy is the people. If the people do not understand or care about intelligence accountability, then there is very little chance that policy-makers will be inclined to pass laws and regulations to adapt the US regime of intelligence accountability. The interested public, if it is sizeable and organised enough, can bridge the 'electoral disconnection' and orient the politics of national security intelligence towards significant change, as congressional committees did in the 1970s following growing public concern about the government's intelligence activities.[3] It is the people who decide what is acceptable in a democratic society, and policy-makers cannot afford to take actions that a vast majority of the population would disagree with. However, intelligence rarely generates so much interest that policy-makers are compelled to act and pass a major reform. A number of commentators have drawn attention to the shortfalls of intelligence outsourcing and contributed to raise the issue on the political agenda.[4] Key accountability holders eventually responded and passed a series of measures to better articulate public-private intelligence collaboration.

Pursuing the government's effort to manage public-private intelligence collaboration and to explain its necessity, scope and administration to the public is crucial, as the US intelligence community will continue to rely extensively on contractors in the coming decades.

Greater involvement of wider society in intelligence affairs, through a long-lasting public debate on the functions and structures of the national intelligence effort, is essential to motivating and empowering intelligence accountability holders at the political level.[5] To be clear, most modern democracies continue to lack such a platform. For a more mature debate on intelligence to happen, better and wider public access to intelligence information through increased transparency is necessary. Recent research suggests that Western democracies may have entered a new era of transparency, whether they want it or not.[6] The best way for governments to limit unwanted disclosures is to expand authorised disclosures of information and set up the conditions for a more mature debate about intelligence practices in the twenty-first century. Two specific measures could make public-private intelligence collaboration more transparent: the extension of whistle-blower protections for contractor employees (previous attempts have failed), and the expansion of the FOIA to include the disclosure of standard contractual terms.[7] These measures, though welcome, are insufficient on their own.

In an era of fake news, competing narratives and partisanship, greater public access to raw information will not be enough to improve the public debate on intelligence. Educated commentators in government and wider society have an important role to play in setting a constructive public debate about intelligence affairs and encouraging the secret state to explain itself.[8] Blind support of government policies, or sensationalist reporting that simply discards the significant role played by the federal government and its contractors in national security, though they are a part of the democratic debate, are not particularly helpful and can even hurt public-private intelligence relations and capabilities. This book has sought to develop a more balanced discussion on intelligence contractors, exploring how intelligence functions have been reconfigured and distributed across the public-private divide. This approach sheds light on the diversity of actors involved in core intelligence practices, the complexity of their interactions and the responsibility of government for the state of intelligence outsourcing.

There is no silver bullet that can solve the issues affecting the relationship between the intelligence community and its contractors. Intelligence officials, policy-makers, companies and outsiders need to accept this reality and continue to inform themselves and fine-tune their decisions – for as long as contractors and their principals in government are being watched carefully, outsourcing has the potential to benefit national security without damaging the liberal democratic ideals at the basis of the US Republic. This book has shown that the quality of intelligence accountability and outsourcing are inextricably linked, but not (as is popularly believed) in an entirely negative way. Public-private intelligence successes are not always easy to achieve, but this does not mean that they are completely out of reach.

Notes

1. Constitution of the United States, 1787.
2. De Tocqueville, *Democracy in America*, p. 182.
3. Zegart and Quinn, 'Congressional Intelligence Oversight: The Electoral Disconnection'.
4. See Priest and Arkin, *Top Secret America*; Risen, *Pay Any Price: Greed, Power, and Endless War*; Krishnan, 'US Intelligence Outsourcing and Its Future'.
5. Leander, 'Risk and the Fabrication of Apolitical, Unaccountable Military Markets: The Case of the CIA "Killing Program"', p. 2267.
6. Aldrich and Moran, '"Delayed Disclosure"', pp. 7–8.
7. Dickinson, 'Outsourcing Covert Activities', pp. 532–3; Jenna McLaughlin, 'Giving Intelligence Contractors Whistleblower Protections Doesn't Have to Be "Complicated"', *The Intercept*, 6 November 2015, available at <https://theintercept.com/2015/11/06/giving-intelligence-community-contractors-whistleblower-protections-doesnt-have-to-be-complicated/> (accessed 29 May 2018).
8. Aldrich and Richterova, 'Ambient Accountability: Intelligence Services in Europe and the Decline of State Secrecy', p. 3.

Bibliography

Archives and Primary Source Databases

The Black Vault
CIA Records Search Tool
Cryptome
Declassified Documents Reference System
Digital National Security Archive
Electronic Frontier Foundation
Every CRS Report
Federal Procurement Data System
Federal Register
Federation of American Scientists
Freedom of Information Act
Government Attic
Library of Congress
National Archives, UK
National Archives and Records Administration, United States
National Security Archives, George Washington University
Public Access to Court Electronic Records
US Declassified Documents Online
Wikileaks

Various unclassified documents from the US Congressional Budget Office, Department of the Army, Department of Defense, Department of the Interior, Department of Justice, the Executive Office of the President, the General Service Administration and the Office of the Director of National Intelligence are available online on the websites of these institutions.

Primary Sources (Printed)

Clinton, Bill, and Al Gore, *Putting People First* (New York: Basic Books, 1992).
Dulles, Allen, *The Craft of Intelligence* (New York: Harper & Row, 1963).
Goldman, Lawrence (ed.), *The Federalist Papers* (Oxford: Oxford University Press, 2008).
Lindsey, Robert, *The Falcon and the Snowman: A True Story of Friendship and Espionage* (New York: Simon and Schuster, 1979).
Prince, Erik, with Davin Coburn, *Civilian Warriors. The Inside Story of Blackwater and the Unsung Heroes of the War on Terror* (New York: Portfolio/Penguin, 2013).
Scheuer, Michael, *Imperial Hubris: Why the West Is Losing the War on Terror* (Washington, DC: Potomac Books, 2005).
Stimson, Henry L., *On Active Services in Peace and War* (New York: Harper, 1948).
Tenet, George, *At the Center of the Storm: My Years at the CIA* (London: Harper Press, 2007).
Zelikow, Philip et al. (eds), *The 9/11 Commission Report: Final Report of the National Commission on Terrorist Attacks Upon the United States* (New York: W.W. Norton, 2004).

Secondary Sources

Books

Abrahamsen, Rita, and Michael Williams, *Security Beyond the State: Private Security in International Politics* (Cambridge: Cambridge University Press, 2010).
Adams, Gordon, *The Politics of Defense Contracting: The Iron Triangle* (New York: Council on Economic Priorities, 1981).
Aid, Matthew, *The Secret Sentry: The Untold History of the National Security Agency* (New York: Bloomsbury Press, 2010).
Andrew, Christopher, *For the President's Eyes Only: Secret Intelligence and the American Presidency from Washington to Bush* (New York: Harper Perennial, 1995).
Andrew, Christopher, *The Defence of the Realm: Authorized History of MI5* (London: Allen Lane, 2009).

Bibliography

Andrew, Christopher, and Vasili Mitrokhin, *The Mitrokhin Archive: The KGB in Europe and the West* (London: Allen Lane, 1999).

Arquilla, John, and David Ronfeldt, *Networks and Netwars: The Future of Terror, Crime, and Militancy* (Santa Monica, CA: RAND, 2001).

Avant, Deborah, *The Market for Force: The Consequences of Privatizing Security* (Cambridge: Cambridge University Press, 2005).

Bamford, James, *The Shadow Factory* (New York: Doubleday, 2008).

Becker, Carl, *The Declaration of Independence: A Study in the History of Political Ideas* (New York: Peter Smith, 1933).

Behn, Robert D., *Rethinking Democratic Accountability* (Washington, DC: Brookings Institution, 2001).

Belko, Michael E., *Government Venture Capital: A Case Study of the In-Q-Tel Model* (Wright Patterson Air Force Base, OH: Air Force Institute of Technology, 2004).

Bell, William G., *Secretaries of War and Secretaries of the Army: Portraits and Biographical Sketches* (Washington, DC: Center For Military History, 1992).

Best, Jacqueline, and Alexandra Gheciu (eds), *The Return of the Public in Global Governance* (Cambridge: Cambridge University Press, 2015).

Born, Hans, and Ian Leigh, *Making Intelligence Accountable: Legal Standards and Best Practice for Oversight of Intelligence Agencies* (Oslo: Publishing House of the Parliament of Norway, 2005).

Brodie, Bernard, *Strategy in the Missile Age* (Santa Monica, CA: RAND Corporation, 1959).

Bruneau, Thomas, *Patriots for Profit: Contractors and the Military in US National Security* (Stanford: Stanford University Press, 2011).

Chesterman, Simon, *One Nation Under Surveillance: A New Social Contract to Defend Freedom Without Sacrificing Liberty* (Oxford: Oxford University Press, 2011).

Craig, Campbell, and Fredrik Logevall, *America's Cold War. The Politics of Insecurity* (London: Belknap Press of Harvard University Press, 2009).

de Tocqueville, Alexis, *Democracy in America*, edited by Bruce Frohnen (Washington, DC: Regnery Publishing, 2003).

Dempsey, John S., and Linda S. Forst, *An Introduction to Policing* (New York: Delmar Cengage Learning, 2009).

Dickinson, Laura, *Outsourcing War and Peace* (London: Yale University Press, 2011).

Donahue, John D., *The Privatization Decision: Public Ends, Private Means* (New York: Basic Books, 1989).

Dunigan, Molly, *Victory for Hire: Private Security Companies' Impact on Military Effectiveness* (Stanford: Stanford University Press, 2011).

Dunlay, Thomas W., *Wolves for the Blue Soldiers: Indian Scouts and Auxiliaries with the United States Army, 1860–90* (Lincoln: University of Nebraska Press, 1982).

Durbin, Brent, *The CIA and the Politics of US Intelligence Reform* (Cambridge: Cambridge University Press, 2017).

Durie, Bruce (ed.), *The Pinkerton Casebook* (Edinburgh: Mercat Press, 2007).

Elkins, Dan, *Managing Intelligence Resources* (Alexandria, VA: DWE Press, 2004).

Engelbrecht, H. C., and F. C. Hanighen, *Merchants of Death: A Study of the International Armament Industry* (New York: Dodd, Mead & Company, 1934).

Epstein, Edward Jay, *How America Lost Its Secrets: Edward Snowden, the Man and the Theft* (New York: Alfred A. Knopf, 2017).

Feigenbaum, Harvey, Jeffrey Henig, and Chris Hamnett, *Shrinking the State: the Political Underpinnings of Privatization* (Cambridge: Cambridge University Press, 1998).

Fine, Sidney, *Laissez-faire and the General-Welfare State* (Ann Arbor: University of Michigan Press, 1956).

Finnegan, John Patrick, *Military Intelligence* (Washington, DC: Centre of Military History, 1998).

Fishel, Edwin C., *The Secret War for the Union: The Untold Story of Military Intelligence in the Civil War* (Boston, MA: Houghton Mifflin, 1996).

Foley, Michael, *American Credo: The Place of Ideas in US Politics* (Oxford: Oxford University Press, 2007).

Forcade, Olivier, and Sébastien Laurent, *Secrets d'Etat: Pouvoirs et renseignement dans le monde contemporain* (Paris: Armand Colin, 2005).

Forrer, John J., James Edwin Kee, and Eric Boyer, *Governing Cross-Sector Collaboration* (San Francisco: Jossey-Bass, 2014).

Fox, J. Ronald, *Defense Acquisition Reform, 1960–2009: An Elusive Goal* (Washington, DC: Center of Military History, 2011).

Goldman, Zachary K., and Samuel J. Rascoff, *Global Intelligence Oversight: Governing Security in the Twenty-First Century* (Oxford: Oxford University Press, 2016).

Goldsmith, Stephen, and William D. Eggers, *Governing by Network* (Washington, DC: Brookings Institution Press, 2004).

Hanks, Christopher H., et al., *Reexamining Military Acquisition Reform: Are We There Yet?* (Santa Monica, CA: Rand Arroyo Center, 2005).
Herbig, Katherine L., *The Expanding Spectrum of Espionage by Americans, 1947–2015* (Seaside, CA: Defense Personnel and Security Research Center, 2017).
Hougan, Jim, *Spooks: The Haunting of America – The Private Use of Secret Agents* (New York: William Morrow and Company, Inc., 1978).
Hughes, Owen E., *Public Management and Administration: An Introduction* (New York: Palgrave Macmillan, 2012).
Hughes, Solomon, *War on Terror, Inc.: Corporate Profiteering from the Politics of Fear* (London: Verso, 2007).
Javers, Eamon, *Broker, Trader, Lawyer, Spy: Inside the Secret World of Corporate Espionage* (New York: Harper, 2010).
Jeffery, Keith, *MI6: The History of the Secret Intelligence Service 1909–1949* (London: Bloomsbury, 2010).
Jeffreys-Jones, Rhodri, *American Espionage: From Secret Service to CIA* (New York: The Free Press, 1977).
Jeffreys-Jones, Rhodri, *The CIA and American Democracy* (New Haven and London: Yale University Press, 2003).
Jeffreys-Jones, Rhodri, *The FBI: A History* (New Haven and London: Yale University Press, 2007).
Jeffreys-Jones, Rhodri, *The American Left: Its Impact on Politics and Society since 1900* (Edinburgh: Edinburgh University Press, 2013).
Johnson, Loch K., *A Season of Inquiry: The Senate Intelligence Investigation* (Lexington: The University Press of Kentucky, 1985).
Johnson, Loch K., *National Security Intelligence: Secret Operations in Defense of the Democracies* (Cambridge: Polity, 2012).
Jones, Wilbur D., Jr., *Arming the Eagle: A History of US Weapons Acquisition Since 1775* (Fort Belvoir, VA: Defense Systems Management College Press, 1999).
Jordan, Amos, et al., *American National Security* (Baltimore, MD: John Hopkins University Press, 2009).
Kahn, Herman, *The Nature and Feasibility of War and Deterrence* (Santa Monica, CA: RAND Corporation, 1960).
Kalifa, Dominique, *Naissance de la Police Privée. Détectives et agences de recherches en France. 1832–1842* (Paris: Plon, 2000).
Kaplan, Fred, *The Wizards of Armageddon* (Stanford: Stanford University Press, 1983).

Kingdon, John, *Agendas, Alternatives, and Public Policies* (New York: HarperCollins, 1995).
Kinsey, Christopher, *Corporate Soldiers and International Security* (London: Routledge, 2006).
Kinsey, Christopher, and Malcolm Hugh Patterson (eds), *Contractors and War: The Transformation of US Expeditionary Operations* (Stanford, CA: Stanford University Press, 2012).
Krahmann, Elke, *States, Citizens and the Privatization of Security* (Cambridge: Cambridge University Press, 2010).
Laurent, Sébastien, *Politiques de l'ombre. État, renseignement et surveillance en France* (Paris: Fayard, 2009).
Ledbetter, James, *Unwarranted Influence: Dwight D. Eisenhower and the Military Industrial Complex* (New Haven, CT: Yale University Press, 2011).
Leites, Nathan, *The Operational Code of the Politburo* (New York: McGraw-Hill Book Company, Inc., 1951).
Lester, Genevieve, *When Should State Secrets Stay Secret?* (Cambridge: Cambridge University Press, 2015).
Lewis, Adrian R., *The American Culture of War: The History of US Military Force From World War II to Operation Iraqi Freedom* (New York: Routledge, 2006).
Lewis, Jonathan E., *Spy Capitalism: ITEK and the CIA* (New Haven, CT: Yale University Press, 2002).
Lipsky, Michael, *Street-level Bureaucracy: Dilemmas of the Individual in Public Services* (New York: Russell Sage Foundation, 1980).
Lowenthal, Mark, *Intelligence: From Secrets to Policy* (Washington, DC: CQ Press, 2015).
Lustgarten, Laurence, and Ian Leigh, *In From the Cold: National Security and Parliamentary Democracy* (Oxford: Clarendon Press, 1994).
McGroddy, James C., and Herbert S. Lin, *A Review of the FBI's Trilogy Information Technology Modernization Program* (Washington, DC: The National Academies Press, 2004).
MacKay, James, *Allan Pinkerton: The Eye Who Never Slept* (Edinburgh: Mainstream Publishing Company, 1996).
McKay, David, *American Politics and Society* (Oxford: Blackwell, 1997).
McNeill, William H., *The Pursuit of Power* (Chicago: The University of Chicago Press, 1982).
Mahnken, Thomas G., *Technology and the American Way of War since 1945* (New York: Columbia University Press, 2010).

Maogoto, Jackson, Virginia Newell, and Benedict Sheehy, *Legal Control of the Private Military Corporation* (Basingstoke: Palgrave Macmillan, 2009).

Mara, Andrew S., *Maximizing the Returns of Government Venture Capital Programs* (Washington, DC: National Defense University, 2011).

Margetts, Helen, *Information Technology in Government* (London: Routledge, 2003).

Marone, James A., *Hellfire Nation: The Politics of Sin in American History* (New Haven, CT: Yale University Press, 2004).

Meyer, Thomas, *The Theory of Social Democracy* (Cambridge: Cambridge University Press, 2007).

Morgan, Richard E., *Domestic Intelligence: Monitoring Dissent in America* (London: University of Texas Press, 1980).

Morn, Frank, *The Eye That Never Sleeps: A History of the Pinkerton National Detective Agency* (Bloomington: Indiana University Press, 1982).

Morton, James, *The First Detective: The Life and Revolutionary Times of Eugène-Francois Vidocq, Criminal, Spy and Private Eye* (London: Ebury Press, 2004).

Nagl, John, *Learning to Eat Soup with a Knife: Counterinsurgency Lessons from Malaya, Vietnam, and Iraq* (Chicago: Chicago University Press, 2005).

Nagle, James F., *A History of Government Contracting* (Washington, DC: The George Washington University, 1992).

Nemfakos, Charles et al., *Workforce Planning in the Intelligence Community* (Santa Monica, CA: RAND, 2013).

Neustadt, Richard E., *Presidential Power and the Modern Presidents: The Politics of Leadership from Roosevelt to Reagan* (New York: Free Press, 1990).

O'Toole, George, *The Private Sector: Private Spies, Rent-a-Cops, and the Police-Industrial Complex* (New York: W. W. Norton & Company, Inc., 1978).

Overholser, Genevar, and Kathleen Hall Jamieson, *Institutions of American Democracy: The Press* (New York: Oxford University Press, 2005).

Pedlow, Gregory W., and Donald E. Welzenbach, *The CIA and the U-2 Program, 1954–1974* (Langley, VA: Central Intelligence Agency, 1998).

Peltier, Thomas R., *Information Security Policies, Procedures, and Standards* (Boca Raton: CRC Press, 2016).

Pelton, Robert Young, *Licensed to Kill: Hired Guns in the War on Terror* (New York: Three Rivers Press, 2007).
Percy, Sarah, *Mercenaries. The History of a Norm in International Relations* (Oxford: Oxford University Press, 2007).
Pocock, Christopher, *The U-2 Spyplane: Toward the Unknown, A New History of the Early Years* (Atglen, PA: Schiffer Military History, 2000).
Polanyi, Karl, *The Great Transformation: The Political and Economic Origins of Our Time* (Boston, MA: Beacon Press, 1968).
Polenberg, Richard, *The Era of Franklin D. Roosevelt, 1933–1945: A Brief History with Documents* (New York: St Martin's Press, 2000).
Posner, Richard A., *Uncertain Shield: The US Intelligence System in the Throes of Reform* (Oxford: Rowman and Littlefield, 2006).
Prados, John, *Presidents' Secret Wars: CIA and Pentagon Covert Operations from World War II through Iranscam* (New York: William Morrow, 1986).
Priest, Dana, and William Arkin, *Top Secret America: The Rise of the New American Security State* (New York: Little, Brown and Company, 2011).
Proxmire, William, *Report from Wasteland: America's Military-Industrial Complex* (New York: Praeger, 1970).
Ratcliffe, Jerry, *Intelligence-led Policing* (Cullompton: Willan Publishing, 2008).
Richelson, Jeffrey, *A Century of Spies* (Oxford: Oxford University Press, 1995).
Risen, James, *Pay Any Price: Greed, Power, and Endless War* (New York: Mifflin Harcourt, 2014).
Roland, Alex, *The Military-Industrial Complex* (Washington, DC: American Historical Association, 2001).
Rostker, Bernard D., *A Call to Revitalize the Engines of Government* (Santa Monica, CA: RAND, 2008).
Rovner, Joshua, *Fixing the Facts: National Security and the Politics of Intelligence* (Ithaca: Cornell University Press, 2011).
Ruffner, Kevin C., *CORONA: America's First Satellite Program* (Washington, DC: Center for the Study of Intelligence, 1995).
Savas, E. S., *Privatization and Public-Private Partnerships* (New York: Chatham House Publishers, 2000).
Scahill, Jeremy, *Blackwater. The Rise of the World's Most Powerful Mercenary Army* (New York: Nation Books, 2008).

Seldes, George, *Iron, Blood and Profits* (New York: Harper and Brothers, 1934).

Shorrock, Tim, *Spies for Hire: The Secret World of Intelligence Outsourcing* (New York: Simon and Schuster, 2008).

Sims, Jennifer E., and Burton Gerber, *Transforming US Intelligence* (Washington, DC: Georgetown University Press, 2005).

Singer, Peter W., *Corporate Warriors: The Rise of the Privatized Military Industry* (New York: Cornell University Press, 2003).

Snider, L. Britt, *The Agency and the Hill: CIA's Relationship with Congress, 1946–2004* (Washington, DC: Center for the Study of Intelligence, 2008).

Sparks, David S. (ed.), *Inside Lincoln's Army. The Diary of Marsena Rudolph Patrick, Provost Marshal General, Army of the Potomac* (New York: A. S. Barnes & Company, 1964).

Stanger, Allison, *One Nation Under Contract: The Outsourcing of American Power and the Future of Foreign Policy* (London: Yale University Press, 2009).

Sulick, Michael J., *American Spies: Espionage against the United States from the Cold War to the Present* (Washington, DC: Georgetown University Press, 2013).

Thomson, Janice E., *Mercenaries, Pirates and Sovereigns: State-Building and Extraterritorial Violence in Early Modern Europe* (Princeton, NJ: Princeton University Press, 1994).

Tudda, Chris, *The Truth is Our Weapon: The Rhetorical Diplomacy of Dwight E. Eisenhower and John Foster Dulles* (Baton Rouge: Louisiana State University Press, 2006).

Verkuil, Paul, *Outsourcing Sovereignty: Why Privatization of Government Functions Threatens Democracy and What We Can Do about It* (Cambridge: Cambridge University Press, 2007).

Voelz, Glenn J., *Managing the Private Spies: The Use of Commercial Augmentation for Intelligence Operations* (Washington, DC: MNIC Press, 2006).

Wagner, Arthur L., *The Service of Security and Information* (Washington, DC: James L. Chapman, 1893).

Warner, Michael, and J. Kenneth McDonald, *US Intelligence Community Reform Studies Since 1947* (Washington, DC: Center for the Study of Intelligence, 2005).

Weigley, Russel F., *The American Way of War: A History of United States Military Strategy and Policy* (Bloomington: Indiana University Press, 1973).

Wilford, Hugh, *The Mighty Wurlitzer: How the CIA Played America* (Cambridge, MA: Harvard University Press, 2008).
Wohlstetter, Albert, *Delicate Balance of Terror* (Santa Monica, CA: RAND Corporation, 1958).
Wolff, Leon, *Lockout! The Story of the Homestead Strike of 1892* (New York: Harper & Row, 1965).
Wood, Gordon S., *The Creation of the American Republic, 1776–1787* (London: University of North Carolina Press, 1993).
Zegart, Amy B., *Spying Blind: The CIA, the FBI, and the Origins of 9/11* (Princeton: Princeton University Press, 2007).
Zoller, Élisabeth, *Introduction au Droit Public* (Paris: Dalloz, 2006).

Academic Journal Articles, Book Chapters and Papers

Ackerman, Robert K., 'Intelligence Tries a New Public-private Partnership', *Signal*, 15 October 2009: 53–5.
Aid, Matthew M., 'Prometheus Embattled', in Loch K. Johnson (ed.), *Strategic Intelligence: Vol.2* (London: Praeger Security International, 2007), pp. 41–60.
Aldrich, Richard, 'Beyond the Vigilant State: Globalisation and Intelligence', *Review of International Studies* 35/4 (2009): 892–902.
Aldrich, Richard, 'Regulation by Revelation? Intelligence, Transparency and the Media', in Robert Dover and Michael Goodman (eds), *Spinning Intelligence: Why Intelligence needs the Media, Why the Media Needs Intelligence* (New York: Columbia University Press, 2009), pp. 13–36.
Aldrich, Richard, and Christopher Moran, '"Delayed Disclosure": National Security, Whistle-Blowers and the Nature of Secrecy', *Political Studies* (early online publication 2018): 1–16.
Aldrich, Richard, and Daniela Richterova, 'Ambient Accountability: Intelligence Services in Europe and the Decline of State Secrecy', *West European Politics* 41/4 (2018): 1003–24.
Andén-Papadopoulos, Kari, 'The Abu Ghraib Torture Photograph: New Frames, Visual Culture, and the Power of Images', *Journalism* 9/1 (2008): 5–30.
Anderson, Evan E., and Joobin Choobineh, 'Enterprise Information Security Strategies', *Computers & Security* 27 (2008): 22–9.
Armstrong, Matt, 'In-sourcing the Tools of National Power for Success and Security', *Small Wars Journal*, 3 January 2008.
Baber, Walter F., 'Privatizing Public Management: The Grace Commission and Its Critics', in Steve H. Hanke (ed.), *Prospects for*

Privatization (New York: The Academy of Political Science, 1987), pp. 153–63.

Barthélemy, Jérôme, 'The Seven Deadly Sins of Outsourcing', *Academy of Management Executive* 17/2 (2003): 87–100.

Bean, Hamilton, 'Privatizing Intelligence', in Rita Abrahamsen and Anna Leander (eds), *Routledge Handbook of Private Security Studies* (New York: Routledge, 2016), pp. 79–88.

Berteau, David, et al., 'DoD Workforce Cost Realism Assessment', Report of the CSIS Defense-Industrial Initiatives Group, May 2011.

Betts, Richard K., 'The New Politics of Intelligence: Will Reforms Work This Time?', *Foreign Affairs* 83/3 (2004): 2–9.

Born, Hans, and Ian Leigh, *Democratic Accountability of Intelligence Services*, DCAF Policy Paper no.19 (2007), pp. 1–20.

Bovaird, Tony, 'Public-Private Partnerships: From Contested Concepts to Prevalent Practice', *International Review of Administrative Sciences* 70/2 (2004): 199–215.

Bovens, Mark, 'Analysing and Assessing Accountability: A Conceptual Framework', *European Law Journal* 13/4 (2007): 447–68.

Bowman, Marion E., 'Legal Issues of Outsourcing Military Functions in Wartime', in John Moore and Robert F. Turner (eds), *Legal Issues in the Struggle Against Terror* (Durham, NC: Carolina Academic Press, 2010), pp. 411–35.

Bradley, Omar, 'Address at the Third National Industry Army Day Conference', *The Antiaircraft Journal* 92/3 (1949): 13.

Bruce, James B., 'Laws and Leak of Classified Intelligence: The Consequences of Permissive Neglect', *Studies in Intelligence* 47/1 (2003): 39–49.

Bruneau, Thomas C., 'Contracting Out Security', *Journal of Strategic Studies* 36/5 (2012): 638–65.

Bukharin, Oleg, 'US Atomic Energy Intelligence against the Soviet Target, 1945–1970', *Intelligence and National Security* 19/4 (2004): 655–79.

Busch, Nathan E., and Austen D. Givens, 'Public-Private Partnerships in Homeland Security: Opportunities and Challenges', *Homeland Security Affairs* 8 (2012): 1–24.

Butt, Stephen, *Outsourcing Intelligence: The Relationship Between the State and Private Intelligence in Post-Apartheid South Africa*, masters thesis, University of Cape Town, South Africa, 2010.

Caldwell, Christopher M., 'Privatized Information Gathering: Just War Theory and Morality', *International Journal of Intelligence Ethics* 1/2 (2010): 32–45.

Camm, Frank, 'How to Decide When a Contractor Source Is Better to Use than a Government Source', in Kinsey and Patterson (eds), *Contractors and War*, pp. 233–54.

Caparini, Marina, 'Applying a Security Governance Perspective to the Privatisation of Security', in Alan Bryden and Marina Caparini (eds), *Private Actors and Security Governance* (Geneva: LIT & DCAF, 2006), pp. 263–83.

Caparini, Marina, 'Controlling and Overseeing Intelligence Services in Democratic States', in Born and Leigh (eds), *Democratic Control of Intelligence Services* (2007), pp. 3–24.

Carver, George A., 'Intelligence in the Age of Glasnost', *Foreign Affairs* 69/3 (1990): 147–66.

Central Intelligence Agency, 'Breaking through Technological Barriers', available at <https://www.cia.gov/library/center-for-the-study-of-intelligence/csi-publications/books-and-monographs/a-12/breaking-through-technological-barriers.html> (accessed 28 May 2018).

Central Intelligence Agency, 'Intelligence in the Civil War', available at <https://www.cia.gov/library/publications/intelligence-history/civil-war> (accessed 28 May 2018).

Central Intelligence Agency, 'Intelligence in the War of Independence: Intelligence Operations', available at <https://www.cia.gov/library/publications/intelligence-history/intelligence> (accessed 28 May 2018).

Central Intelligence Agency, 'Saving Mr Lincoln', in 'Intelligence in the Civil War', available at <https://www.cia.gov/library/publications/intelligence-history/civil-war> (accessed 28 May 2018).

Chatterjee, Pratap, *Outsourcing Intelligence in Iraq: A CorpWatch Report on L-3/Titan*, December 2008.

Chesterman, Simon, '"We Can't Spy if We Can't Buy": The Privatization of Intelligence and the Limits of Outsourcing "Inherently Governmental Functions"', *The European Journal of International Law* 19/5 (2008): 1055–74.

Chesterman, Simon, and Angelina Fisher, 'Conclusion: Private Security, Public Order', in Simon Chesterman and Angelina Fisher (eds), *Private Security, Public Order* (Oxford: Oxford University Press, 2009), pp. 222–6.

Churchill, Ward, 'From the Pinkertons to the PATRIOT Act: The Trajectory of Political Policing in the United States, 1870 to the Present', *The New Centennial Review* 4/1 (2004): 1–72.

Cohen, Raphael S., 'Putting a Human and Historical Face on Intelligence Contracting', *Orbis* 54/2 (2010): 232–51.

Corn, Geoffrey S., 'Contractors and the Law', in Christopher Kinsey and Malcolm Hugh Patterson (eds), *Contractors and War: The Transformation of US Expeditionary Operations* (Stanford, CA: Stanford University Press, 2012), pp. 157–83.

Crampton, Jeremy W., Susan M. Roberts and Ate Poorthuis, 'The New Political Economy of Geographical Intelligence', *Annals of the Association of American Geographers* 104/1 (2014): 196–214.

Daniel Zelik, Emily S. Patterson and David D. Woods, 'Understanding Rigor in Information Analysis', Proceedings of the Eighth International NDM Conference, Pacific Grove, CA, June 2007.

Davies, Philip H. J., 'Intelligence and the Machinery of Government: Conceptualizing the Intelligence Community', *Public Policy and Administration* 25/1 (2010): 29–46.

DCAF Intelligence Working Group, 'Intelligence Practice and Democratic Oversight – A Practitioner's View', *DCAF Occasional Papers No.* 3 (2003): 1–80.

de Nevers, Renée, '(Self) Regulating War? Voluntary Regulation and the Private Security Industry', *Security Studies* 18/3 (2009): 479–516.

Dickinson, Laura, 'Public Law Values in a Privatized World', *The Yale Journal of International Law* 31 (2006): 383–426.

Dickinson, Laura, 'Outsourcing Covert Activities', *Journal of National Security Law & Policy* 5/2 (2012): 135–237.

Dickson, Brice, 'Counter-Insurgency and Human Rights in Northern Ireland', *Journal of Strategic Studies* 32/3 (2009): 475–93.

Driessnac, John, and David King, 'An Initial Look at Technology and Institutions on Defense Industry Consolidation', *Acquisition Review Journal* 35 (2004): 63–77.

Dujmovic, Nicholas, 'Getting CIA History Right: The Informal Partnership between Agency Historians and Outside Scholars', *Intelligence and National Security* 26/2–3 (2011): 228–45.

Duke, Misty, and Damien Van Puyvelde, 'The Science of Interrogation: What Research Tells Us about "Enhanced Interrogation"', *International Journal of Intelligence and CounterIntelligence* 30/2 (2017): 310–39.

Elrington, C. R. (ed.), 'Paddington: Paddington Green', *A History of the County of Middlesex: Volume 9: Hampstead, Paddington* (1989), pp. 185–90, available at <http://www.british-history.ac.uk/report.aspx?compid=22663> (accessed 28 May 2018).

Gailmard, Sean, 'Accountability and Principal-Agent Theory', in Mark Bovens, Robert E. Goodin, and Thomas Schilemans (eds), *Oxford*

Handbook of Public Accountability (Oxford: Oxford University Press, 2014), pp. 90–105.

Gale, Jacob B., 'Intelligence Outsourcing in the US Department of Defense: Theory, Practice, and Implications', thesis submitted to the Faculty of the Graduate School of Arts and Sciences of Georgetown University in partial fulfilment of the requirements for the degree of Master of Arts in Security Studies, 15 April 2011, Washington, DC.

Gill, Peter, 'Not Just Joining the Dots But Crossing the Borders and Bridging the Voids: Constructing Security Networks after 11 September 2001', *Policing and Society* 16/1 (2006): 27–49.

Gillard, Emanuela-Chiara, 'Business Goes to War: Private Military/Security Companies and International Humanitarian Law', *International Review of the Red Cross* 88/863 (2006): 525–72.

Grant, Ruth W., and Robert O. Keohane, 'Accountability and Abuses of Power in World Politics', *American Political Science Review* 99/1 (2005): 29–43.

Greer, Kenneth E., 'Corona', *Studies in Intelligence* 17 (1973): 6–9.

Guttman, Dan, 'Public Purpose and Private Service: The Twentieth Century Culture of Contracting Out and the Evolving Law of Diffused Sovereignty', *Administrative Law Review* 52/3 (2000): 859–926.

Guttman, Dan, 'Government by Contract: The White House Needs Capacity to Review and Revise the Legacy of 20th Century Reform', National Academy of Public Administration, Issue Paper on Presidential Management Capacity to Respond to 21st Century Challenges, August 2008.

Haines, Gerald K., 'The Pike Committee Investigations and the CIA: Looking for a Rogue Elephant', *Studies in Intelligence* (1998), pp. 81–92.

Hansen, Morten, 'Intelligence Contracting: On the Motivations, Interests, and Capabilities of Core Personnel Contractors in the US Intelligence Community', *Intelligence and National Security* 29/1 (2013): 58–81.

Harris, Shane, 'Spider and the Flies', *Government Executive* 37/4, 15 March 2005: 62.

Harris, Shane, 'Intelligence Incorporated', *Government Executive* 37/8, 15 May 2005: 46.

Hastedt, Glenn, 'Foreign Policy by Commission: Reforming the Intelligence Community', *Intelligence and National Security* 22/4 (2007): 443–72.

Hastedt, Glenn, 'An *INS* Special Forum: Implications of the Snowden Leaks', *Intelligence and National Security* 29/6 (2014): 798–9.

Henig, Jeffrey R., 'Privatization in the United States: Theory and Practice', *Political Science Quarterly* 104/4 (1989): 649–70.

Hillebrand, Claudia, 'The Role of News Media in Intelligence Oversight', *Intelligence and National Security* 27/5 (2012): 689–706.

Hogg, Bernard, 'Public Reaction to Pinkertonism and the Labor Question', *Pennsylvania History* 11/3 (1944): 171–99.

Hoogenboom, Bob, 'Grey Intelligence', *Crime Law and Social Change* 45/4–5 (2006): 373–81.

Horwitz, Morton J., 'The History of the Public/Private Distinction', *University of Pennsylvania Law Review* 130/6 (1982): 1423–8.

Issacharoff, Samuel, 'Political Safeguards in Democracies at War', *Oxford Journal of Legal Studies* 29/2 (2009): 189–214.

Johnson, Loch K., 'The Contemporary Presidency: Presidents, Lawmakers, and Spies: Intelligence Accountability in the United States', *Presidential Studies Quarterly* 34/4 (2004): 828–37.

Johnson, Loch K., 'Accountability and America's Secret Foreign Policy: Keeping a Legislative Eye on the Central Intelligence Agency', *Foreign Policy Analysis* 1/1 (2005): 99–120.

Johnson, Loch K., 'Governing in the Absence of Angels: On the Practice of Intelligence Accountability in the United States', in Hans Born, Loch Johnson and Ian Leigh (eds), *Who's Watching the Spies? Establishing Intelligence Service Accountability* (Dulles, VA: Potomac Books, 2005), pp. 57–78.

Johnson, Loch K., 'A Shock Theory of Congressional Accountability for Intelligence', in Loch K. Johnson (ed.), *Handbook of Intelligence Studies* (London: Routledge, 2009), pp. 343–60.

Johnson, Loch K., 'Intelligence Shocks, Media Coverage, and Congressional Accountability, 1947–2012', *Journal of Intelligence History* 13/1 (2014): 1–21.

Johnson, Loch K., 'A Conversation with James R. Clapper, Jr., The Director of National Intelligence in the United States', *Intelligence and National Security* 30/1 (2015): 1–25.

Jones, Calvert, 'Intelligence Reform: The Logic of Information Sharing', *Intelligence and National Security* 22/3 (2007): 384–401.

Kahn, David, 'The Intelligence Failure of Pearl Harbor', *Foreign Affairs* 70/5 (1991): 136–52.

Khattab, Mohab Tarek, 'Revised Circular A-76: Embracing Flawed Methodologies', *Public Contract Law Journal* 34/3 (2005): 469–520.

Kim, Yong Woon, and Trevor L. Brown, 'The Importance of Contract Design', *Public Administration Review* 72/5 (2012): 687–96.

Koistinen, Paul A. C., 'The "Industrial-Military Complex" in Historical Perspective: World War I', *Business History Review* 41 (1967): 375–403.

Koistinen, Paul A. C., 'The "Industrial-Military Complex" in Historical Perspective: The InterWar Years', *The Journal of American History* 56/4 (1970): 819–39.

Krishnan, Armin, 'US Intelligence Outsourcing and Its Future', *Brown Journal in World Affairs* 18/1 (2011): 195–211.

Lahneman, William, 'Outsourcing the IC's Stovepipes', *International Journal of Intelligence and CounterIntelligence* 16/4 (2003): 573–93.

Lavallee, Tara, 'Globalizing the Iron Triangle: Policy-making within the US Defense Industrial Sector', *Defense & Security Analysis* 19/2 (2003): 149–64.

Leander, Anna, 'The Power to Construct International Security: On the Significance of Private Military and Security Companies', *Millennium: Journal of International Studies* 33/3 (2005): 803–26.

Leander, Anna, 'Risk and the Fabrication of Apolitical, Unaccountable Military Markets: The Case of the CIA "Killing Program"', *Review of International Studies* 37/5 (2011): 2253–68.

Lerner, Josh et al., 'In-Q-Tel', *Harvard Business Review*, 25 May 2005: 1–20.

Lotz, George B., 'The United States Department of Defense Intelligence Oversight Programme: Balancing National Security and Constitutional Rights', in Hans Born and Marina Caparini (eds), *Democratic Control of Intelligence Services: Containing Rogue Elephants* (London: Aldershot, 2007), pp. 109–24.

Louie, Gilman, 'Panel: Intelligence and the Private Sector', transcript from the *Ethos and Profession of Intelligence* conference held at Georgetown University, 11 June 2014, Washington, DC.

Manget, Frederick F., 'Intelligence and the Rise of Judicial Intervention: Another System of Oversight', *Studies in Intelligence* 39/5 (1996): 43–53.

Mashhadi, Omid, Matthew Riggins, Teezar Firmansyah, Ari Kantrowitz and Roger London, 'In-Q-Tel as an Early Stage Investment Model', *Chesapeake Crescent Initiative* (2009), pp. 1–14.

McCubbins, Mathew D., and Thomas Schwartz, 'Congressional Oversight Overlooked: Police Patrols and Fire Alarms', *American Journal of Political Science* 28/1 (1984): 165–79.

McIvor, Arthur, '"A Crusade for Capitalism": The Economic League, 1919–39', *Contemporary History* 23/4 (1988): 631–55.

Michaels, Jon D., 'Beyond Accountability: The Constitutional, Democratic, and Strategic Problems with Privatizing War', *Washington Law Review* 82/3 (2004): 1001–127.

Michaels, Jon D., 'All the President's Spies: Private-Public Intelligence Partnerships in the War on Terror', *California Law Review* 96/4 (2008): 901–66.

Michaels, Jon D., 'The (Willingly) Fettered Executive: Presidential Spinoffs in National Security Domains and Beyond', *Virginia Law Review* 97/4 (2011): 801–98.

Mistry, Kaeten, 'Narrating Covert Action: the CIA, Historiography and the Cold War', in Christopher Moran and Christopher Murphy (eds), *Intelligence Studies in Britain and the US: Historiography since 1945* (Edinburgh: Edinburgh University Press, 2013): 111–28.

Molzahn, Wendy, 'The CIA's In-Q-Tel Model: Its Applicability', *Acquisition Review Quarterly* (2003): 47–61.

Mugan, Richard, '"Accountability": An Ever-Expanding Concept?', *Public Administration* 78/3 (2000): 555–73.

Nguyen, Vinh, 'Current Trends in Intelligence Outsourcing Affect Work Force Stability', *Signal* 62/4 (2006): 77.

Page, Benjamin I., and Robert Y. Shapiro, 'Effects of Public Opinion on Policy', *American Political Science Review* 77/1 (1983): 175–90.

Parmar, Inderjeet, 'Conceptualising the State-Private Network in American Foreign Policy', in Helen Laville and Hugh Wilford (eds), *The US Government, Citizen Groups and The Cold War: The state-private network* (London: Routledge, 2006), pp. 13–28.

Percy, Sarah, 'Regulating the Private Security Industry', *Adelphi Paper* 384 (2006): 1–76.

Perrin, Benjamin, 'Promoting Compliance of Private Security and Military Companies with International Humanitarian Law', *International Review of the Red Cross* 88/863 (2006): 613–36.

Petersen, Karen Lund, 'Terrorism: When Risk Meets Security', *Alternatives: Global, Local, Political* 33/2 (2008): 173–90.

Pillar, Paul R., 'Intelligence, Policy, and the War in Iraq', *Foreign Affairs* 85/2 (2006): 15–27.

Pillar, Paul R., 'Adapting Intelligence to Changing Issues', in Loch K. Johnson (ed.), *Handbook of Intelligence Studies* (New York: Routledge, 2009): 148–62.

Powers, Richard Gid, 'Introduction', in Daniel P. Moynihan, *Secrecy: The American Experience* (London: Yale University Press, 1998), pp. 1–58.

Price, David E., 'Private Contractors, Public Consequences: The Need for an Effective Criminal Justice Framework', in Kinsey and Patterson, *Contractors and War*, pp. 205–30.

Radsan, A. John, '*Sed Quis Custodiet Ipsos Custodes*: The CIA's Office of General Counsel?', *Journal of National Security Law & Policy* 2/2 (2008): 201–55.

Reinders, Robert, 'Militia and Public Order in Nineteenth-Century America', *American Studies* 11/1 (1977): 81–101.

Ricchiardi, Sherry, 'Missed Signals', *American Journalism Review* 26/4 (2004): 22–9.

Romzek, Barbara S., and Melvin J. Dubnick, 'Accountability in the Public Sector: Lessons from the Challenger Tragedy', *Public Administration Review* 47/3 (1987): 227–38.

Roper, James E., 'Using Private Corporations to Conduct Intelligence Activities for National Security Purposes: An Ethical Appraisal', *International Journal of Intelligence Ethics* 1/2 (2010): 46–73.

Rose, P. K., 'The Founding Fathers of American Intelligence', available at <https://www.cia.gov/library/center-for-the-study-of-intelligence/csi-publications/books-and-monographs/the-founding-fathers-of-american-intelligence/art-1.html> (accessed 28 May 2018).

Rosenbach, Eric, and Aki J. Peritz, 'Confrontation or Collaboration? Congress and the Intelligence Community: The Role of Private Corporations in the Intelligence Community', Intelligence and Policy Project of Harvard Kennedy School's Belfer Center for Science and International Affairs, July 2009.

Rothkopf, David J., 'Business versus Terror', *Foreign Policy* 130 (2002): 56–64.

Schooner, Steven L., 'Fear of Oversight: The Fundamental Failure of Businesslike Government', *American University Law Review* 50/3 (2001): 627–723.

Schwab, Stephen Irving Max, 'We're In It for the Money', *International Journal of Intelligence and CounterIntelligence* 24/1 (2011): 201–5.

Scott, James M., and Jerel A. Rosate, 'Such Other Functions and Duties: Covert Action and American Intelligence Policy', in Loch K. Johnson (ed.), *Strategic Intelligence, Volume 3: Covert Action: Behind the Veils of Secret Foreign Policy* (London: Praeger Security International, 2007), pp. 83–106.

Shalhope, Robert E., 'The Ideological Origins of the Second Amendment', *The Journal of American History* 69/3 (1982): 559–614.

Snider, L. Britt, 'Recollections from the Church Committee's Investigation of NSA', *Studies in Intelligence* (Winter 1999): 45–50.

Soroka, Stuart, 'Media, Public Opinion, and Foreign Policy', *The International Journal of Press/Politics* 8/11 (2003): 27–48.

Stanley, Jay, 'The Surveillance-Industrial Complex: How the American Government is Conscripting Businesses and Individuals in the Construction of a Surveillance Society', ACLU report, 2004.

Steele, Robert D., 'National Security and National Competitiveness', *Bulletin of American Society for Information Science* 19/3 (1993): 20–2.

Stiens, Kevin P., and Susan L. Turley, 'Uncontracting: The Move Back to Performing In-House', *Air Force Law Review* (2010): 145–78.

Stone, Christopher, 'Corporate Vices and Corporate Virtues: Do Public/Private Distinctions Matter?', *University of Pennsylvania Law Review* 130/6 (1982): 1441–509.

Stone, Geoffrey R., 'Judge Learned Hand and the Espionage Act of 1917: A Mystery Unravelled', *University of Chicago Law Review* 70/1 (2003): 336–7.

Strachan-Morris, David, 'The Future of Civil-Military Intelligence Cooperation Based on Lessons Learned in Iraq', *Intelligence and National Security* 24/2 (2009): 257–74.

Szajnfarber, Zoe, Matthew G. Richards and Annalisa L. Weigel, 'Implications of DoD Acquisition Policy for Innovation: The Case of Operationally Responsive Space', American Institute of Aeronautics and Astronautics, San Diego, CA, September 2008.

Taylor, Stan A., and David Goldman, 'Intelligence, Reform: Will More Agencies, Money, and Personnel Help?', *Intelligence and National Security* 19/3 (2004): 416–35.

Tenet, George, 'The U-2 Program: The DCI's Perspective', *Studies in Intelligence* 42/5 (1999): 1–4.

Tingle, Michal Laurie, 'Privatization and the Reagan Administration: Ideology and Application', *Yale Law and Policy Review* 6/1 (1988): 229–57.

Tromblay, Darren E., 'Information Technology (IT) Woes and Intelligence Agency Failures: The Federal Bureau of Investigation's Troubled IT Evolution as a Microcosm of a Dysfunctional Corporate Culture', *Intelligence and National Security* 32/6 (2017): 817–32.

Trouteaud, Alex R., 'Civil Liberties', in John G. Geer (ed.), *Public Opinion and Polling Around the World: A Historical Encyclopedia* (Santa Barbara, CA: ABC-CLIO, 2004), pp. 171–6.

Turner, Michael A., 'Intelligence Reform and the Politics of Entrenchment', *International Journal of Intelligence and CounterIntelligence* 18/3 (2005): 383–97.

Turner, Michael A., 'Covert Action: An Appraisal of the Effects of Secret Propaganda', in Loch K. Johnson (ed.), *Strategic Intelligence, Volume 3: Covert Action: Behind the Veils of Secret Foreign Policy* (London: Praeger Security International, 2007), pp. 110–13.

Valero, Larry, '"We Need Our New OSS, Our New General Donovan, Now": The Public Discourse over American Intelligence, 1944–53', *Intelligence and National Security* 18/1 (2003): 91–118.

Van Puyvelde, Damien, 'Médias, responsabilité gouvernementale et secret d'Etat: l'affaire Wikileaks', *Le Temps des Médias* 16/1 (2011): 161–72.

Van Puyvelde, Damien,'Intelligence Accountability and the Role of Public Interest Groups in the US', *Intelligence and National Security* 28/2 (2013): 139–58.

Van Puyvelde, Damien, 'Qualitative Research Interviews and the Study of National Security Intelligence', *International Studies Perspectives* 19/4 (2018): 375–91.

Van Puyvelde, Damien, Stephen Coulthart and M. Shahriar Hossain, 'Beyond the Buzzword: Big Data and National Security Decision-Making', *International Affairs* 93/6 (2017): 1397–416.

Voelz, Glenn J., 'Contractors and Intelligence: The Private Sector in the Intelligence Community', *International Journal of Intelligence and CounterIntelligence* 22/4 (2009): 586–613.

Wall, Robert, and Craig Covault, 'Trouble at NRO', *Aviation Week & Space Technology* 159/7, 18 August 2003: 25.

Waller, J. Michael, 'Private Intelligence Contracting Is Here to Stay', *Serviam Magazine* (July–August 2008), available at <https://www.iwp.edu/news_publications/detail/private-intelligence-contracting-is-here-to-stay> (accessed 29 May 2018).

Warner, Michael, 'The CIA's Office of Policy Coordination: From NSC 10/2 to NSC 68', *International Journal of Intelligence and CounterIntelligence* 11/2 (1998): 211–20.

Warner, Michael, 'Wanted: A Definition of "Intelligence"', *Studies in Intelligence* 46/3 (2002): 15–22.

Warner, Michael, 'Sources and Methods for the Study of Intelligence', in Loch K. Johnson (ed.), *Handbook of Intelligence Studies* (New York: Routledge, 2006), pp. 17–27.

Weber, Edward P., 'The Question of Accountability in Historical Perspective: From Jackson to Contemporary Grassroots Ecosystem Management', *Administration and Society* 31/4 (1999): 451–94.

Weber, Max, 'Politics as Vocation', in H. H. Gerth and C. Wright Mills (eds), *From Max Weber: Essays in Sociology* (Abingdon: Routledge, 1998).

Willis, Henry H., Genevieve Lester and Gregory F. Treverton, 'Information Sharing for Infrastructure Risk Management: Barriers and Solutions', *Intelligence and National Security* 24/3 (2009): 339–65.

Wiltz, John Edward, 'The Nye Committee Revisited', *Historian* 23/2 (1961): 211–33.

Wirtz, James J., 'A Review of: "Bureaucracy Does Its Thing",' *International Journal of Intelligence and CounterIntelligence* 21/3 (2008): 578–80.

Wright, Ginger Ann, 'Procurement Authorities of the CIA', *Administrative Law Review* 53/2 (2001): 1198–229.

Yannuzzi, Rick E., 'In-Q-Tel: A New Partnership between the CIA and the Private Sector', *Defense Intelligence Journal* 9/1 (2002): 25–37.

Zegart, Amy B., 'September 11 and the Adaptation Failure of US Intelligence Agencies', *International Security* 29/4 (2005): 78–111.

Zegart, Amy B., 'The Domestic Politics of Irrational Intelligence Oversight', *Political Science Quarterly* 126/1 (2011): 1–25.

Zegart, Amy B., and Julie Quinn, 'Congressional Intelligence Oversight: The Electoral Disconnection', *Intelligence and National Security* 25/6 (2010): 744–66.

Newspapers and Media

Baltimore Sun
British Broadcasting Corporation
Business Week
Business Wire
Copley News Service
Daily Beast
Defense Daily
Financial Times
Government Executive
Guardian
Huffington Post
KMWorld
Los Angeles Times
Mother Jones
New York Times
New Yorker
Newsbytes
Newsweek
Politico
PR Newswire US

Propublica
Public Broadcasting Service
Salon
San Diego Union Tribune
San Francisco Chronicle
Secrecy News
The Hill
The Intercept
Time
Vanity Fair
Wall Street Journal
Washington Post
Washington Technology
Weekly Standard
ZDNet

Index

A reference in *italics* indicates a figure.

EU Authorised Representative:
Easy Access System Europe Mustamäe tee 50, 10621 Tallinn, Estonia
gpsr.requests@easproject.com

Printed and bound by CPI Group (UK) Ltd, Croydon, CR0 4YY
24/08/2026
02202645-0002